The Princess
&
The Package

Exploring the Love-Hate Relationship
Between Diana and the Media

Michael Levine

RENAISSANCE BOOKS

Los Angeles

Interns interested in working in Mr. Levine's Los Angeles office should contact:

Intern Coordinator
Levine Communications Office, Inc.
5750 Wilshire Blvd., Suite 555
Los Angeles, CA 90036
Tel: 213-692-9999 ext. 13
Fax: 213-692-9988
E-mail: levinepr@earthlink.net

Library of Congress Cataloging-in-Publication Data

Levine, Michael
    The princess and the package : exploring the love-hate relationship between
    Diana and the media / Michael Levine.
        p.   cm.
    ISBN 1-58063-028-6 (hc. : alk. paper)
    1. Diana, Princess of Wales, 1961–1997.   2. Princesses—Great Britain—
    Biography.   3. Mass media—Great Britain.   I. Title.
DA591.A45D538 1998
941.085'092
[b]—DC21   98-26672
                                                                        CIP

10 9 8 7 6 5 4 3 2 1

Design by Lisa-Theresa Lenthall

Distributed by St. Martin's Press
Manufactured in the United States of America
First Edition

To my publishing mentor, Bill Hartley

Acknowledgments

To my encouraging associates at Renaissance Books.

To my father, Arthur; stepmother, Marilyn; and sister, Patricia.

To my loyal and hardworking staff: Kristina Bullard, Sharma Burke, David Dillon, Michelle Dolley, Derek Esplin, Jill Henry, Phillip Kass, Kelly Kimball, Melody King, Michael Norton, J. T. Steele, and Jennifer Trauth.

To my wonderful friends: Bill Calkins, Adam Christing, Richard Impresscia, Karen Karsian, Megan Mandeville, Nancy Mager, John McKillop, Cable Neuhaus, Rick Rosenthal, and Mitchell Schneider.

To Jacqueline Saviano for her help and support in developing this book.

To Ann Hartley, my heartfelt appreciation for her dedication to excellence, which can be seen on every page. Her tireless effort went endlessly beyond her role as copy editor and for that she has my gratitude forever.

To my editor Arthur Morey who brought forward my ideas in a way that gave them clarity, force, and shape. I was blessed by his trenchant mind, hard work, and brave leadership. I was lucky to have found Arthur Morey.

P A R T   I
The Princess

Introduction 9

CHAPTER 1: The Chess Game 19

CHAPTER 2: A Natural Actress 37

CHAPTER 3: First Role: Seductress 51

CHAPTER 4: The Royals 63

CHAPTER 5: Television Star, Princess Bride 71

CHAPTER 6: The Shadow Bridegroom 83

CHAPTER 7: Media Product, Media Toy 93

CHAPTER 8: Many Masks 105

CHAPTER 9: The Princess Speaks 125

CHAPTER 10: Confessor 153

CHAPTER 11: Liberation 185

CHAPTER 12: Paris 211

P A R T   I I
The Package

CHAPTER 13: The Audience of Mourners 223

CHAPTER 14: The Coverage 241

CHAPTER 15: Diana, the Investigation 251

CHAPTER 16: Cause Célèbre 265

CHAPTER 17: Queen of the Media Age 277

CHAPTER 18: Diana, the Movie 289

CHAPTER 19: The Princess Was the Package 303

Source Notes 317

Bibliography 329

Interviews 345

Index 347

PART I

The Princess

Introduction

Like many people, I learned of Diana's fatal car accident on the radio. The difference was, I was on-air when I heard the news.

Late Saturday afternoon, August 30, 1997, I'd been writing at home when the phone rang. It was the news director from the all-news radio station in Los Angeles, saying, "We need you. You're on-air live."

At the time, I was the station's official media commentator, hired because I had written extensively about the media and because of my history as a public relations crisis-communications authority. In the past I had represented Nancy Kerrigan through the Tonya Harding debacle, Michael Jackson through the child-molestation accusations, and, when the so-called trial of the century took over America's airwaves, I'd found myself speculating about the public's reaction to O. J. Simpson, in everything from *Newsweek* to *Nightline*.

Now my home phone was patched into a live broadcast, and the news director was saying that Diana Princess of Wales and her body-guard Trevor Rees-Jones had been critically injured in a car accident. Her new boyfriend, Dodi al Fayed, and the driver, Henri Paul, had been killed. And he wanted my comments.

I'm sure that if I were to listen to an air-check of that broadcast, my shocked gasp would be clearly audible. Still, my response must have made some sense, because the news director asked if the station could call back every ten minutes. Yes, of course, I said. No sooner did I hang up the phone than it rang again. This time it was CNN. They wanted commentary too, and were sending a camera crew. During their interview, CNN not only asked my opinion of the media ramifications of the tragedy, but also wanted to know if I had any personal insights I could share about Dodi al Fayed.

That question was my first personal brush with the microscopic scrutiny that the media brought to bear on even the most peripheral aspects of Diana's life.

Dodi had long dabbled in the movie business and, in fact, had co-financed the Oscar-winning feature *Chariots of Fire*. In the early 1990s he was producing the film *F/X 2: The Deadly Art of Illusion,* and during that time I had represented him to help raise his profile within the entertainment industry. Apparently even a modest busi-ness relationship with Diana's lover was considered enough to get your name on an assignment editor's speed-dial.

After that, the interviews and questions were almost nonstop: Why was there so much interest in the romance between the Princess and Egyptian-born Dodi al Fayed? What would the romance with a "foreigner," also reputed to be a playboy, mean to Diana's reputation? Should laws be passed to forbid dangerous and threatening behavior by paparazzi, who at that time were assumed to have caused the acci-dent through their hot pursuit of the couple for candid photographs?

When Diana's passing was announced that Saturday evening, a new question surfaced: What will this mean to the royal family? The interview requests increased exponentially. *Dateline. The Today Show.* BBC Radio. In two weeks I granted fifty interviews. My staff calculated that we declined several times that many requests.

Within a week of Diana's death the story, short on hard evidence, had become almost entirely self-sustaining. The event fed on itself. Here was the media (them) asking the media (me) about the impact of the media (them and me) on the story (Diana and Dodi), and what I (now not only the media but also part of the story) had to say about it. Strange times we live in. It has been said that the media created the story or that it created a public appetite for the story. Whether that perception is true is one of the subjects this book will discuss. My experience was only a small example of the convoluted and incestuous relationship that existed between the media and the story. Undeniably there was a kind of institutional media narcissism that seemed to be accepted and tolerated. The media kept one eye on the ball while the other eye remained gazing at its own navel.

MSNBC dubbed the nonstop coverage of Diana's death and funeral during the week of August 31, 1997, "the mother of all stories." It was one of the few times I didn't cringe when I heard the over-used play on Saddam Hussain's characterization of Operation Desert Storm as "the mother of all battles." I agreed. The intensity of interest was unprecedented in my experience.

Early in the following week, my instant analysis had a chance to become less instant and more analytical. Why should we care so much about these two people? After all, they weren't heads of state or wielders of great power whose passing would have significant worldwide consequences. To me, the Diana-Dodi love affair that dominated airwaves and water-cooler conversations started to become less interesting than the other love affair: the unending, love-hate relationship between the media and Diana Princess of Wales. I began writing down my thoughts.

As the week progressed, I debated constitutional attorneys and tabloid journalists. It was my position that in the last fifteen years the tabloid media had increased in number to an alarming degree, and their reporting tactics had begun to resemble professional wrestling. Though I had been shocked by the accident, I was not surprised; the high prices being paid for intrusive, exclusive pictures rewarded photographers for breaking the law. At that time, I called for a law monitoring newsgathering behavior that would be an expanded version of the Son of Sam law: If a media person committed a crime while in the process of obtaining a photograph, he or she could not benefit monetarily from that photograph.

Then Diana's brother, Charles Spencer, delivered his powerful eulogy at the funeral. In a particularly moving moment, he claimed that his sister had been murdered by the media who incessantly pursued her: "A girl given the name of the ancient goddess of hunting was, in the end, the most hunted person of the modern age."

Diana's death provoked many questions: Did the media, in some sense, "create" the Princess and so persecute her in its appetite for more stories, more photos, more action and scandal? Was Diana, like other celebrities, trained and primed as a sort of sacred victim for a bored, voyeuristic public? In periodic bouts of grandiose introspection, TV news commentators and newspaper columnists blame themselves for many of the world's troubles. It is their way of reminding themselves and us how powerful they are. Their self-importance is fed further by the habit of politicians, clergy, and moralists to blame all senseless acts of violence (like the schoolyard shootings of late 1997 and early 1998) on the media.

But the image of Diana as an innocent victim is false. Like Prince Charles and the royal family, like the pundits, photographers, and press lords, Charles Spencer underestimated the Princess. She was not pathetic. She was not merely a victim. From the time she was in her teens she had systematically courted, ever more skillfully, the very media that many people, including her brother, believe were responsible for her death.

The thought that she had worked with the media suggests that Diana might share responsibility for many of the trials of her personal life. If she was aware of her media presence and the power that came with it, if she used it to good purpose in her charity work, can it be said that she "manipulated" the media? Did she control her media appearances for her own ends—as a tool in her ongoing battles with the royal family, for example? Or to feed a neurotic need for attention? If that is so, then it might be fair to conclude that Diana played a high-stakes game and lost. Even if the ugliest scenario were true— that Diana, her lover, and their driver were killed while fleeing paparazzi—it could be argued that the Princess was herself partly to blame. Was Diana used by the media or vice versa?

The deeper I got into the research, the more I found myself seeking answers to other questions: How and why did this young woman of modest accomplishments become virtually canonized? How could the cynical media that many believe drove Diana to her death be transformed overnight into the sycophantic media that fed the frenzy of grief surrounding her funeral? What does Diana's relationship with the press teach us about the media, its impact on society, and ourselves as individuals? More than any other event of modern times, the death of the Princess raises fundamental issues about the relationship between fame and those who merchandise fame. These issues touch on the way we look at contemporary society. They force us to reexamine our feelings about heroism, saintliness, leadership, and truth. This relationship permeates our politics. The public wants great leaders, but such greatness is only believable at a distance. The more closely we watch our leaders and the more continuously we watch them, the less great they appear to be. If that person is not good, we'll find someone else.

None of our famous political leaders—Washington, Jefferson, Franklin, Roosevelt—could have sustained this level of intense attention.

As I began to look through books and articles on Diana, and our media culture, I quickly realized that there were a number of writers and social commentators whose insights and opinions would help to supply answers. Each of the more than fifty authors, journalists, psychologists, and communications advisers that I interviewed offered missing pieces of a puzzle that, when put together, complete a larger picture that, until now, has not been fully revealed.

The title, *The Princess and the Package,* is meant to convey a sense of the larger picture that emerged from my research and interviews. First, it alludes to Diana the packaged commodity. This was the Diana with whom the media collaborated because her ever-changing images and soap-opera-life story sold newspapers, magazines, merchandise, and even causes. The title also speaks to the way in which Diana herself gift-wrapped her media image for her own ends, from Shy Di who seduced the press to win Charles to Diana the Beneficent who aided charitable causes.

Why did people buy the package? Why did so many people throughout the world feel that when she died they had lost a personal friend, even a benefactor? Most only saw her image. But that was enough. In our media culture, it seems that style has actually become substance, and image is everything. In my book *Guerrilla PR,* I coined the term "The Tiffany Theory." Simply stated, if a gift is given in a Tiffany box, it will be perceived to possess a higher value than if not boxed or if boxed with a less prestigious label. That is how our culture thinks. Our politicians, corporate heads, film and television stars, like our toilet paper, is gift-wrapped for our consumption. It is no less true for princesses.

Diana kept wrapping herself in whatever bows and ribbons she thought the public would like. The media packaged and re-packaged her as whatever they thought would sell the most. It is both interesting and disturbing that neither thought that what was inside the package was good enough for the public to buy plain-wrapped. And it is equally disconcerting that so many of us kept buying each new package without ever stopping to realize that we'd been had.

Marshall McLuhan said "the medium is the message." With Diana that was eminently true. Today's multi-channel, visual media thrives on beauty, youth, and drama. Diana provided the look and the plot line to fill the media's need. Her youth and extraordinarily photogenic face made her perfect for our image-conscious age. The woman who became famous simply for marrying into the right family was written about and photographed incessantly, which made her more famous, which led to more coverage, which made her even more famous—but famous for what?

Diana's relationship with the media epitomizes modern fame as propounded by cultural historians Daniel Boorstein and Leo Braudy. Both contend that today there need be little or no correlation between achievement and fame, which was not the case as recently as fifty years ago. Modern fame has become more a function of visibility than credibility. Today someone can become a celebrity simply because they are well-known for their image—the frequency of their appearances and the spin of their press agents. My own dealings with the media confirm this daily. Andrei Codrescu, editor of *Exquisite Corpses* and commentator for NPR, puts it in a nutshell when he says that celebrities are people who are famous for being famous.

In media circles today, there is no topic that is more discussed and debated than the concern for what technology is doing to news reporting. Where once there were three major television networks in America, there are now five or six networks, all with international affiliations; there are multi-national media conglomerates that supply programming; and there are twenty-four-hour-a-day cable news channels. Where once there were only two or three weekly public affairs programs, now not an evening goes by without at least one such program vying for ratings with a seemingly endless slate of tabloid and talk shows. To compound the problem, they are all competing for viewers with the Internet news services, many of which are owned by newspapers and magazines that are pre-empting their own publications for fear they might be scooped by television.

In large measure, it is this rapidly changing media technology and the competition it has engendered that turned Diana into an icon. To use a simple analogy, which is more important: a letter or a fax? Obviously there is no right answer without knowing the contents of each, but the fax *seems* more important. There is a perceived correlation between urgency and importance. Just as the fast fax makes the message seem more important, the new high-speed media technology created an illusion of Diana's importance. The photos that were instantaneously transmitted then splashed in banner headlines across newspapers and magazines around the world, the satellite feeds of almost every public appearance she made that were up-linked, down-linked, sound-bited, and Web-paged to every corner of the globe—all this made Diana seem bigger than she really was.

Technology has a double edge. Technology is the enemy of reverence, and tabloid media the bane of civility. In the last fifteen years the media has been preoccupied with the private lives of public figures. Because a telephoto lens can capture an intimate moment between a celebrity couple on a beach, it becomes news. Is it news or is it simply commerce—valuable because it is rare? And if rarity is the measure by which we judge news, we are all on a very slippery slope, descending to where? Where do you go after broadcasting wiretapped conversations? Why not photos taken through a bedroom window? And if you're going to show photos, why not a live television feed from a camera hidden over the bed?

The media's increasingly intrusive view of the world is one-dimensional, and it distorts. It focuses on the trivial, therefore ignores the important, and turns the public into voyeurs.

The media and the celebrities it reports on are formidable adversaries in a symbiotic relationship. Each needs the other in order to exist. They come into conflict over privacy. Celebrities need to maintain the media's interest in them in order to remain in the public eye. At certain times, however, they wish to live like private citizens. Members of the media, on the other hand, do everything they can to expose and then to sensationalize celebrity lives. Ordinary persons expect that, should they be embarrassed by drug abuse, eating disorders, or extracurricular sexual affairs, these matters can be kept quiet and personal. The press seems to believe that for celebrities the price of fame is the loss of privacy. It is apparently impossible for the courts to define privacy rights clearly. This conflict of interests and forces makes the relationship between the rich and famous and those who pursue them volatile and combustible.

In the "good old days" politicians, presidents, and senators could get away with illicit sexual affairs because there was a gentleman's agreement. The government manipulated the press through leaked information to the most cooperative reporters; the members of the press looked the other way when there was potential scandal. No such gentleman's agreement exists in modern times.

As a culture, we watch and worship celebrities. We yearn to transcend our own quiet desperation by living vicariously through their lives. Millions of people tried to fill the black holes in their lives with Diana. In July of 1981, approximately 750 million people sat in front of their television sets to watch this assistant kindergarten teacher marry a prince. The fairy tale fed their emotional fantasies. Her charmed life brought excitement to their less charmed existences. Later, her troubled marriage allowed them to empathize and, in a way, gave them comfort.

When Diana died, more than a billion people watched the coverage and they got the picture: Diana was beautiful. Adored by the masses. A loving mother. A humanitarian. A virgin bride betrayed by her unfeeling, philandering husband. And a victim of ruthless paparazzi that hounded her and drove her to her death in a Paris tunnel.

The Diana that I found was all of that. And she was more. The product of an emotionally deprived upbringing, Diana's psychological makeup drove her to define herself by playing roles and by seeking adulation. She was a perfectly packaged product of our time—photogenic, image-conscious, introspective, confessional, self-absorbed, and manipulative—a media-age phenomenon. A kind of arms race broke out between the Princess and those who would package her. As she became ever more skillful at using the media to advance her causes, the media became ever more adventurous in finding ways to penetrate her defenses. Each formed temporary alliances with the government, the royal family, and even Prince Charles in their attempt to control the other. The death of Diana, with photographers on the scene, has forced the media to reexamine its modes of operation. It must also consider the increasing animosity of the public towards those who invade privacy and embarrass those who are in the public eye. It has amazed political commentators that President Clinton has retained high public-opinion ratings despite alleged sexual scandals. In the post-Diana era perhaps we should recognize that the public has decided that the personal life of a celebrity is not necessarily our business.

The Chess Game

> *"... it was very much a poker*
> *game, chess game ..."*
> —Diana Princess of Wales
> BBC *Panorama* interview

Though the struggle of the Princess of Wales with press lords, television producers, and ravening freelance photographers was explosive, unremitting, and ultimately tragic, it was not the only struggle of Diana's life.

From the beginning of her marriage, Diana was at odds with the royal family. The stakes of that battle were partly personal: Diana demanded the attention of her husband. Important constitutional questions arose when she became dissatisfied with the marriage. Diana insisted on retaining custody of her children—who stand second and third in line of succession to the throne—and she hoped to keep some of the rights and benefits her position had given her. Because she stood up to the royal family and its allies, the Princess found herself at crosspurposes with the elected government, the landed gentry, and the complex, anachronistic, and idiosyncratic British class system.

Diana's struggle with the monarchy did not aim at social revolution. Diana could not have allied herself with the radical MPs who want to do away with the monarchy—as she herself pointed out, her sons have a great deal to gain if the monarchy thrives. And while, on a cultural level, she seemed to succeed the rockstars and the Carnaby Street crowd who had transformed England in the 1960s, she was not a radical. In divorcing Prince Charles, Diana staged what amounted to a Palace coup, a challenge to the system from within. It was a civil war led by an insider, herself a noblewoman, born on an estate owned by the Queen, member of a family associated with the royal family for almost three centuries.

The world first met her as Shy Di, the Princess Bride, a symbol of renewal for Britain in the early 1980s. She had encouraged the press into pressuring Charles to propose. From the time of the courtship and throughout the marriage, Diana developed one-on-one relationships with certain royal correspondents and members of the tabloid press who she believed would show her in a positive light. She used them and other media professionals to advise her on what to say and how to present herself.

By the mid-1980s, she had metamorphosed into Diana the Beneficent, embracing causes and creating a new image as a social advocate for the working classes and have-nots. When this did not earn her the expected acknowledgment from the royal family for a job well done as Princess of Wales, she sought consolation and approval from the media and the public.

As her marriage proved loveless, Diana, as if by intuition, became increasingly enchanted with celebrity and the spotlight. Perhaps, as some said, Diana courted the media for her humanitarian causes. Perhaps, on a psychological level, she simply needed attention.

After almost a dozen years of an increasingly unhappy marriage, and after first securing the approval of the Queen, Diana and Prince Charles agreed to a divorce. As the marriage ended, the machinations of Diana on one hand, and of the royal family and the Prince on the other, became increasingly apparent.

Diana's skill at controlling events became particularly clear in the years spanning 1991–1996. Up to that point, most of what the Princess was becoming, learning, doing was disguised or hidden. Afterward, she had very obviously begun to come into her own. But for a period, beginning in the terrible year of 1992—or the *annus horribilis* as the Queen called it—Diana, Charles, the Court (the family, advisers and attendants of the Queen), and the media had about equal power. They contended with one another.

As the public struggle between the Prince and Princess began, we can see, in microcosm, a pattern of political and psychological infighting that had been going on almost from the beginning and continued until the death of the Princess.

It was fascinating for me, who thinks he knows a little something about public relations, to study and analyze how this untrained young woman was able to manipulate the media in her battles with the royal family. From the beginning, she seemed to have an instinctive ability to make the right move at the right time to turn things to her advantage. And she was never more effective than when she set out to win a divorce from Charles, and to do it on her own terms.

Diana was determined to maintain her virtuous image while systematically painting Charles as the heartless unfaithful who caused her unhappiness, her illnesses, and the failure of their marriage. She insisted on forcing him to seek separation and divorce, which would blemish *his* public standing, not hers.

Her desire for approval may seem understandable, perhaps even familiar, to Americans used to hand-pumping, bear-hugging politicians like LBJ and Bill Clinton. But Diana's claim to a kind of power and legitimacy based on the strength of personal character, style, charisma, and the common touch, is distinctly un-British. The rulers of France, from before Louis XIV through Napoleon through DeGaulle, have had a sense of direct connection to the masses. The authority and legitimacy of English monarchs historically rested on a system of contracts and agreements. Through a series of reforms over the past two centuries, the United Kingdom has become a modern democracy, though the prime minister is not directly elected. In working through the media to take her case directly to the people, Diana challenged the very basis of English government tradition.

None of this is meant to imply that the monarchy operates with no concern for popular support. The royal family, legitimized by both law and tradition, are monarchs in a democracy where there is increasing republican sentiment. For nearly two hundred years the kings and queens have done whatever possible to maintain their popularity among the public, who have come to see them—despite many royals having had all-too-visible weaknesses—as models of behavior. As Diana began to win the hearts of the British people, the royals jealously struggled to win them back.

Thus began a public relations war, a contest of strategy and gamesmanship that played itself out like an epic chess game and riveted the attention of the entire world.

But the contest between Diana and Charles was no ordinary chess game. It was beyond fantasy chess or even chess as Lewis Carroll envisioned it. This game had onlookers who became actively involved. The Court refused to stay in the stands. They insisted on making their own moves to protect Charles and the institution of the monarchy.

The media wouldn't sit quietly on the sidelines either. They confused everyone by backing one side and then the other. They threw new pieces on the board, and even upset the board now and then with sensational revelations about the private lives of the players.

To complicate things further, a secondary competition was being played fitfully between the media and the royals. This was news in itself, since the press had traditionally supported the monarchy until the 1970s.

To see the relationships between the members of the royal family, the media, the government, and the public as a challenge-and-response contest is simplistic. But it is valuable to begin with a glance at that pattern, because it is the one we were presented by the media, especially the tabloids. According to the press, when the Prince took action, the Princess responded. And vice versa. Each took advantage of the other's embarrassing predicaments. Their lives were that simple.

The speed at which the new media can create a story is impressive, but it is not particularly conducive to the reporting of nuance, motivation, or deeper patterns and trends. The media reports life as if it *were* a chess game. The principle players, anxious for media attention because it brings popular support, begin to act as if life were indeed like chess.

Diana's opening strategy was cautious and defensive. It was prompted by a report in *News of the World* about her current confidant, riding instructor Major James Hewitt, from an interview with Hewitt's girlfriend, Emma Stewardson. Two subsequent stories appeared by reputable *Daily Mail* gossip columnist Nigel Dempster—known for impeccable sources, including Princess Margaret and his own wife who is related to the Queen.

Diana's opening gambit: In July of 1991, the Princess refused Charles's offer to stage a ball to celebrate her thirtieth birthday, despite his many attempts to convince her. Diana's goal was to deflect attention away from her relationship with Hewitt and to generate public sympathy. She may have sensed that Charles would seem mean and callous if he did not celebrate her birthday At a fund-raising luncheon for a children's hospice she was asked how she would spend her birthday. Her reply was, "I'm going to celebrate my birthday home alone with the only man in my life tonight—Prince Harry."

Court countermove: Charles's camp immediately leaked to Nigel Dempster that Diana had nixed the planned gala. Regardless, most of the public still saw her as the victim. Charles put the squeeze on Diana by tightening the purse strings. He also ignored her idea to launch a Princess of Wales Trust for her charities because it would compete with his charity trust.

Diana's countermove: The Princess advanced, proposing that she and Lady Sarah Ferguson fly to the Gulf to visit British troops, but Charles said the action was more appropriate for a top-level royal.

Charles's countermove: The Prince responded by taking the trip himself.

The media jumped in: A number of books and articles reviewed the 1991 tenth anniversary of the wedding. They pointed to Diana's immaturity and frivolity as the cause of what was obviously an increasing rift between the royal couple. The audience—the public—was invited to pick a favorite.

The Court joined the combat: The Palace decided to diffuse rumors of a weak husband and a domineering wife about to split up. A PR campaign was launched, focusing on an image of unity. An official photo that captured the Windsors picnicking in the country as a family was issued in January of 1992.

For the moment, superficially, everything seemed in order. In the photos, Charles looks happy and dapper as the lord of his family. Anyone who cared to have a look, however, could have seen that these people barely knew one another.

Diana: By now a master at the use of the photo opportunity, Diana arranged the famed Taj Mahal photo, which showed her all alone in front of one of the world's most powerful symbols of romantic love, built by a Mogul emperor in memory of his wife. The message—I am a woman on my own—was not lost on the media or the public, who had plenty to cluck their tongues about.

Charles: The Prince soldiered on. In public appearances he came across as terribly stuffy and was perceived as being self-indulgent, while Diana seemed earnest and sympathetic.

Diana: In June 1992, *Diana: Her True Story,* a biography by tabloid journalist Andrew Morton, was released. It was a major attack. Morton had the cooperation of Diana's friends, family, and Diana herself—unbeknownst to the Palace. Diana pointed to the dysfunctional, bloodless, and unsupportive Windsors, including an unfaithful Charles with Camilla Parker-Bowles, as the cause of her bulimia, suicide attempts, and failed marriage. Despite all, Diana was on the modern path to self-discovery through spiritual and artistic pursuits.

The story hit the front pages of every newspaper in Britain. The book was serialized in the *Sunday Times.* Excerpts provided a *People* cover that became the magazine's bestseller to that date.

The crowd went wild. Public opinion polls showed overwhelming support for the Princess.

Charles: Stepping out of the game and the glare of publicity, perhaps fearful he was overmatched, Charles went to the Queen to discuss the consequences of a divorce. According to Kitty Kelley's *The Royals,* the Queen expressed concern about the impact of a divorce on the grandchildren, Prince Charles's public image, and the monarchy.

The Court: In the aftermath of Morton's book, the Palace was forced to put aside their hostilities toward Diana. They were under attack and needed to circle the wagons. Sir Robert Fellowes, Diana's brother-in-law and the assistant private secretary to the Queen, urged the self-regulating Press Complaints Commission to issue a statement condemning the coverage of the Waleses' marriage. The Palace drafted a denial, to be released with Diana's approval.

Diana: Making a deliberately weak move, she gave the Court's denial the mildest endorsement possible, stating, "I cannot be held responsible for what my friends say."

Media: The editors of the papers owned by press tycoon Rupert Murdoch, in one of their favorite roles—injured, misunderstood defenders of the public interest—stood up and defended their sources. They called upon Lord McGregor to vouch for their integrity. Before running the excerpts, *Sunday Times* editors had grilled Morton's sources on their own. Both Carolyn Bartholomew and confidant James Gilbey signed affidavits stating that what was said was true. The media felt vindicated.

Diana: She was now having to fight a rear-guard action. Diana needed to signal her support of Morton without contradicting herself. And so she set up a situation in which she could be photographed visiting her old friend Carolyn Bartholomew who was an acknowledged source for Morton's book. Most of the media believed that Diana had surreptitiously staged the photo opportunity to signal her authorization of the book. The apparently innocent visit, with an explanation of its significance, ran in all the papers. It even attracted attention overseas, making it one of the most widely discussed casual social calls of the decade.

There followed a number of insignificant small moves and counter-moves—snubs and innuendoes and royal sightings—subject to the kind of symbol-reading that Kremlinologists used to do.

Charles: Courtiers and friends of the Prince launched a smear campaign against Diana, feeding stories to the media about her mental instability, which newspapers printed daily.

Diana: The Princess loved her children, and William and Harry became pieces in her strategy. She made the best of her outings with them—shopping, movies, visits to amusement parks. She was with William when he required stitches from a golf-club injury to his head, while Charles was absent.

Media: The match was becoming predictable and there may have been a sense that it might end in a draw—bad for newsstand sales. So the media found a way to make things more interesting. On August 24, 1992, *The Sun* published the transcript of a 1989 ham radio operator's recording of the "Squidgy Tape"—a twenty-three-minute conversation between Diana and close friend James Gilbey—four days after the story broke in the Florida-based *National Enquirer.*

Apparently realizing that they couldn't help Charles or control his wife, the Queen and Prince Philip called a time-out to confer. After a private discussion at Balmoral, they agreed that Charles and Diana could informally separate.

Charles, for the first time, was developing a strategy. Broadcaster Jonathan Dimbleby was signed to write Charles's biography, described as a rejoinder to Morton's *Diana: Her True Story.* The press spun an image of Charles as a loyal employer, loving father, and misunderstood public figure. At least he didn't have a silly nickname. Not yet anyway.

Media: Upping the ante, the media kept up the pressure during September. There were published reports about trouble in the marriage. *The Sun* claimed Diana had had a five-year relationship with riding instructor James Hewitt. ITV did a documentary on the collapse of Charles and Diana's marriage.

Charles: He agreed to make a state visit to South Korea with Diana in early November. The trip was sardonically described as "the togetherness tour."

Diana: On the trip, Diana rebuffed Charles's public affection, as she had in India earlier that year. The two had no fun at all. Headlines read "The Glums" and "How much longer can this tragedy go on?" On November 6, the Palace finally admitted there was a rift.

Media: Throwing support to Diana, in November the *Mirror* tipped off the existence of a sixty-minute taped conversation between Charles and longtime confidant and mistress, Camilla Parker-Bowles. Brief quotes were printed: "I love you . . . I adore you . . ." The release of the tape seemed strategic; the paper had held the tape for over a year.

Both parties needed to regroup. Both must have sensed the need for better advice. Diana brought in the big guns. She addressed eight hundred media heavyweights who attended an event to support one of her causes, the prevention and treatment of drug abuse by young people. "Like it or not, I have been quite a provider for the media," she said, "and now I'm asking for your help."

With the players still about even, an official separation was announced on December 9, 1992. Diana got what she wanted: a home and her own staff at Kensington Palace, co-custody of the children, the opportunity to carry out full and separate programs of public engagement—and a chance to be queen "in due course," according to Prime Minister John Major's announcement to the House of Commons.

And then, for a second time, the match was overshadowed by the game going on between the Court and the media.

The Court: To protect the monarchy, Lord Wyatt—identified as a close personal friend of the Queen Mother—commented in the *Sunday Times:* "Princess Diana could never have won a university place, but she won a prince and failed to keep him. She is addicted to the limelight her marriage brought. It's like a drug. . . ."

Media: Editors kept the story of the separation on the front pages.

The Court: In her annual Christmas address, the Queen adopted the "dysfunctional family" motif to shore up support for the beleaguered monarchy. She admitted: "Like many other families, we have lived through some difficult days this year. . . ."

Media: In January of 1993, the tabloids gave the public the "Camillagate" scandal. *The Sun* and *Today* printed extracts from an intimate conversation between the Prince and his lover, Camilla Parker-Bowles. The story was picked up on the front pages in fifty-three countries. Supposedly recorded in December of 1989, the interchange was highly salacious and in faintly bad taste. Camilla says that she wants him day and night, "desperately, desperately, desperately." Charles returns the compliment and now earns himself a number of nicknames. Most are much more descriptive than "Squidgy."

Diana: Looking again like a woman more sinned-against than sinning, Diana regained public sympathy. Charles's prestige dropped. Leading Establishment figures traditionally loyal to the Crown— members of the Church of England, the military, and Parliament— questioned Charles's fitness to rule.

There followed another quick series of moves and countermoves. Charles gave up polo entirely, spending his time instead in public, autographing soccer balls at a London recreation center, cutting ribbons, laying wreaths, inspecting factories. He visited an inner-city housing project, toured troops in Bosnia, and inspected a former concentration camp in Poland. Something in his public manner seemed wrong. His appearances seemed unenthusiastic. He was trying to be a kinder, gentler prince but his heart did not seem to be in it.

Diana visited homeless shelters. She talked to battered wives, toured hospices and orphanages and Red Cross feeding centers, touched untouchables in India, hugged lepers in Nepal, embraced amputees, and ladled soup for starving refugees. Videotapes seem to show a woman genuinely interested in making contact. Her visits were worth reporting. During the first six days of March alone, Diana tallied 3,603 inches of newsprint to Charles's 275 inches, according to a media research firm.

Apparently unable to beat the Princess at her own game, the Palace and Charles tried to weaken her position by pulling Diana out of public life and out of the newspapers, sabotaging her charity work. The tabloids reported the snubs, and editorials cried for more respectful treatment of the mother of the future king. A pettiness crept into Charles's dealings with his wife. She was made to fly business class instead of first class. On a solo visit to Nepal, Diana learned that a band greeting her at the airport had been forbidden to play the British national anthem. Diana was snubbed, she was not invited to royal family functions. It was impossible to know whether the Court hoped to wound her psychologically or believed that it could weaken Diana's hold on the public imagination.

Diana knew how to respond. When snubbed from the Royal Ascot, she took the boys to Planet Hollywood. In the next day's newspaper, photos of a mother in blue jeans, rollicking with her children, was run next to a shot of the royal family waving from their carriage. One headline: "The Hugger and the High Hats." Uninvited to the Queen Mother's birthday party, Diana took William and Harry go-carting. The photographers went with her and Diana and the boys hit the front pages again. Now on a roll, Diana accommodated photographers who accompanied her on vacations with her children.

Charles tried in vain to beat Diana at her own game. He went with the boys on vacations to Italy and Greece. She took the Princes to Disney World in Florida. The public could decide for itself: Which vacation was more fun?

Diana also courted the media privately. She threw cocktail parties for those who wrote about her tours. She became friendlier with them than she had been during her courtship. These meetings seemed to work to her advantage. But though they were apparently sympathetic to the Princess, the press could never be counted on for loyalty.

Media: Exploiting the attention paid by the public to the match between the Prince and Princess, the *Sunday Mirror* on November 7 and 8, 1993, published very candid shots (taken with a hidden camera) of Diana at her gymnasium, in spandex shorts and leotard, pushing a shoulder-press with her legs spread apart. There followed days of coverage about the invasion of privacy and debate about press curbs from the Palace, Parliament, and publishers.

Again a break was called and an alliance built up between Diana and the Court. With the backing of the Queen and Prince Philip, Diana sued the newspaper, the photographer, and the owner of the gym.

Hoping to give momentum to moves for a privacy law, Diana prepared to testify in court. The impending trial was the perfect recipe for a media feast. More than nine hundred reporters had applied for credentials in a courtroom with seventy-five seats.

The Court: While lending legal and financial support, the Court undermined Diana's case. Scheduled as a defense witness, her detective was transferred out of her service. Diana's chauffeur decided that he wanted to work for Charles.

The suit was settled out of court. The Mirror Group issued a public apology, paid $40,000 in damages to a charity in Diana's name, and didn't write about the case. Bryce Taylor, the owner of the gym, publicly apologized, gave up the photos and negatives, and agreed never to discuss the case, but only, it is alleged, after being paid off. Diana now appeared to be in the stronger position.

Diana: The Princess withdrew from public life to regroup and recharge for the next phase of her strategy—getting out of her marriage once and for all, and building a new career.

Media: Pictures of the now-reclusive Princess were rare and, therefore, brought a higher price. Aggressive freelance photographers and paparazzi—the "stalkerazzi"—followed Diana's every step, twenty-four hours a day, never losing her for more than a few minutes. Their game plan was to startle her, face to face, so she would lose her cool.

Charles: The royals stepped up their public relations campaign. In July, a two-and-a-half-hour Independent Television documentary, *The Prince of Wales* by Jonathan Dimbleby, was broadcast on BBC and viewed by 12.7 million people. This was the "charm offensive" that was supposed to portray Charles as a hard-working but very human prince, as he pressed the flesh with Diana's favored underdog constituency and cavorted with sons William and Harry at Balmoral. Making excuses, he admitted to having an affair with Camilla Parker-Bowles. The documentary accomplished none of what the Prince had hoped it would. The tone was interpreted as self-pitying.

Diana: Coming out of seclusion, Diana appeared the night of the documentary at a *Vanity Fair*-sponsored gallery benefit looking particularly glamourous. Later that week, she popped up at Wimbledon and other public places. Diana clearly outdrew Charles as the paparazzi swarmed around her.

Charles: Seizing the opportunity, Charles represented Diana as intellectually vacant, mentally unstable, a media exhibitionist, shallow, and materialistic. Friends of the Prince leaked to tabloids that Diana had lavished $240,000 on personal expenses in one year.

Diana's countermove: She threw back the stone. Diana's camp revealed that Charles had spent $650,000 in the same period for must-haves, including manicures and polo ponies.

Media: Once again a publisher became a player. *A Princess in Love* was published—the kiss-and-tell book by Anna Pasternak about former Life Guards officer James Hewitt, Diana's lover from 1986 through 1991.

Diana: In late September through October of 1994, Diana boldly invited several media bosses to one-on-one teas at Kensington Palace. Her goal was to change the current notion that she was volatile and unbalanced. She wanted to show the top men themselves, up close and personal, that she was an intelligent woman with her feet on the ground. The teas were a successful first-effort at damage control and image reversal.

Charles: An authorized biography of Charles, *The Prince of Wales* by Jonathan Dimbleby, was released in October and excerpted in London's *Sunday Times.* It was meant to set the record straight and convince the public that Charles was a conscientious soul, worthy to wear the crown. The result was as disastrous as Dimbleby's documentary. While the public felt sympathy, they lost respect, further jeopardizing Charles's hope of becoming king, and spurring talk of divorce. Members of Parliament felt that if the Queen should die, it would be a scandal for Diana to be crowned at Charles's side.

Media: In early August 1996, *News of the World* broke the story that a lonely, isolated Diana had been having an eighteen-month-long flirtation with England's national rugby team captain, Will Carling, twenty-nine years old and a married man. The rest of Fleet Street jumped in and painted Diana as a predator.

Diana: Defending herself, Diana called Richard Kay of the *Daily Mail* and assured him that her innocent friendship with

Carling started because of her sons' interest in rugby.

Week by week and month by month, Diana seemed to be winning the match. But after several years of tit-for-tat, it appeared that Diana didn't have an end game. She had no significant advantage over Charles. The sheer accumulation of scandal and the constant intrusions of the media to upset strategies on both sides made it unlikely that Diana could win in the way that she wanted. She needed a bold stroke to beat the Prince.

The media, which had sponsored the match, surely were coming out ahead. They had made significant revenues, and kept writers and photojournalists employed by covering this tournament.

But Diana knew that she needed media attention to fulfill her agenda. And she must have feared that a point would come when either she could not win the loyalty of the press lords or, even worse, she would become boring to them. She needed to do something as decisive as overturning the table and letting the chess pieces roll into whichever corners they might. The time had come for her to make her boldest move: talking.

Lady Colin Campbell wrote in her conclusion to *Diana in Private* that Diana's survival technique throughout the years was to reveal "very little" about the person behind the glossy façade. "She always keeps comments to a sympathetic minimum" with all but her closest friends, and she did not give interviews. But once she had decided to speak, Diana was not about to hold anything back.

It's an old saw that the best defense is a good offense, but among those to whom spin control is a way of life, it goes one step further. In Hollywood, it's not enough for you to have a successful movie, you're only happy if your competitor's picture blows up in the projector on opening night, his wife leaves him, his house burns down, and his dog dies. It would appear that the Princess had more than a passing familiarity with this scorched-earth school of public relations.

After gradually creeping back into public life, Diana agreed to a BBC interview that aired throughout the world in November of 1995. The interview transformed Diana's world forever. It made her divorce inevitable. It defined her as a unique figure in popular culture and gave her a kind of power she had only begun to explore at the time of her death. And it checkmated Charles.

The world became acquainted with Diana incrementally. Over at least a decade, a series of interviews, exposés, photos, tell-all books, and rumors taught us that the fairy-tale marriage of the Prince and Princess of Wales had levels we didn't know about. There were elements of illness, sadness, even sordidness in the marriage (and in those of other royal couples too).

We also discovered that there was more to the Princess than had met the eye. She was not what she had at first seemed to be. She was a paradigmatic woman of the '90s—when women were evolving and transforming themselves at something near the speed of light. We don't know what she might have become.

Following her sudden death, we began a second reappraisal, this time learning something more about ourselves. Many otherwise savvy and worldly people were moved by the death of the Princess. Most of us were surprised that Diana, whatever she represented, had touched the lives of so many people in such a serious, positive way. How did she do it?

In this book we will undertake a third reevaluation of Diana's life, one that credits her craft, her skill in building a public image and using it to advance her causes. In retrospect, it seems surprising that we didn't acknowledge her skills sooner. Some of the reasons we could not see the Princess and those around her clearly will be discussed in later chapters. But unlike conventional biographies, this book does not promise to reveal the true Diana beneath the surface. My intention is to take the surface of this very public person seriously. I believe that the surface—the package—was very much a part of Diana's intrinsic being. And I am fascinated by and impressed with the skill she showed in creating herself.

A Natural Actress

> *"Here was a situation which hadn't ever happened before in history, in the sense that the media were everywhere. Here was a fairy story that everybody wanted to work."*
>
> —Diana Princess of Wales
> BBC *Panorama* interview

The later successes of Diana the grand master, Diana the general, Diana the politician come from the paradoxical fact that she was ignored and underestimated by everyone for the first three decades of her life. First as a shy, gawky child, then as a trophy wife, then as a pop-culture star, Diana always seemed easy to control and no particular threat. Even those who knew her best, remembering her afterwards, describe her keen sense of how to take advantage, how to appear on the world stage, how to gain the spotlight to advance herself and her career. They comment on her good instincts, her intuitive grasp of affairs. Few acknowledge that she consciously used the media to win the hearts of the world.

There were, of course, some early signs that Diana was skilled at public performance. Those who had seen the Princess at official functions were immediately struck by how well she assumed her role.

She undoubtedly liked what she was doing and was pleased by the attention of the press and the public. She insisted that she failed to understand the public's interest in her through a self-deprecating sense of humor, a subtle way of drawing even more attention to herself. In *Hamlet,* Queen Gertrude, commenting on the Player Queen's overheated refusal of the Player King's marriage proposal, says, "The lady doth protest too much, methinks." The excessive denial divulges the Player Queen's true desire for him, even though she is still married. In the process, she whets his appetite more. Like the Player Queen, Diana teased with temperance.

She often said that she couldn't understand why the media was so fascinated with her. Such false modesty was glaring in the *Panorama* interview when she stated to the world: "I never encouraged the media. . . . I still to this day find the interest daunting and phenomenal, because I actually don't like being the center of attention." *Newsweek* astutely cautioned that these two statements should be taken with "a bucketful of salt."

"There is no question she loved her celebrity," asserts Richard Stolley, creator/founding editor of *People* magazine which to date has published in excess of fifty cover stories on Diana, more than triple that of number-two cover girl, Elizabeth Taylor. "There were times when she was not in control of the media that she normally adored."

Stolley, interviewed for this book, witnessed Diana in action in June 1997 at a Chicago fund-raiser for breast cancer and AIDS, co-hosted by *People* and Northwestern University. "She had become extremely skillful and polished," recalled Stolley, now senior editorial adviser for Time Inc. "She was beautifully gowned and made-up, and moved slowly with elegant, deliberate gestures. She had a slightly distant graciousness, but for those few seconds she was shaking your hand, she was totally focused on you. You see this among politicians. LBJ was a genius at that."

For a few days, Diana was Queen of Chicago. She wore a purple (one of the colors of Northwestern University) Versace dress, and whatever her official status she looked royal in it. She knew how to play to the crowds in the North American heartland.

Diana was gifted at changing roles to suit the situation, much like a chameleon; perhaps a more telling comparison might even be made to such pop divas/actresses as Madonna or Cher. Indeed, in addition to her public role as Princess, Diana seemed to essay many different personas, which suggests the kind of psychological makeup that has been commonly associated with actors and performers.

Acting is a skill difficult to master. But those who become actors often exhibit a temperament, a sense of self, that attracts them to the profession. Psychoanalyst and human-development expert Erik Erikson, author of *Identity and the Life Cycle,* hypothesized that actors displayed symptoms of "identity diffusion," an ego identity problem that was dealt with by performing on stage. Diana seemed to have been grappling with this sort of identity problem until shortly before her death.

The facts and circumstances of her early life strongly suggest that the young, formless Diana was psychologically primed to seek identity and healing through the fantasy role of Princess of Wales and its requisite celebrated stature. Many performers come from troubled childhoods. They seem to feel a desire to redress some past hurt, to heal some part of childhood—to make real, actually, something that is a fantasy. The performer is emotionally immature. He or she may have a predilection to narcissism. It goes with being dominantly right-brained.

When she was six, Diana had been emotionally wounded by her parents' divorce. At the time, she was, effectively, abandoned by her mother. But she may have felt rejected by her parents from the day she was born.

After giving birth to two daughters, Sarah and Jane, in January of 1960 Frances Spencer delivered a son, a very desired heir to carry on the noble Spencer name and inherit the family's vast estate. Deformed and sickly, the infant boy died within ten hours. Parents John and Frances tried for another son. Instead, eighteen months later on July 1, 1961, they produced a third girl: Diana.

Assuming there was something wrong with her because she kept producing girls, older family members pressured Frances, then only twenty-three, to be examined at London clinics. In his 1997 biography, *Diana, Her True Story—In Her Own Words,* Andrew Morton reports that the experience was humiliating, especially for the proud, tough-minded woman. Diana's younger brother, Charles, has said that the rift between his parents was created during this period and was the root of their divorce. As will be apparent from the following brief sketch of her childhood, Diana, like her sister Sarah, possessed an outspokenness that appears to have been similar to her mother's. And Diana's marriage had many of the same problems that her parents' marriage had. Like many people who grew up in troubled families, Diana may have spent her adult life trying to avoid the same mistakes made by her parents.

The shame felt by her mother was a burden Diana bore as a child and as an adult. "While she was too young to understand, Diana certainly caught the pitch of the family's frustration," wrote Andrew Morton in his biography, "and, believing that she was a 'nuisance,' she accepted a corresponding load of guilt—and failure for disappointing her parents and family. . . ."

Diana's loss of innocence came early. She was not the boy her parents wanted but she was a cheerful child until age six, when her parents entered into ugly, public divorce proceedings. From that time on, snapshots of loneliness and unhappiness crowded her early memory: "Her mother's tears, her father's lonely silences, the numerous nannies she resented, the endless shuttling between parents, the sound of her brother, Charles, sobbing himself to sleep . . ." wrote Morton. "It was a childhood where she wanted nothing materially but everything emotionally."

After the divorce—during which her effervescent and loving mother lost custody of the children to her boring and emotionally closed father—Diana, very early, adopted controlling habits and role-playing patterns to provide structure for herself in an environment of emotional chaos, neglect, and desperation.

In *Diana: An Intimate Portrait,* author Ingrid Seward quotes Diana's nanny Mary Clarke saying afterwards that Diana developed her nervous blush, her habit of always looking down, at the time of her parents' divorce.

She became deeply attached to her younger brother and looked after him. Such a bond is a symptom of identity diffusion; one suffering from "an early identity hunger" is "apt to attach himself to one brother or sister," Erikson wrote in *Identity and the Life Cycle.* To find out who one is and how that self-conception fits into society, a person naturally tries on different roles during and after adolescence. Role experimentation ends when one feels "a sense of inner continuity."

But Erikson found the process had been unsuccessful among actors. Confused about where to draw boundaries because they don't know who they are, they struggle with intimate relations for fear of being swallowed by another when they feel close, and they have difficulty planning appointments and showing up on time.

This behavior is often masked by people who have found an identity that allows them to function within society. The confusion they feel over their true identity does not disappear, but is hidden or buried. Angry because they cannot express themselves, many actors and other performers become subversive. They seem convinced that the world would be a richer place without fences. They often haven't matured psychologically and emotionally. And frequently they are willing to go to ludicrous ends in a persistent, militant refusal to grow up.

As a young girl, Diana tried to develop herself through activities suited to her natural performer's winning personality: social, charming, fun-loving, and sexy. She studied and enjoyed playing the piano. Always athletic, Diana excelled in tennis and dancing.

Unfortunately, Diana's social upbringing did not allow her sufficient freedom of exploration and expression to complete her journey of self-discovery. An aristocrat raised to have impeccably good manners and never to behave badly in public, Diana learned early and well to hide her true feelings behind a façade of cheerfulness and grace. But the tools traditionally used by nobility to keep their feelings hidden simply weren't enough for Diana. Whether she was motivated by her psychological demons, or forced to action by the circumstances in which she grew up, Diana's frustrations seemed to lead to a desperate need for an audience. Very much like many successful actors and politicians, Diana had been wounded by the family misfortunes that she experienced in childhood, and she craved attention.

Missing their mother, indeed suspicious that the nannies were going to take their mother's place, Diana and her siblings tried to get rid of them with vicious tricks—putting pins in chairs, throwing clothes out the window, locking them in the bathroom.

Diana also showed a tendency to "invent" the truth. Her brother, Charles, confirms this habit. "I don't know whether a psychologist would say it was the trauma of the divorce, but she had real difficulty telling the truth purely because she liked to embellish things."

Even at this early age, escaping into fantasy was a salve for her emotional wounds.

As M. Scott Peck, M.D. says in his best-selling *The Road Less Traveled,* "Life is difficult." We are here on earth to grow and growth is painful, he explains. But many performers seek to avoid that pain and return to their Eden, the womb, through pretending in what he calls "a drama."

There, ironically but logically, Erikson noted, they find a temporary inner peace because the role draws parameters that they need but haven't yet developed for themselves. They are told what to say, what to do, what to feel, where to stand—from the script, from the director—which real life does not provide. There's a chance to rehearse again and again until the performance is right—which life also does not provide. And then the director tells the performer whether he or she fits the role.

"Between acts and plays, there is a sense of nothingness and emptiness about who they are, but when they are on stage, they get to fill a void by playing a role that gives them the structure to know who they are," explains Dr. Alan Entin, a family psychologist in private practice in Richmond, Virginia, who has studied the Erikson theory.

Her spirits suppressed in school, her personality cramped by her position in the family, and raised to mask emotions, Diana was known to use manipulation to get what she wanted.

While we cannot know how conscious the young Diana was of the pressure, the history of her family suggests that there must have been heavy demands made on her to conform to the standards of the British ruling class.

A centuries-old family whose fortune was made through sheep ranching, the Spencers had plenty of illegitimate ties with the Stuart line: three of Diana's antecedents were mistresses of King Charles II, another was mistress of his younger brother James II, and another of

George IV. The Duchess of Marlboro was First Lady of the Bedchamber to Queen Anne. All but one produced royal bastards. "When they weren't being romanced by the Royal Family," writes Ingrid Seward in *Diana: An Intimate Portrait,* "the Spencers were usually to be found serving it and being honored in return." Queen Elizabeth II became godmother to Diana's brother, Charles.

More recent Spencer history had been less happy. Prince Charles is quoted as having said, ". . . before you marry the daughter you should first look at the mother." He seems not to have followed his own advice when he married Diana. Frances Spencer was spirited; her husband, quiet and dull. She began an affair with the extroverted wallpaper heir Peter Shand Kydd in 1966. Lord Althorp was shattered. The divorce became ugly and in the end, because she had taken the first step, Frances did not win custody of her children.

In that day and age, having a liaison was not uncommon, but being found out broke the first cardinal rule within aristocratic circles. Private matters were to remain just that. Frances paid the price when Janet Shand Kydd sued for divorce, citing adultery as grounds and listing Frances as a corespondent. Newspapers reported this—Diana's first insight into the media's power to negatively influence the outcome of people's lives. This highly public airing of adultery embarrassed Frances's own mother, Ruth Fermoy, who for thirty years was one of the Queen Mother's Women of the Bedchamber and possessed a rigid courtier mentality. Fermoy joined forces with John Spencer to deprive Frances of custody. The lives of Diana and her brother (Sarah and Jane were away at school) were thereafter dominated by their father, a decent man loved by his daughter, though he was as cold and remote as the man she later married.

When trying to understand Diana's motives in controlling the press we shouldn't overlook the obvious. The story of her own mother taught her that a father's status could prove more important in a custody battle than a mother's love. It also showed that free expression—especially when manifested through a sexual liaison—could take away a woman's rights. In Diana's chess game with Prince Charles, her furious courting of the media may have seemed to her the only way to escape the fate of her mother with whom she identified.

But on a deeper psychological level, the young Diana may have believed that loss of reputation was synonymous with lost love and abandonment. If you aren't a good girl, if you aren't the mother and wife that people expect you to be, then you will be punished. And your children will be punished as well. Diana learned early that playing to a prescribed image would deflect emotional pain.

It is true of actors and narcissists as well that they resent and sometimes oppose authority. It is not so much a political position as a response to real differences in world views. Accountants, who are governed by the left brain, and poets, who are dominated by the right brain, can look at the same world and see it differently. The left-brainer would say, "What a beautiful world, if there were only less chaos, if there were more fences and rules to protect this beautiful place. How dare those chaotic anarchists ruin our beautiful world!" The poet will say, "If we only didn't have so many fences, so many regulations. Why are they poisoning our beauty?" Diana clearly had right-brain orientation. She was governed by a creative soul and spirit. On some level she was bound to feel constrained by a group of people dominated by a cold, logical approach to living.

By her very nature, Diana was almost certain to become an adversary—a formidable adversary—of the royal family. The famous British ideal of civilized behavior is certainly a kind of packaging. British reserve hides all personal idiosyncrasy, all real feeling, within a standard of appropriate behavior. Diana had that sort of packaging bred into her. She learned a female version of aristocratic packaging—

an untiring cheerfulness—from her mother. Diana had all the tools to be an exemplary noblewoman. She had them in excess. She took the traditional packaging concept, magnified it, made it colorful, and used that revised package to win hearts and challenge the monarchy.

When Diana was fourteen, her grandfather Spencer died, leaving her father, John, a two-million-pound debt on the Althorp estate, which included a splendid mansion on thirteen thousand acres, six miles northwest of Northampton.

After her father remarried, Diana's natural jealousy of her stepmother, Raine, was compounded by the fact that Raine, later the Countess de Chambrun, was, as Morton says in *Diana: Her True Story,* "a phenomenon": gushing, colorful, and politically rigid as a member of the London County Council. To put her husband's affairs in order, Raine sold off the family art. She opened Althorp to tourism, with a gift shop that peddled souvenirs and organized dinners. To refurbish the estate, she and John raised more capital by selling off some of its cottages.

The children felt violated by the sale of their heritage. Perhaps they disapproved of their father's new life as proprietor of a gift shop. Charles's valet, Stephen Barry, wrote: "There is not a great deal of love lost between the Princess and her stepmother."

Simon Blow, a society journalist popular among the landed gentry, wrote an article for *Connoisseur* about the rape of Althorp—the selling of irreplaceable items for capital that would be spent immediately. The children were secretly pleased.

It is a curious paradox that Raine's mother is Barbara Cartland, the writer of the romance novels that Diana read with great pleasure. It's been suggested that romantic novels contributed to the expectations she had going into her marriage. But when the wedding was being planned, Diana struck Cartland's name from the list of those invited. It was an indirect rebuff to her stepmother.

A number of psychologists have noted that many celebrities have been either deprived or spoiled. They received either little affection or approval, or too much without having earned it. All of this creates an emotional "black hole" that they try to fill by seeking adulation or escaping into fantasy.

The term "narcissistic vulnerability" explains this type of wound. This particular pattern of self-involvement can often be part of an actor's psychological makeup, believes narcissism expert Dr. Marion F. Solomon, author of *Narcissism and Intimacy*. Interviewed for this book, she said that those with narcissistic vulnerability crave highly validated feedback from others—publicly or privately—to repair their wounds from early emotional failures. The causes range from failure to meet parents' expectations of idealized perfection to lack of emotional care-taking due to parents' depression, alcoholism, emotional withdrawal, or physical illness.

These injured individuals often first seek this healing approval by playing a role, "selecting an image of themselves to fuse with another," and acquiring the power and strength the other represents, often within an idealized romantic relationship that they believe will "capture paradise lost," Solomon writes.

Many performers say that they feel more alive in their roles than as themselves. That's because play-acting fills the holes in their souls. Often, the image is what they would like to be.

To bear the pain of their lives or a lack of core identity, those with identity diffusion and narcissistic vulnerability escape into either fantasy and imagination or compulsive, self-destructive behaviors that distract attention from required tasks. Hints of these patterns began to surface in Diana's youth as well.

Though her teachers deemed her of average intelligence, after her parents' divorce the young Diana couldn't concentrate on school work and later simply lacked intellectual curiosity, unlike her siblings. Diana herself admitted: "At the age of fourteen, I just remember thinking that I wasn't good at anything, that I was hopeless. My brother was always the one getting [passing] exams at school and I was the dropout."

The classic lack of self-definition manifested more clearly in Diana during her days as a young noblewoman, a time of floating and floundering. She had no clear goals and didn't stick with anything.

After failing her exams, thus ending higher education, Diana attended finishing school in Switzerland at age sixteen, then returned to London. She took cookery classes, then dabbled for a month at becoming a dance teacher at Vacani Dance School in South Kensington. Her only real ambition in life thus far had been to become a dancer—an unattainable goal because she was too tall. After that, she worked part-time as her sister Sarah's maid. She filled the rest of her time as an assistant kindergarten teacher and nanny.

Many thought Diana nothing more than another frivolous, self-absorbed "Sloane Ranger"—a young, upper-class girl with the right breeding and right family, who lived and socialized around the posh Sloane Street and Sloane Square. These young women were expected only to marry well, someone companionable, not necessarily for love. To find that appropriate match, one had to party well—go on the right ski trips, country weekends, hunting and debutante balls. Drinking was a regular activity, but cultural activities were not.

Diana lived in the Knightsbridge area and was part of the scene but seems not to have fit in. Morton claims she was really a loner.

She was the classic little girl lost. She hadn't a clue as to what made her unique. All the elements of her life, however, pushed her toward a role that would give her structure, make her feel special, fill that emptiness, heal her wounds, and recapture paradise lost.

Instead of seeking the London stage, she chose the royal arena to play out her fantasies. Psychologist Alan Entin believes that Diana's lack of goals or direction, and her own sense of herself, are what spurred her to "quickly fall into the role of Princess of Wales. She knew she could do it well." Love and romance was also an emotional cure-all.

Diana's focus was fueled by circumstances, as well as by a desire to redeem the family name and image, and realize the longstanding Spencer family ambition to become part of the royal family. When her sister Sarah began to date Prince Charles, the family was ecstatic. Charles, meanwhile, dawdled, and Sarah, in an attempt to snap him into a decision, told a reporter she would turn him down because she didn't love him, humiliating Charles and violating the upper-class protocol of keeping things within your circle. (This was the same protocol, note, that her mother had broken.) The relationship ended, but the stage was set for Diana's entrance.

But what Diana brought to her relationship with Prince Charles—the psychological scars, the family tradition, the memory of her mother's misfortunes (all leading to an innate talent for performance)—are only part of her story. Equally important, the times were changing. A generation of tragedy and scandal in the United States had helped create a new journalistic attitude. The growth of an entertainment industry capable of producing supercelebrities had encouraged a public fascination with gossip. Technology had begun, in fact, to fashion the "global village" first imagined in the '60s. And the rise of powerful media lords like Rupert Murdoch and Ted Turner had radically changed the lives of public figures, for better and for worse.

It is usual to disparage this trend as tawdry. But, as noted by Gail Collins, a member of the *New York Times* editorial board, gossip "also serves a deep psychological need. . . . It helps people to understand how things really work in the mysterious world behind closed doors. People express their hidden fears through gossip, imposing on others the anxieties they haven't resolved in their own lives." Whether by nature or because she was more closely in touch with the real world, Diana Spencer had a better understanding of the new environment than did the Prince she had her eye on.

While living with flatmates in London, Diana made it clear in comments that she wanted to become a member of the royal family. After a party at Kensington Palace—the residence of her sister Jane who married Queen Elizabeth's assistant private secretary, Sir Robert Fellowes—Diana commented to a friend: "It would be wonderful to live at KP."

The impression of the Charles-and-Diana romance was of an apple-cheeked innocent swept away by an ardent prince into a fantasy life. But she wasn't as innocent as she appeared. Charles wasn't the pursuer. He was the pursued. During a skiing trip, she said to a friend: "It would be nice if I could be a dancer—or the Princess of Wales."

She won that role by cleverly inhabiting another role: seductress. Diana seduced Charles—and herself—with the fantasy. Moreover, she shrewdly used the media to do it—without daring to protest the media attention at all. Yet.

First Role: Seductress

> *"All charming people have
> something to conceal, usually
> their total dependence on the
> appreciation of others."*
> —Cyril Connoly
> *Enemies of Promise*

When her affair with Prince Charles began, Diana was still so young, so artless, that it is difficult to see in her the self-packaging genius that she became. Still, all young people in love package themselves in order to win their object of desire. Tolstoy remarked that geniuses are only a little bit more gifted than commonplace talented people. Diana was not yet a celebrity, but she had good skills as a young woman in love. Maybe genius.

On the first two occasions that Charles and Diana crossed paths, the Prince was simply cordial and nice to the then-schoolgirl— once at Sandringham for a shooting weekend and another time at Balmoral. Charles, who had his eyes open, saw that Sarah's sister was becoming an attractive young woman. Surely he was not infatuated, but he was interested enough in Diana to arrange an invitation to Balmoral for Sarah Spencer and her sister.

At that time, Diana apparently knew he did not see her as an object of desire. At Balmoral, a friend says, the then-eighteen-year-old Diana developed a crush on the Prince "from a mixture of him being the Prince of Wales and actually taking the trouble, yet again, to be nice to her." Charles may have been vulnerable. He was attracted to powerful women like Davina Sheffield, Jane Wellesley, Anna Wallace, and Sarah Spencer. But he resented it when they showed too much spirit. Disconsolate over losing his great passion, Anna, and the death of his great-uncle and mentor, Lord Mountbatten, who had been recently murdered by the Irish Republican Army, Charles floundered morosely in the summer of 1980. Sister Jane knew that Diana wanted to get to know Charles, so she invited her up to Balmoral in July of 1980.

Diana went, sensed an opportunity, and began her pursuit of Charles. In the A&E *Biography* "Diana, the True Story," James Whitaker, a reporter on the royal family who also made friends with Diana during her courtship, says: "She set out to get Prince Charles and, in my opinion, he was easy meat for her. She not only was very flattering to him, she was very sympathetic to him. She was very supportive to him. She talked about the awfulness of his misery over Earl Mountbatten's death. She had all the right things. And I think he was enchanted. I don't think, to begin with, that he could contemplate that she was going to be his wife. I think she did, that he was going to be her husband."

In the same documentary, a piano teacher of Diana's claims that she had admired the Prince long before she met him, keeping copies of photos of him all over her bedroom. At what point she crossed the line from schoolgirl with a crush to woman on the make is unclear.

She hooked him with time-honored feminine strategies: visible adoration, sensuality, and then elusiveness. Tactics were regularly discussed with flatmates. Recalled Carolyn Bartholomew: "It was pretty normal procedure that goes on between girls, 'Make sure you do this or that.' It was a bit of a game."

She made herself utterly available and sent out very clear messages of worship. The Prince was flattered.

By redeveloping a childhood friendship with Princess Margaret's daughter, Lady Sarah Armstrong-Jones, Diana got herself invited to join the family for Cowes Week on the royal yacht *Britannia.*

A week later, Charles invited her to a small dinner party at Buckingham Palace. "She was clearly determined and enthusiastic about him," remembered Patti Palmer-Tomkinson, according to Kitty Kelley's *The Royals,* "and she very much wanted him."

Years afterwards, Diana told the media and the public that her unhappiness was due to Charles's betrayal. According to Andrew Morton, she was the artless youth wooed by a man clearly interested in her. At the time of their engagement, "I thought he was very much in love with me, which he was. . . ." But then, according to Morton, during their marriage he kept her down, ignored and undermined her, and cheated on her.

In reality, her misery was also brought on because she wasn't true to herself during the courtship and her engagement to Charles.

A critic or a moralist might argue that Diana hadn't taken the time or painful effort to form herself. As M. Scott Peck says, self-discovery requires dedication to reality at all costs, a stark honesty with yourself and others. Diana traveled the road of self-denial. Like an actress, she pretended to be someone other than herself during the courtship in order to win the role of Princess of Wales. She had betrayed herself. But she was nineteen, without a meaningful career, and he was destined to be king of England. If Diana was naïve or cunning, she was not much more so than many young people starting out in life.

Romantic and surprisingly ambitious, looking for a purpose in life, Diana interpreted Charles's initial courtesies as interest. This allowed her to justify falling madly in love with him, a man she barely knew.

She played the courtesan to entice him. At the same time, Diana beguiled the press. Her interaction with the media might have seemed unsophisticated on the surface, but on closer examination it was extremely shrewd—and instrumental in enticing Charles to court her and ultimately propose.

While she may not have been a candidate for Mensa, this young lady had intuition, a sixth sense, a remarkably well-developed instinct. Early in the relationship one sees that she courted the media with the same skill she used in pursuing the Prince. She had an actress's innate sense of timing and response to the cues of a situation.

The media fueled the attraction into a relationship before Charles was ready. Following the Prince as he fished on the River Dee at Balmoral, the media noticed a female companion who fled when she saw them and stood behind a tree. Through their binoculars, they saw a hand appear, with a compact that allowed the woman to see where they were, then use it to walk away, keeping the tree between her and them.

Diana's flirtation with the media had begun.

On September 8, 1980, Harry Arnold of *The Sun* broke the news of Charles's latest romance. Publicity made the romance more serious than it might have been. A relative of Charles's said, "It removed some of the element of choice, from the Prince of Wales's point of view."

Diana, according to friends, was ecstatic. Thereafter, the press's interest in Diana, as with no girlfriend before, was sustained and excessive. Morton reported that the media rented a nearby flat from which they could peer into her bedroom with binoculars. They'd call her directly at home to confirm or deny stories.

If she was disingenuous, even self-deceived in her wooing of Prince Charles, she was more so in her courtship of the press. While actually helping them to get photos of her, she claimed at first that she tried to outrun the media. In tapes given to Andrew Morton in 1991, she says: ". . . I always made sure that I was going through the lights just as the light was turning red, so they were stuck. When I got into my car, they'd chase me everywhere. You're talking about thirty of them—not two." It is the kind of caper that looks like flirting of a fairly intense kind. Did Diana Spencer believe that a red light would thwart an eager press corps? Or did she know that they would be enticed further?

Within weeks, Diana had set up cordial relationships with regular reporters. Her innocence, her natural sweetness, brought out the best in journalists and photographers. Morton quotes her speaking with utter innocence about reporters: "I was constantly polite, constantly civil. I was never rude. I never shouted."

They assumed her cooperation and politeness—which dignified them in a way that few celebrities ever did—was youthful innocence rather than guile. The moral here is that while the media pontificates about being objective and fair, they are human—and, as humans competing and working under pressure-cooker deadlines day in and day out, they can be roped in by flattery and succumb to laziness. And they will write and speak more warmly about those who make their jobs easier by giving them stories or by simply being available for comment and photos. In this regard, Diana was perfect.

Soon thereafter, Whitaker admits, he and other colleagues decided that Diana was a suitable choice for future queen—and told the public so.

When Charles asked her how she put up with them, she responded: "I love working with children, and I have learned to be very patient with them. I simply treat the press as though they were children."

Her close friendships with reporters bordered on cahoots. James Whitaker, for example, advised her on what she should and should not say. If she said something compromising, they didn't use it, because they wanted her to marry Charles. "Little did they know," wrote Lady Colin Campbell in *Diana in Private*, "that she got them to join her in achieving her goal."

In October, *The Sun* ran a presumptuous headline: "Charles Set to Make Lady Di His Bride Next Year."

Whenever the press asked her directly about Charles, she smiled engagingly and was noncommittal. When the *Sunday Mirror* reported that Charles and Diana had an overnight liaison on the royal train in November 1980, the relationship was thrown onto a higher level. Because Diana's family members were part of the royal Court, the Queen actually demanded a retraction (which was denied) to protect both the reputation of Diana as an unsoiled innocent and the esteem of Charles who would not love and leave such a young flower. He was fond of Diana, but not in love. Yet, such actions showed how serious his family was about the romance and the impression it made on the press and the public.

Kay King, a friend from the Young England School where Diana taught kindergarten, claims that the press became so annoying that a decision was made to buy them off. The school would permit them one photo session with Diana Spencer if they would go away.

What emerged was the famous picture of Diana's long legs beneath the transparent voile skirt as she held two children in the gardens of St. George's Square. For a possible future princess it might seem a risqué shot. On the other hand, it demonstrated that the teacher had very nice legs. Was the session naïve or calculated? Diana had said that she would hate to be known as a girl who doesn't wear a slip. Yet, she didn't, and she posed outdoors in the light anyway. How could she not have known the effect? Cunningly coy?

Here again we are in dangerous territory. Probably the worst that could be said of the young Princess is that she flirted with her husband-to-be and with the members of the media who were interested in their relationship. Is flirting a type of manipulation? Many women will justifiably object to the idea that cunning or coyness plays a part in the way women represent themselves. On the other hand, it is a truism that in many traditional families very young women are encouraged to develop social skills, to learn charm. Is there anything harmful or manipulative in this? Few would say so. But when a celebrity, a star, exaggerates these skills to woo reporters or photographers we feel uncomfortable. The young Princess was always pushing the envelope of charm. Certainly she seemed willing to go further than other royals to play to the camera lens, to reveal her humanity to a wide public.

This provocative photo, the first of many pivotal images that would come to comprise the Diana lore, may have simultaneously prodded Charles toward commitment. Charles admired the picture. Lady Colin Campbell reports an ex-girlfriend of the Prince saying "Like most men, he's chuffed when people admire his woman."

From the media's point of view, Diana seemed to like the attention during this period, certainly more than Charles's previous flames had.

In November, Diana had revealed to Roger Tavener of the highly regarded Press Association News Agency that she'd like to marry soon, maybe the following year. "I don't think nineteen is too young. It depends on the person." He astutely followed up and asked if Charles had proposed. When her sister Sarah had been asked a similar question, she had said she'd turn Charles down. Diana knew better. Giggling and blushing, she replied: "I can't confirm or deny." The story was filed and spread to other news outlets like wildfire.

Shy Di. Already she was learning to pique the curiosity of the press. Recalled the sister-in-law of one of the courtiers at that time: ". . . the role of Princess of Wales required acting skills. Diana is a performer to put all the great divas in the shade."

Diana had carelessly shown her cards, which could have alienated the royal family and killed her chances with Charles. On the advice of her ambitious family, Diana denied the story, which in and of itself would not carry a lot of weight against the word of a respected journalist. But before the royal family's misgivings toward Diana could turn to ostracism, her mother, Frances—renowned for her public relations acumen—promptly penned an indignant letter to *The Times* of London, eviscerating Tavener's report and declaring Diana's innocence, while also subtly referring to her daughter's suitability as a royal bride.

Charles felt boxed in. "He could not get to know Diana better unless he saw more of her. And he could not see more of her without feeding the public's expectations as well as Diana's," wrote Lady Colin Campbell.

While touring India for eight weeks in November and December of 1990, Charles spoke off the record with British royal reporters about Diana. From a very early age, Charles had been aware that he must be extremely careful in his choice of a wife. Interviewed on television in his teens, he explained that his wife must do her job well or be criticized, reflecting badly on him and on the monarchy. But then, in his early thirties, there had been so many women in his life that making a choice must have seemed impossible.

Charles did not ardently court Diana. Was he temperamentally cold? He was himself a victim of the system. In the A&E *Biography* of Prince Charles, a friend, David Starkey, points out, "Most previous Princes of Wales were serial adulterers." Summarized a cousin of Charles's: "If it hadn't been for the press, the Prince of Wales would never have married Diana. They turned a perfectly ordinary, though attractive girl, with a pleasing but quite unexceptional personality, into a media superstar. To give her her due, she rose to the occasion magnificently." But playing to that image was the critical audition that landed Diana a role in the Windsor family's decades-long performance for the public.

At the time, the royal family was convinced that Diana fit the role for the Windsors' drama. Credentials: noble birth. Character: silent and compliant. Image: motherly. Look: stately (Prince Philip felt she would breed height into the family).

From the media's point of view, Diana suited another need: news. "She was clearly different than Charles's other loves," says Martin Lewis, a British-born television and radio commentator/humorist/writer/producer, now based in America, who has been a correspondent for the BBC and who co-anchored and co-produced *The Farewell to a Princess* live telecast of Diana's funeral for E! Entertainment Television. At the time of the courtship and engagement, Lewis was producing the first rock concert benefit for Amnesty International at Westminster Abbey.

Interviewed for this book, Lewis says: "Charles had been romancing women for ten years, but his girlfriends had been society debutantes, very hoity-toity, starchy, more like from the Tricia Nixon school. But this girl was young, pretty, and natural. The media seized on her with more fervor. They fanned the flames."

Diana was also swept up in the wave of the tabloids' coverage of the royals. "When Princess Margaret's marriage to Lord Snowden broke up, the media became titillated with their lives," Lewis explains. "When the rendezvous between Charles and Diana on the train was reported, the media was piqued more because having sex could now be implied. The British Press Commission admonished them, but from then on, another Pandora's box was open."

Finally, Diana's entry was perfect timing for what the public, the working class that read the tabloids in particular, needed from the monarchy. The fresh-faced girl who could be a queen-in-waiting was interpreted as a "metaphor for renewal" for the royal family itself and the country it symbolized, a country suffering from a lengthy economic depression. Diana nicely counterbalanced the strict, arch-conservative prime minister, Margaret Thatcher, who had come to power in the late 1970s.

After the 1960s' youthful boom, which included the worldwide Beatles craze, the 1970s were fraught with an oil crisis, a miners' strike that toppled a government, riots, and perennial debt. The working class gravitated to the punk movement, which reflected the stagnant and negative mood. In 1979, people were initially euphoric when Margaret Thatcher was elected prime minister. By the end of 1980, optimism waned as unemployment hit an all-time high (2.5 million and rising) and the longstanding gap between upper and lower classes widened further.

In Diana, the public—in particular the lower socio-economic class—saw hope for their own dreams to overcome their bleak lives and social status, according to Carole Willcocks, a former *People* and current *Entertainment Weekly* staffer. She lived in Cambridge, England, with her British husband between 1975 and 1978, and was visiting relatives there during the week of the wedding. In an interview for this book, she said: "In England, there is always this doom-and-gloom undertone about being less than royalty, aristocracy, or upper class. In America, you can transcend class distinctions. There aren't people to put a label on you. You can have a label, but you can wear it off. But in England you are branded forever, like a sheep. They knew Diana was a noblewoman, but she was young and not educated. She was a nanny and preschool teacher, not a graduate of Oxford or Cambridge. She was popular because she was unexceptional at that time. They looked at her and thought, 'I'm not special, but maybe I can have good luck too.'"

Diana's emergence resonated across the Atlantic as well. Unlike the British media and the royal family, America's national press almost immediately sensed a powerful media force. They saw in Diana a surface ordinariness, a requirement for popularity in a democracy, and a deeper star-power, a necessary quality for fame and celebrity—anyone's ticket into the upper echelons, despite birth.

"Think of her as the Girl Next Door, a blue-eyed blonde with peaches and Devonshire cream complexion," read the first words ever printed about Diana in *People* in an article about her engagement, announced on February 24, 1981.

The sentence was naïve, as was the girl—neither could have predicted the media icon. By April, *Time* magazine began to pick up the sensation she would become: "Center stage right now in history's longest running show is Lady Diana, who entered as an ingénue and was already a star before she got to the footlights."

Already, they were entranced with her illusion.

Diana was spellbound too, but by her own dreams. Incidents throughout the courtship and engagement should have alerted her to the reality of marriage with Charles.

Any woman with a clearer and stronger sense of self, including the right to be loved for who she is, would have heeded the messages and dumped Charles then. Previous girlfriend Anna Wallace had done just that. A girl with a strong spirit and direction, Anna wasn't taken with the status that came with being Princess of Wales.

Virtually everything one reads suggests that Diana was deeply, deeply in love with Charles. Was she in love with the illusion, with the fantasy? Who knows. Aren't we all trying to find wholeness, a way home, a way to transcend our past? To repair our past? Of course we are. And was she insightful enough to know it? Probably not. Diana mistook the drama taking place around her for the trappings of true affection. It looked like a fairy-tale romance: somewhere inside, true love must reside. It is sadly ironic that the same sort of packaging that Diana Spencer did so well herself is what confused her during her courtship with Charles.

These are common sentiments and motives of those with a narcissistic vulnerability, Dr. Solomon writes in *Narcissism and Intimacy*. They seek that perfect state, that existed only in the womb, in their relationships. "When there is a history of narcissistic failure or injury, a pathological state may arise in which there is a turning to others for a reparative experience, in a desperate longing for fusion and mirroring, for idealized love and romance."

Warning bells that this relationship was not to be the expected balm were ringing from the beginning. But having fallen in love with her fabrication of a marriage, an idealized picture that would suit her true needs for attention, nurturing, and support, Diana denied the signs. She ignored Charles's inattentive, even self-absorbed, behavior and tuned out her own inner voices and physical illness From the beginning, she was involved in substantial self-denial.

During her first official public engagement, Diana wore what felt natural and fashionably smart for a girl of her age and background—a black, silk taffeta ball gown, strapless, backless, and plunging. Charles chastised her for being inappropriate. She wore it anyway. Unknowingly, she broke royal protocol with the color and daring. Their altercation over this issue was an omen of the dynamics to come—his disapproval of her self-expression, her rebellion, and her subsequent seeking of attention and approval elsewhere. That night and thereafter, the media and the public found her breathtaking.

It was a grand illusion, one that the world clamored for, beginning with a wedding that was staged as a modern fairy tale.

CHAPTER 4

The Royals

> *"The British public want
> the Royal Family to continue
> in their conventional role as
> symbols of the national
> identity . . . [But] they no
> longer wish to be "led"
> by their leaders."*
>
> —Lady Colin Campbell
> *The Royal Marriages*

What was the illusion Diana was buying into when she married Charles? As a member of an old, noble family, Diana Spencer should have known as well as anyone the strengths and weaknesses of the monarchy and the royals. Her mother had been accused of breaking upper-class protocol by going public during her divorce proceedings. But Diana had been brought up to know how royalty behaves. However much the British public identified with her, she was as deeply a member of the ruling class as the Prince himself.

I've suggested that Diana could marry Charles only by denying her true nature. But though Charles would not make a good husband for her, she was well-matched to the royal family. Fundamentally she was not very different from them.

Diana adopted from the royals a great deal of what she knew about being a public figure. Her notion of public service—the importance of charity, the value of personal contact—was like theirs even after her divorce. But Diana had an ability to make personal contact with strangers and a need to act upon that ability. The idea of genuinely reaching out to members of a crowd had never occurred to members of the royal family.

The package that the Princess created for herself had many similarities to those that the royal families have created for themselves over the fifteen hundred years the British monarchy has existed.

The power of British monarchs was first compromised in the thirteenth century when the English king made a pact guaranteeing rights to freemen. During the English Renaissance, Tudor kings found that they had to accommodate the growing urban middle class. Members of the royal family began to be public figures as sovereign authority was being questioned by political, religious, and cultural forces. In his landmark book, *The Frenzy of Renown: Fame and Its History*, cultural historian Leo Braudy documents how, beginning with Henry VII, rulers who were previously born into power that went unquestioned began to find that they had to court their subjects in order to exalt their stature and hold on to their position.

The Tudor king consolidated his military defeat of rebels with extensive propaganda supporting his dynastic claims, as well as expanded royal administration and new economic policies. Son and successor, Henry VIII, used ceremony and spectacle to symbolically set himself up as the head of state over the Church of England during the Reformation. When Elizabeth I inherited the throne in 1558, she took to walking among the people, even attending plays to maintain her popularity and solidify her power. Before her accession to the throne, questions surfaced about her legitimacy. These doubts, fed by conflicts between Roman Catholics, Puritans, Presbyterians, and members of the new institutional Church of England, fueled Mary

Queen of Scots' claims to the throne. Furthermore, Queen Elizabeth I contended with the growing notion of democratic rule. She tried to censor the popular history play *Richard II,* in which Shakespeare dramatizes the human impossibility of being a monarch. "Kingship in Shakespeare's theater is always a role. Some play their parts well, others badly, depending on their personal nature and their grasp of how a king ought to act," Braudy writes. By the seventeenth century, a monarch would hold on to his or her seat only by convincing the public of fitness, not just by dazzling them.

Thus began what Braudy terms the "democratization of fame." Power is attained and maintained through public approval of the monarch's command of the part. As an image-maker, Elizabeth I identified herself with England. Her successor in 1603, James I, disseminated his own writings and propaganda about divine rule. Caught up in struggles with Parliament over finances and the establishment of the Church of England, Charles I was beheaded in 1649 and the monarchy was replaced by a commonwealth led by the Lord Protector, Oliver Cromwell. Monarchy was restored in 1660 in the person of the colorful King Charles I. But when Charles's brother, King James II, was removed from the throne in 1688, Parliament once more exerted control. Struggles for power between the kings and Parliament continued throughout the reigns of William and Mary and Queen Anne. These ended in 1714, when Queen Anne died without issue and the German prince, George I, came to the throne as the first member of the House of Hanover. Elizabeth II is a direct descendant of George I.

Though the name of the royal family has changed through marriage and for political expediency (the royal family adopted the very English name Windsor during World War I), the character of the family has remained remarkably the same. George I was a German princeling from the small state of Hanover who spoke no English when he came to the throne. A Scottish folk song of the period says, in translation:

> Oh what the devil have we gotten for a king
> but a wee, wee, German lord?
> And when we went to bring him home
> he was digging in his yard.
> Shucking kale
> and laying leeks
> in his long hose and his britches
> —his beggar's duds.

It goes on for four or five more unflattering verses. The English monarchs from that time on have maintained the appearance of modesty, rootedness, ordinariness. To be sure, George III was flamboyant if not completely crazy. Edward VII was colorful and sophisticated but personally corrupt. The model English monarch of the past three centuries was Queen Victoria—dour, sober, unflamboyant, and matriarch of a huge family. Even after she became Empress of India, she continued to work hard to establish herself as the quintessential English wife.

From the beginning, the House of Windsor was built on a carefully constructed illusion.

To make the monarchy appear even less imperial, George V decided to project the Windsors as the family next door, only enlarged, given the size of their house. He allowed the royal children to marry commoners, meaning anyone outside of royalty, with noble titles or not. The first such marriage was between his second-born son, Albert (King George VI), and Elizabeth Bowes-Lyon, a daughter of a Scottish earl. George V was well-liked because of his simplicity, decency, and plain tastes. The empire expanded during his reign.

It was required that royal brides be virgins. A constitutional crisis was precipitated when King Edward VIII expressed his wish to marry a divorcée. In 1936, Edward abdicated so he could marry his beloved Wallis Simpson. He was rejected by the family and by the public because she was a garish, unabashedly high-living American—and twice divorced. The monarchs were expected to embody family virtues. Divorce was antithetical to family stability.

Charles was old enough to remember how Edward VIII, his great-uncle, was essentially exiled from the family for marrying Wallis, even after he stepped down. The new King George VI wanted to keep Edward, who had been a beloved heir, out of England to avoid a competing Court. Edward was assigned to be governor of the Bahamas and titled Duke of Windsor, but Wallis—at the insistence of George's wife, the new queen consort (today's Queen Mother)— was denied the title Her Royal Highness because her divorced status forbade entry into the royal circle. The Duke and Duchess of Windsor were banned from Princess Elizabeth's wedding. Neither attended Queen Elizabeth II's coronation.

The coldness shown by the royal family toward the Duke and Duchess of Windsor has often been represented as a sort of priggishness, proof that the royals couldn't tolerate something so revolutionary as true love. It is often overlooked that after his abdication Edward was very friendly with many Britons and Europeans who sympathized with the Nazis. It is probable, in fact, that out of pique or stupidity, the former king may have been a traitor. In any case, Queen Elizabeth knew that her uncle was a troubled if not dangerous man. And later, when the marriage of Diana and Charles was dissolving, she may have been aware of the danger of having any sort of Court in exile.

The Queen Mother, Elizabeth Bowes-Lyon, became the master myth-maker for the family once her husband, George VI, ascended the throne in 1936 after his brother's abdication. Though she cultivated a dull, middle-class, domestic image by posing for pictures serving tea and walking dogs, Elizabeth also used pageantry—feathers, a radiant smile, soft voice, curtsies, uniforms, horses—to move hearts. She would wave at crowds as she drove by with the comfortable affability of a film star. In earlier times, the royal family had often relied on public ceremony to strengthen its position. Bowes-Lyon translated old-style pageantry for the age of radio and film. She worked against the royal family's institutional dowdiness, cultivating the fantasy of royalty, which was to behave splendidly.

She showed considerable courage during the Blitz. Instead of fleeing to the countryside, the royal family set an example of courage and loyalty by staying at Buckingham Palace. The King and Queen even made public appearances. Princesses Elizabeth and Margaret spoke on the radio. In photographs they wear sweaters and look like bourgeois schoolchildren.

The media, part of the Establishment in England as in America, kept quiet about the problems of the royal family (drinking, gambling, shady politics).

In the late 1940s, in an economic recession, weakened by the war, with a Labour government overseeing the dismantling of the empire, the royal family was put to the test of keeping up morale. Again, they relied on public relations, producing an extravagant pageant for the wedding of Princess Elizabeth and Prince Philip in 1947.

When Princess Elizabeth became Queen Elizabeth II in 1952 after the death of her father, George VI, she ushered the monarchy into the media age. Her 1953 coronation was televised, the first time the ceremony had been seen by ordinary people. Though still adored from afar, the new Queen was nevertheless closer to the people.

Despite an onslaught of newspaper and magazine photo spreads of the young Queen and her family, later in the 1950s the image began to crack a little. Following Princess Margaret's escapades with a divorced man, Group Captain Peter Townsend, the media reported that her marriage to a divorced man would damage the institution of the monarchy, a national symbol of proper family life. Margaret ended the affair. Meanwhile, the Queen was being criticized for being elitist and out of touch. In 1957, she responded by televising her annual Christmas message to the nation for the first time.

The royal family image was further altered in the 1960s when Margaret married photographer Anthony Armstrong-Jones. Clubbing and mixing with actors, artists, and rockstars, she was considered cool, glamorous—the Diana of her day. Paparazzi followed her, even photographing her in bathing suits. Editors obliged when the Palace instructed them not to buy the pictures, but some media began to satirize the awe in which the royal family had long been held.

In 1969, to further promote the family image, the Queen decided to open up to the people even more with a documentary about the royal family's daily life at home—decorating the Christmas tree, enjoying picnics, and the like. That same year, Charles's investiture as Prince of Wales was televised. In 1972, to celebrate her twenty-fifth wedding anniversary, the Queen and her family walked outside Westminster Abbey, where a commemorative service was held, and mingled and talked with the crowds outside—the first royal walkabout since the war. The Queen spoke about the importance of family life. (Shortly thereafter, she asked for a pay raise—which is subsidized by taxes—even though a million people were out of work.) The next year, Princess Anne married Mark Phillips.

A flaw in the exemplary royal performance surfaced with Princess Margaret's affair and subsequent divorce. But, by the end of the 1970s, that was passed over, the family became humdrum again, and the people were bored. "Charles was getting balder, Princess Anne was married, Prince Andrew wasn't doing a lot. There was no real royal who was particularly interesting," recalls Richard Stott, former *Daily Mirror* editor.

"Come 1979 or so . . . the Queen was going on a royal tour—I think to Scandinavia—and no one went at all. No one. No television, no newspapers, not even the Press Association. And this was seen as terrible because there's one thing worse than having yourself pried into and that's not being bothered about at all."

Into this vacuum, as if in answer to the needs of the British public, stepped Diana. Her public had been waiting for her for a long time. They were eager and forgiving. Their affection for her instructed her—as did the examples of the royal family—as to what kind of princess she should be.

Television Star, Princess Bride

July 29, 1981. Scenes of a royal wedding: The monarchy is staging its first major event in the era of modern media. The virgin bride is riding in a glass coach, waving at the nearly one million cheering celebrants lining the two-mile processional route past monuments and buildings that mark Britain's historical triumphs and tragedies.

This was a worldwide promotional event for Britain, with its royal family as central symbol. The Commonwealth spared no expense. The royal Court worked with the BBC and ITV to set up 120 cameras rigged by 750 miles of cable at strategic locations (twenty-one in St. Paul's Cathedral alone). Three communications satellites over the Indian and Atlantic oceans beamed the BBC's feed of the images to eighty-one foreign broadcasting companies, from Sweden to Japan to Zambia. For almost eight hours, the airwaves were saturated with commentary in thirty-four languages.

Though the three U.S. networks shared the BBC feed, the competition remained fierce to capture the attention of the fifty-five million Americans expected to watch the nuptials. At a reported cost of $5 million, the networks dispatched some 450 staffers, including top commentators, correspondents, producers, and technicians, and deployed two dozen cameras at carefully selected positions along the route to get exclusive shots of in-your-face arresting moments. NBC's *Today Show* built an open-air studio across from Buckingham Palace and broadcast from there for an entire week.

In an attempt to match the stunning visual story, the print press came out en masse too. Almost one thousand foreign journalists operated out of the Overseas Press Center on St. James's Street, which was equipped with fifty typewriters, 126 telephone lines, and eleven telex machines—a far cry from today's technology but a feat for the time. Calling itself *The Royal Sun* for the big week, *The Sun* stationed forty reporters with walkie-talkies along the processional route. *Die Aktuelle,* the West German women's magazine, ferried its reporters and photographers around in two planes, two helicopters, two speedboats on the Thames River, and a fleet of cars and bicycles.

Here's what we saw:

An ivory taffeta gown of handsewn silk (spun by worms at the only silk farm in England) with romantic poufed sleeves, pearls, and antique lace. An aerial view of the twenty-five-foot-long train—the longest in royal history—stretching over the steps of the 271-year-old St. Paul's Cathedral where Diana was about to take her vows. A joyous and moving program comprised of the music of Handel, Purcell, and Jeremiah Clarke, and performed by three orchestras, three choirs, and Royal Opera soprano Kiri Te Kanawa. After conducting the rites, the Archbishop of Canterbury rejoicing to a congregation twenty-five-hundred strong, with most of the monarchs of Europe, multitudes of government leaders, and diplomats from around the world: "Here is the stuff of which fairy tales are made. . . ." The Princess leaning forward to kiss the Prince on the balcony of Buckingham Palace, where they also posed for official wedding-day pictures; Charles in his admiral's uniform leaning down to kiss an adoring Diana, her billowing skirt accenting a bowed position.

These are the images that were satellited to television viewers in seventy-four countries on the cusp of high noon that day in London, making the wedding of the Prince and Princess of Wales the most watched event in history to that date. Roughly 750 million tuned in, about one-fifth of the world's population at the time. *Time*'s Jay Cocks dubbed the occasion "the century's greatest, grandest nuptial, the sort of love story Hollywood doesn't make anymore and the kind of spectacle it can't even afford anymore." Declared actor Richard Burton: "No Hollywood production could have matched what I saw today."

The wedding captured front-page headlines worldwide. It also generated news within the discipline and business of print journalism. Japan's *Yomiuri Shimbun,* the largest newspaper in the world (circulation: eight million), deemed the wedding story important enough to rush in a color photo midway through its evening press run. *The Economist* had a color news page for the first time in its 138-year history. Even the London *Times,* long known as the Gray Lady for its predominance of copy, published a color photograph of the royal couple as a souvenir front page on the Thursday, the day after the wedding.

Why the media rage and audience demand worldwide? For one thing, weddings in general mark a timeless, common, human feeling of new beginnings, new hope. What Walter Bagehot, the eminent British economist and journalist, wrote almost one hundred years previously apparently still held true: "A princely marriage is the brilliant edition of a universal fact, and as such it rivets mankind."

The event was produced as a fairy tale, and fairy tales speak to the human desire to transcend the tedium of everyday life. Our weariness and discontent come from buying into fear and not moving beyond our inertia to make a difference in our own lives and the lives of others. That's why we go to the movies, to see people act out what we wish we had the courage to do, to see the ordinary attain the extraordinary. Diana was the protagonist in this familiar, inspirational tale of transcendence.

The pageantry—with the Prince, the coaches, the gown, the jewels—hearkened back to the medieval lore of King Arthur's Camelot, the ideal of chivalry. It represented a golden age far removed from the squalor and meanness of twentieth century life. In fact, as I pointed out earlier, the wedding celebrated traditional values: elderly women aristocrats like Ruth Fermoy had picked a bride for Charles because it was time he settled down. They picked a pretty virgin, one who seemed unlikely to make demands. The demands and opportunities of Prince Charles's life aren't like those of most. But, in his bowing to social pressure to give up his bachelorhood, many could identify with him.

Why would Britain splash the royal nuptials around the globe? One answer was less obvious to the viewer, but made good business sense to the Crown and the government: to advance the country's enormous tourist trade, upwards of $10 billion annually—a substantial sum for a country in economic straits. The royal historical sites—the Tower of London and the Crown Jewels, to name a few—and quaint ceremonies surrounding the royal life, such as the changing of the guard, attract visitors from around the globe. London is a top destination for flush Americans in particular. The wedding alone was expected to bring in $200 million from souvenirs and $440 million more in tourism.

A second, even less apparent reason was to bolster the badly wounded British pride. During the previous generation, Britain, for centuries the most powerful nation on earth, had ceased to exert much economic or political influence anywhere. The country had had to settle for less wealth as it dealt with aging industrial plants, war-depleted natural resources, and an agricultural base that produced only half the nation's food needs. In rebuilding, it did not fair well compared with competitors like West Germany, France, and Japan. Even traditional British luxury goods, such as autos, liquor, and clothing, faced strong competition.

Time's Jay Cocks described the wedding as "a fairy tale of present pomp and past glory, a last page from the tattered book of empire with the gold leaf still intact." But no one put it more succinctly than Mike Burgneay, then twenty-one and of Forest Hill, who camped overnight outside Buckingham Palace to ensure a good sightline: "We may be down, but if we can put on a wedding like this, we certainly aren't finished. This shows the rest of the world that Britain can still pull it off."

Diana, in particular, emerged as Britain's new world star, the best since the Beatles—something not anticipated by the royal family. This was partly because the bride at any wedding is automatically considered the main attraction. But *People*, which launched celebrity journalism in America in the 1970s, saw her as more than a bride—she was a celebrity. She was "a godsend antidote to a dysfunctional royal family," said *People* creator Richard Stolley when interviewed for this book.

Britain anointed Diana its star too. As the first English noblewoman to marry an heir apparent since 1660, Diana was viewed as a rare, if not extinct, English commodity at the time. Her children would also be the first royals to combine the disparate threads of the Stuart and Hanoverian lines, thereby fusing the old and new royal families.

But from the time of the wedding onward, it was clear that Diana's popularity would exceed that of the royal family. Could they have co-opted and controlled her? Apparently they didn't think to try.

Entertainment Weekly's Carole Willcocks, also a trained psychotherapist, explains the sociopolitical-economic psychology behind the public sentiment at that time: "Britain may have lost its world status, but it could still deal with what was under its own feet, what grew on its land. For example, England was always proud of its big, very round apples. But when it joined the European Common Market in 1973, there was a standard that the apples had to conform to. Suddenly, the apples had to be a certain size—smaller. Another blow to the pride. Not only did it lose control of its empire, but it lost control of its own backyard. Britain had to adapt its products to the Common Market regulations if it wanted to make money. The royal wedding was something the British could toot their own horn about. And Diana was a British product that no one could touch—or so people thought. She was their well-rounded apple."

The romantic pageantry—with the new bride and queen-in-waiting as the reason for its being—infused the British with a badly needed sense of continuity, escape, and hope during tumultuous times.

Americans are often enamored of the exterior glamour of royalty and its elite position. But they are generally mystified by the importance placed on an inherited institution that holds little political power, yet consumed in 1980, for example, an estimated $25 million to support royal households and other expenses, such as yachts, jets, and helicopters.

For the British, however, the monarchy has always represented continuity and stability, a "gold filling in a mouthful of decay," as playwright John Osborne wrote. "Governments may go, leaders may change, but the royal family is forever," says writer-broadcaster Martin Lewis. Decades earlier, economist and journalist Walter Bagehot defined the Court's role: to set an example of how to live, a mirror of national virtues. As "head of society," the Court should be the center for congregation of interesting people other than politicians, those from the literary, scientific, and philosophical worlds. As the "head of our morality," the Court should set a standard of personal behavior.

At the time, the Windsors, and in particular the Queen, were viewed with tremendous respect, even if the aristocracy was derided for resting and living on unearned laurels. A survey published in the liberal *Guardian* newspaper the week before the wedding showed that seventy-six percent of those polled felt the advantages of the monarchy outweighed its costs; sixty-seven percent considered the bundle being lavished on the wedding to be money well spent.

Many still remembered and admired the royal family's courage and loyalty during World War II. Furthermore, Queen Elizabeth II was thought to have some political clout. Reading all government papers thoroughly, she gave her opinions on policy to the prime minister at weekly private meetings, even though the royal family believes it must avoid all political controversy in public. British journalist and author Charles Douglas-Home calls this potential for power the Queen's "presence," enhanced by her long reign of twenty-eight years. In that time, she had gained considerable experience in government affairs, while prime ministers, a total of eight in her time, had come and gone.

"In a modern age of social dislocation," wrote Carole Willcocks in her wedding coverage for the *National Catholic Register* in the United States, "the British monarchy is somewhat like the papacy— it's a spiritual and emotional anchor."

Actor Peter Ustinov described the enthusiasm for the royal family and the day's events as a primal need for public pomp and ceremony. When NBC's anchorman John Chancellor asked Ustinov, a hired commentator, why the British people loved the royal family so, he quipped that it was the same drive that makes them "rip out seats at football matches. I think they're trying to find their origins."

The joining of Charles and Diana offered the British a chance to band together as well, despite hardships, renewing their spirits. Those hardships were economic; almost three million, or twelve percent of the work force, were unemployed. There was also social unrest. Just that week, rioting in Liverpool's Toxteth district had erupted, and one youth was run down by a police van and killed—the most recent example, at that time, of months of frightening rioting, looting, and arson in industrialized urban centers fraught with youth unemployment hovering at fifty percent. "It looked like civil war for two or three days," Martin Lewis recalls.

Finally, the hardships were political uncertainty. That week, in Northern Ireland, a seventh Irish Republican Army hunger-striker died in an anti-British-rule protest that had been going on for a month and a half.

Within this context, says Martin Lewis, "the wedding was a beacon of hope. Because of the timing, it was imbued with greater significance in Britain."

The wedding also proved a seminal event in modern media culture. Everything that Diana represented suited the criteria for a global icon that the masses would embrace and the media could exploit.

To begin with, Diana was beautiful. She looked like a fairy princess. The value of physical beauty is timeless and universal. In addition to its purely sexual appeal, beauty nourishes the creative, intuitive, and spiritual needs of human nature.

Moreover, beauty is becoming an emotional lifeline in the impersonal information and technology age. In the 1980s, the personal computer put emphasis on speed and data over human contact. Beauty, then—especially in the form of a visual image on the television screen and in newspaper and magazine photographs—is all we have to delight and invigorate the heart and soul. And it is fleeting.

"Beauty feeds us," says Nancy Friday, author of *The Power of Beauty*. In her book, Friday discusses how pretty babies, the Gerber babies with dimpled cheeks and puckered lips, get picked up first, are held more, and have their needs attended to before other babies, citing studies with professional caregivers in day-care centers and pediatric wards. Come adolescence and the rage of hormones, pretty children get picked up first, again . . . and this continues until the fading of youth.

Diana possessed the right kind of beauty to satisfy the appetites of the contemporary masses worldwide: accessible—to men, women, and children. "She was pretty in a pristine, virginal way, like a butterfly emerging," Friday told me. "What allowed men and women to dote on her was that she had no sexual element. She was not erotic, she didn't have big breasts. She didn't arouse envy. Nothing divides, especially women, more than high sexual quotient. We love that winsome, fragile beauty more. Diana had that pure beauty."

Howard Dickman, assistant managing editor for *Reader's Digest*, expressed the same sentiment to me: "A huge amount of her appeal was due to her good looks, and I would add non-threatening good looks. She didn't have the kind of Hollywood-star looks that would piss women off. As for men, she was attractive but she wasn't so attractive that you would say 'Give me a break!'"

Diana also reflected a democratic quality that characterized modern fame. Before the American and French revolutions, fame in authoritarian societies was reserved for those born and bred in the upper reaches of social hierarchies—royalty and nobility. But with the advent of governments by the people, and more equal opportunity to make a better life for oneself, one could rise from obscurity and become famous through individual achievement that is acknowledged as worthy—and this is crucial—by the populace. Audience acceptance of the famous person as one of the crowd is key to the longevity of a famous person in modern times, because it supports the aspiration of the individual in the audience to have his or her own piece of the pie. We first got to know Diana as an assistant kindergarten teacher living with a couple of friends. Giggly and naïve. In a way, she succeeded by failing. Some of her success was just luck and timing and the forces of a complex universe.

By bridging the old and new standards, Diana became and remained an intriguing character on the world stage. "Even though she was an aristocrat, her relationship with Charles was a Cinderella story. She was an assistant kindergarten teacher plucked out by the Prince to be married," said cultural historian and author Leo Braudy when interviewed for this book. "She maintained this popularity even though she came from a family with a longer lineage in England than the Windsors. She had the mystique of wealth, yet was one of us."

Time's president E. Bruce Hallett also noted this blend of contradictory qualities. Writing about the wedding for the magazine, he said, "Diana stole one of the grandest shows of the century in a wedding that marked her as both impossibly glamorous and a kind of universal Every Woman."

Rich in heritage while possessing contemporary celebrity traits, Diana became the icon of an event that also represented the best of the past and present. Wrote Tom Shales in the *Washington Post:* "Even if one felt satiated by coverage of the wedding before the telecast began, something about this merger of 20th century technology and age-old tradition was captivating and moving."

In addition, Diana proved at the wedding to have tremendous merchandising value, another way to gauge the audience's embrace of a famous person in our celebrity culture. If the masses are willing to spend money on products associated with the person, then that person has hit the jackpot of modern stardom.

The prime example that foreshadowed the Diana commodity craze: the fascination swirling around her wedding dress and the meteoric business success of the designers, David and Elizabeth Emanuel.

In business only three years and located in a small shop at 26A Brook Street in London, the married couple had been known for their custom-made evening dresses and wedding gowns for British nobility. Hardly couture. They had designed the black, silk taffeta, strapless dress that Diana wore for her first public appearance with Charles.

After the announcement that Diana chose the Emanuels to design her gown, crowds began gathering on the street below their second-story shop. As a precaution against enterprising photographers with long lenses who would steal a shot of the dress in progress, they kept their window shades lowered until the day of the wedding.

Nevertheless, in the heat of competition to scoop a story that could sell a lot of newspapers, *Women's Wear Daily* printed a drawing of the gown the day before the wedding. The sketch turned out to be a fraud, but publisher John Fairchild didn't care: "We said this could be a hoax before we ran it," he said. "I thought it made a very amusing story."

As soon as they saw the dress, London bridal designers began to make knockoffs. A polyester version was in a Debenhams department store by early afternoon the day of the wedding.

Beauty. A democratic image. Merchandising value. All were qualities evident at the wedding, and all met the criteria for a global icon. Signs that Diana's popularity and somewhat trivial life story would perfectly suit the modern media age were apparent throughout the television coverage of the wedding.

Wedding commentary hinted at the future trend toward behind-the-mask coverage of celebrities' personal lives, which would ultimately turn Diana's life into a public soap opera. NBC anchorman John Chancellor rebuffed a BBC interview with Charles and

Diana, days before the wedding, in which they revealed little more than gratitude "for all the kind wishes." He said, "Correspondents tend to tiptoe through interviews with royalty in this country." When asked about the in-your-face shots along the processional route, then ABC News executive producer Robert Siegenthaler explained: "The British feed tends to be stately rather than close-up and personal. Ours has a more 'people' feel to it."

Like so much of today's media coverage, a lot of the wedding coverage was trivial, inane, silly, and in poor taste, in attempts even by the most heavy-duty journalists to be entertaining. But the photos were beautiful and affecting.

July 28 and 29, 1981. Bonfires blazing on a hundred and one hilltops across the kingdom. Skyrockets of gold, silver, red, and blue shooting through the London sky. Thousands in Hyde Park agog over Britain's largest pyrotechnic display in two centuries, modeled on the show staged in 1749 to mark the end of the War of the Austrian Succession. A finale that consumed two and a half tons of explosives in eighteen minutes, and included a gigantic Catherine wheel that rose 170 feet above the park, spurting multicolored fire from its rim. Campers sleeping overnight along the processional route. Strangers of all colors dancing in the streets around St. Paul's, and a Maori singer trilling to rapt East End youths through the loud speakers from a parish church. Grand soirées, hotel wedding galas, festive pub parties—in London and all through England.

And Diana saying "I do."

The Shadow Bridegroom

> *"The most daunting aspect*
> *was the media attention,*
> *because my husband and I, we*
> *were told when we got engaged*
> *that the media would go*
> *quietly, and it didn't."*
>
> —Diana Princess of Wales
> BBC *Panorama* interview

There was a third, perhaps equal partner in the royal wedding. The shadow bridegroom, which ultimately became more important to Diana than Charles, was the media, personified by Rupert Murdoch.

Owner of the tabloids *News of the World* and *The Sun* since 1969, Murdoch bought *The Times* and the *Sunday Times* in 1981, making him the most powerful press baron in Britain. To many, it seemed that his mandate to editors must have been to undermine the fuddy-duddy Britain and its monarchy, which represented a stratified class system that withheld opportunities from everyone and thus economically harmed the country. The Murdoch press's attacks on the monarchy influenced the tone of all the tabloid press coverage.

For decades, royals had maintained their power through mystery; they never talked to reporters. But to lay the groundwork for a royal pay raise, Queen Elizabeth opened the door for intrusion in

1969 with the first "informal" royal documentary. That same year, Murdoch also directed his editors at *The Sun* and *News of the World* to "stop worshipping these people, stop treating them as gods. They are ordinary human beings and will help sell newspapers," recounts Harry Arnold, former *Sun* reporter.

Through the 1970s, coverage of the royals became increasingly personal. The press diligently reported on Princess Margaret's failing marriage and romantic affairs. Prince Philip participated in an authorized 1971 biography, Basil Boothroyd's book *Philip: An Informal Biography.* In the 1980s, royal family members appeared on talk shows and cooperated with authors. Princess Margaret collaborated with gossip columnist Nigel Dempster on the 1981 bestseller about her loves and marriage, and royal books by Charles, Andrew, Princess Michael, and Fergie also came out in the 1980s. Once Princess Anne had separated from Mark Phillips in 1989, and Fergie's toe-sucking and topless shenanigans were reported in the early 1990s, "there was no way to put the genie back in the bottle," British-born writer-broadcaster Martin Lewis adds.

"Diana was the antithesis of the punk movement," explains Martin Lewis. "And Diana had a glamour. She was also the same age as [the popular bands of the time, such as Culture Club with lead singer] Boy George, who was [a] flamboyant [cross-dresser]; Wham, with their fantastic clothes; and the globetrotting Duran Duran. She became a part of that culture. She wore low-cut dresses, she was sexy. The media went crazy and swept her up in this. They treated her like a pop singer, a member of a pop aristocracy, and I think she enjoyed it." Certainly no public figure in the Thatcher years could match her style.

Throughout the decade Murdoch's *Sun* and *Daily Mirror* were battling for readership. Their usual currency had been stories about bishops caught with actresses in salacious situations, and the like.

They had never been celebrity-driven, except when it came to the Beatles. "But Diana's rise coincided with the new boom in tabloid journalism," Lewis explains, noting that by 1992 London had eleven daily newspapers. Competition grew stiff. "Her mass awareness and popularity was due to repetitive coverage. She became an icon by repetition. Diana was the first MTV-generation royal."

Time's Jay Cocks, when describing her appeal as early as the wedding, noted how Diana's image had bridged the trendy and the traditional: ". . . Diana's seemingly paradoxical quality of patrician funkiness has caught the spirit of a generation that fancies itself a little more romantic than those of the '70s and '60s and acts, at least outwardly, a good deal more conservatively."

From the wedding onward, the media made a haul on Diana and her every move—positive and negative—without a hint of remorse. The gold mines were the rumors about the troubled marriage and Diana's health, which the media had been reporting as early as 1982.

In the late 1980s, the Palace chastised the press for harming the marriage. Media reaction was that of incredulity. In the PBS *Frontline* documentary "The Princess and the Press," Simon Jenkins, former editor of *The Times*, recalls: "Our response at the time was, 'You invited massive, blanketed, intrusive publicity into this relationship. Now that it is going wrong, you say 'lay off'? As a human being you say yes, but on behalf of the press pool . . . the only better thing than a love story is a love story gone wrong."

In trying to justify their relentless pursuit of celebrities, the media moguls typically took the high ground, arguing that the public had "a right to know." Rupert Murdoch's tabloid *Daily Telegraph* pointed out that given the perception that the public desired "every morsel of information about her life," the craving for images of her in the world marketplace was voracious.

Diana's ascendancy coincided with a period of radical change in media practice. The scramble to hold on to viewers, combined with limited real news, generated more fallout: tabloidization of the mainstream media.

Lance Morrow writes in the *Columbia Journalism Review:* "More and more competitive with one another, harassed by bottom-lining business offices, hungrier and hungrier for material, they are increasingly tempted to plunge profitably into the emotional goo, as with Diana, or else, as with Marv Albert, to elevate private pornographic moments to the status of public events."

Several decades ago, the media knew President Franklin Delano Roosevelt was paralyzed and used a wheelchair and was having an affair, but photographers didn't steal shots of him obviously seated in his wheelchair or meeting with Lucy Mercer, nor did reporters write about details of his personal life. They were preoccupied with bread lines, unemployment, the New Deal, and war-torn Europe. Newspapers and magazines made money covering those issues. *Life,* in particular, profited handsomely reporting on World War II. Survival at home and abroad were widespread concerns. Not quite twenty years later, despite the added competition of television and satellite technology, the media kept silent about President John F. Kennedy's rampant sexual liaisons, which were widely known. That's because they were immersed in the U.S./Soviet tensions: the space race, Bay of Pigs, the Cuban missile crisis. Survival concerns remained keen.

But times, values, media economics, and media technology have changed seismically, prompting "many heretofore 'respectable' media to stop raking the muck and start playing in it," *Los Angeles Times* media critic David Shaw told the *Columbia Journalism Review.*

The preoccupation with the private lives of celebrities—the willingness to treat such stories as "news"—was introduced into the tabloid media in Britain and Australia by Rupert Murdoch in the 1970s and became even more prominent in the 1980s when he bought *The Times*. Murdoch brought his brand of journalism to the United States when he purchased the *New York Post* in 1976. That, along with the launch of tabloid television here, began to change the landscape for the mainstream media.

Murdoch's political and personal agenda is complicated. He's Australian by birth, conservative, antimonarchical. His marriage to the same woman lasted for decades, but in business he is a risk-taker. In *Newsweek*, Bill Powell and Carolyn Friday define him as a typical tycoon: "Think of tycoons as the stunt men of commerce." Routinely, when he acquires a paper like the *New York Post* or the *Chicago Sun Times*, veteran journalists resign. (The late columnist Mike Royko, who defected to the *Chicago Tribune*, wrote that "no self-respecting fish would be wrapped in a Murdoch newspaper.") Both in his acquisitions (which also include Twentieth-Century Fox) and in the editorial policies of his newspapers, Murdoch doesn't draw a hard-and-fast line between entertainment and news.

There is little dispute about the way Murdoch's papers have operated in Great Britain. *Time* magazine reported that the editor of a rival paper said in 1984, "It gets worse editorially and better commercially. Fleet Street knows they pinch stories and put words in people's mouths, and their intrusion into privacy, particularly of the Royal Family, is second to none."

The rude treatment of the royals soon spread elsewhere. Beginning in the mid-1980s, a host of sensational stories made their way into the mainstream media after their initial splash in the tabloids. Among them: Bill Clinton and Gennifer Flowers, Erik and Lyle Menendez, Tonya Harding and Nancy Kerrigan, John and Lorena Bobbitt, Amy Fisher and Joey Buttafuoco, William Kennedy Smith, Heidi Fleiss, Michael Jackson.

The turning point came with the O. J. Simpson story. That's when mainstream journalists "were ready to plunge into the fray, to try to be first rather than rushing frantically to be second after having waited in stately silence while the tabloids broke the stories," wrote media critic David Shaw in the *Los Angeles Times*. It was, he continued, *The Star* and *Hard Copy* that first reported the contents of O. J. Simpson's statement to the police days after the murders of his ex-wife, Nicole Brown, and her friend Ronald Goldman.

The O. J. Simpson story proved a ratings and circulation bonanza. Some one hundred million Americans watched the reading of the verdict in 1996. In 1998, television screens, newspapers, magazines, radio waves, and the Internet were awash in the latest on Monica Lewinsky and Kathleen Willey and their alleged sexual encounters with President Clinton at the White House. And in February 1998, the king of spectacle, the *Jerry Springer Show*—known for on-air brawls and the display of fetal sonograms—became the first syndicated talk show to beat out *The Oprah Winfrey Show* since Oprah became number one in 1987. This is significant, given that Oprah Winfrey made a conscious decision to take the high road in content in the last few years.

In *Time* magazine, James Collins attempted to explain the success: "No doubt someone has a Theory of All Squalor stating that as politics becomes entertainment, and entertainment becomes reality, and reality becomes politics, then the leap from Monica Lewinsky to Jerry Springer is, well, something or other."

Crime and sex. That's what captures people's attention. That's what media across the board have learned in the last two decades, attests Howard Rosenberg of the *Los Angeles Times*. "People give lip service to wanting more quality information, yet how can one blame the media for putting out crime and sex if people have shown an interest in it?"

Time Inc.'s Dan Okrent concurs. It's the 11:00 P.M. local news, he says, that sets the agenda for even the national news more than anything else because the foreign news is not there and the networks and major newsmagazines don't think the audience is interested.

In 1965, when Okrent was a copy boy at the *Detroit Free Press,* he recalls that "every daily newspaper in America prepared their list of stories by whatever was above the fold of the front page of the *New York Times.* Today, local television sets the agenda. And that is determined by what people want to talk about at the water cooler. It's not important news like interest rates, balance of payments, health care, primary education. That's boring. Rather, it's scandal and mayhem."

Fundamentalist religion and science fiction do well, Time Inc. editor-in-chief Norman Pearlstine told me. This doesn't mean journalism as a whole is deteriorating these days, Pearlstine adds. "It is always on a slippery slope. There are always examples of media excess and unprofessionalism and so forth. But why has *Time* not had a cover story on Bosnia in the last year? Is Diana really worth two covers when Bosnia got none? Why has *Newsweek* done Paula Jones twice? To a large degree, media is responsive to public demand, sure. With its five international editions, *Time* probably hosts sixty to seventy pages of world-class international news that it doesn't run domestically. That's not because the [domestic] editors are tawdry, immoral, or irresponsible. It is because in business you make judgments to some degree on what your customers are."

This is not necessarily good, editors admit. But the audience preference should not be surprising either, for these types of stories have touched a primal chord for centuries. *Entertainment Weekly*'s Richard Sanders reminded me when I asked for his opinion: "Sensationalism goes back to the Greek tragedies, which were about murder, crime, lust, fate—basic emotional stories—not about policy or taxes. People are fascinated by stories that touch on life-and-death issues. Reflection on their own mortality arouses interest and holds them."

The audience's choices also reflect their own decline in values, believes Cindy Adams, a columnist for Murdoch's *New York Post.* Interviewed for this book, she said: "Society has changed. The world has evolved a separate morality. People are having babies without being married. People talk about their drug problems. People are doing on screen and in public what I have never seen my husband do in private. There is no refinement left. No privacy. So the art in every society mirrors the society. Did you ever see people naked in the news before? Or four-letter words in Broadway shows? Or people without clothes on the stage?"

But doesn't the media's attention to these base drives further corrupt morals? Maybe, maybe not. Hard to know who started the cycle. Senior editor Bruce Handy, who writes the pop-culture column, Spectator, for *Time* magazine, explained it to me this way: "It takes two to tango. You can't blame the media. Society has changed and the media reflects that. The two sort of drive each other a little bit. The media isn't this complete innocent thing that has been dragged down by a degraded society. At the same time, society hasn't been dragged down by the media."

Many in the media point out two key reasons to report the secrets of the famous. First, people want to know the real person under the packaged image—very important when determining what political candidate to vote for. Bernie Weinraub, entertainment reporter for the *New York Times,* told me: "Twenty-five, even fifteen years ago, people abided by what the government said and took everything hook, line, and sinker, and now there's much more self-questioning, and much more doubt, and I think that is very healthy."

Second, the reporting on private lives gives people a way of further connecting with a person or an image of a person they already feel they know from watching them on the big or little screens.

In our conversation, *People* contributing editor Mitchell Fink said: "People all over the world identify with famous people, so they want to know them, to know about them, but most of all, they want to know that they are human. And the only way that famous people are humanized is when they make a mistake. The public wants to know that their lives are not problem-free, which is why it becomes front-page news when someone you least expect is suddenly accused of wild things."

But Howard Kurtz, media reporter for the *Washington Post,* gave me a more cynical explanation for tabloidization: "The media love to create and destroy because we get easily bored with the same story line. Someone arrives on the scene and we gush. Inevitably, the white-hot spotlight reveals flaws. Just as inevitably, the press subconsciously believes that the superstar has gotten too big for his britches. It's more interesting to say a marriage is in trouble, or someone is bulimic—whatever helps you write the new story."

Diana could not know—who could?—that the excesses of the media were just down the road. In fact, Princess Di, as they called her, was one of a handful of figures who fueled the change. Had the new Princess known that her shadow bridegroom would prove to be such a fickle companion, would she have been more cautious?

It is doubtful she could have put the brakes on the media. Journalism is driven by market forces at every level. Because Diana rarely if ever played members of the media against one another, I have, in this book, treated the media as monolithic. In fact, there is fierce competition among writers, photographers, and editors. In his book *Spin Cycle,* Howard Kurtz describes Mike McCurrey, the White House press secretary, undergoing a particularly heated press conference on tobacco legislaton: "The tobacco story was the only chance for these esteemed television correspondents to get on the air that night. They were trying to goad him [McCurrey] into making some news." The news does not just happen; it is, as Kurtz says, "made."

I have suggested that Diana's desire to express herself was a powerful, driving force behind everything she did. And in the war that was to come between herself and the royal family, the media was the only ally powerful enough to help Diana get what she wanted. Once the press had become involved in the romance, there was no turning back for the Princess. Diana's marriage to the press was a shotgun wedding in which the bride had no choice.

Media Product, Media Toy

> *"I seemed to be on the front of a newspaper every single day, which is an isolating experience, and the higher the media put you, place you, is the bigger the drop."*
>
> —Diana Princess of Wales
> BBC *Panorama* interview

They needed space. "They have a marriage to build and a family to make. They, their advisers, the press and the public should give them room to do it." That was the tone of a London *Times* editorial at the end of the wedding week. Unfortunately, that did not happen. When conflicts arose between the Prince and Princess they were carefully concealed. (It would be more than ten years before there was official acknowledgment of their problems.) But it was clear from the outset that her relationship with the media was going to be tempestuous.

Instead of abating, the attention to Diana accelerated after the wedding. Crowds were mesmerized by the new queen-in-waiting as she attended her official engagements. The fiercely competitive tabloids turned each scoop on Diana into a trophy—a commodity that increased profits at the newsstands. Her sense of style began to resurrect Britain's fashion industry.

To the people, the Princess was almost like a religious icon. By 1983, her portrait hung everywhere. Her radiant face graced all the tourist places—hotels, restaurants, shops. Her picture even held a place of honor on the mantels of people's homes, as if she were a family member—or an inspirational force.

When we see public figures on the street or in the market, we think at first that we know them because they appear in our living rooms, on our TV sets, three feet from our heads. Public figures, used to being recognized, learn to respond to people who make eye contact with them. The public is easily confused about what it means to know someone.

Whenever I am interviewed frequently on television, I often run into people who mistake me for, say, a friend's cousin. They don't realize the degree to which television creates that familiarity in their minds, so they feel that they know me in a more personal way. We love that which we know and that with which we spend time. Most Americans spend seven hours a day watching TV, so we have created a culture of intimate friends through the media. And we feel that we have connections with them. Diana was one such friend.

This is not an absolutely new phenomenon. During the Great Depression, Americans displayed portraits of President Franklin Delano Roosevelt in their homes and shops. In the midst of bread lines, mortgage foreclosures, and bank closures, FDR inspired hope with his New Deal and the rallying call "We have nothing to fear but fear itself." Similarly, Diana was a ubiquitous presence, a symbol of restoration for a country that continued to suffer through tough times. To say that England was intoxicated with her, especially after she had given birth in 1982 to Prince William, the future king, would be an understatement. England acted like a love-struck teenager.

Like Hollywood stars whose power and thus salaries are determined by their ability to open a movie—that is, pull in the number-one box office on the first weekend, regardless of the movie's overall quality—Diana quickly became the Helen of Troy of the modern global media age. Her face launched the sales of thousands of magazine issues. Her appearances, or stories about her, skyrocketed the ratings for television shows. Memorabilia, such as Diana dolls and wedding plates, blossomed into a worldwide industry.

It's true of all stars that the longer one looks at them the more their radiance seems to fade. The process is aided by the media, which obscures the light with negative stories. They focus on the stars' foibles and run unflattering, candid paparazzi shots to maintain the readers' interest, which keeps sales strong.

This focus on the negative was especially true with the British media dominated by Rupert Murdoch. No one who works for Murdoch ever worried about killing the goose that lays the golden eggs. They knew there would always be another goose.

The period of rapid expansion in Murdoch's empire, and Diana's career as a public figure, both coincided with extraordinary technological changes that have radically transformed the workplace and the home throughout the industrialized world. At the beginning of the 1980s there were no fax machines and no personal computers. The world did not have *USA Today*, CNN, FedEx, VH1. MTV had barely started. The metabolism rate of business has unalterably changed. The rate of information transfer has increased more in the last fifteen years than perhaps in the previous two hundred. Any bit of news, word or photo, can be transferred anywhere almost instantly. Public figures must be ready for rapid response. A rumor unanswered in twenty-four hours becomes truth. A minute is a year. In many ways, ordinary people live their lives differently. They spend more time alone. In the age of the Internet, old social controls don't work as they once did.

Diana was tossed about like a toy boat caught in the ebb and flow of the media tide. A media darling in her early years, she bore the brunt of late '80s media criticism that questioned the sincerity of her involvement in controversial charities. And, of course, the tabloids wrote about rifts in her marriage.

Becoming ever wiser to the game over the years, Diana continued to use the media to advance her own causes, as she had first done to push Charles to propose. The obvious causes were her charities. The less obvious was her reputation, which she protected and molded.

From the beginning, Diana's star power was an intriguing mix of contradictory factors: An inborn magnetism coupled with a calculated presentation groomed by directors and acting coaches. A dignified look and a democratic manner. A natural style aided by the best designers, cosmeticians, and hairstylists. A heartfelt compassion for the down and out, but a cunning manipulation of those she wanted to win over.

Who would have guessed that this simple assistant to a kindergarten teacher would become the leading lady in the drama of the Windsor family? And yet, the evidence was right in front of our eyes from the very beginning. All we had to do was look at early photographs of Diana, her bob soft and casual and her line elegant, while the Windsors were tight-lipped and laced-up. Thoroughly contemporary Diana stood out like an exquisite piece of modern art in a timeworn and traditional frame. That juxtaposition had not been seen since Princess Margaret's clubbing days in the '60s.

In addition, Diana had charisma—something nobody in the royal family was blessed with except for the Queen Mother, who kept a low profile because of her age. This aura seems to be inborn. Some have it, some don't. Diana did. Prince Charles didn't. There are countless good, decent people in the world who lack charisma and many scoundrels and liars who have it in spades. There's absolutely no correlation between character and charisma.

But charisma does compel and intrigue. And it invited favoritism from the public and media from the start. Prince Charles was known for his humane approach, but his manner was "grimacing reserve" while Diana's was outgoing, eager, open, and glamorous. During her first official engagement, a carefully planned three-day tour of Wales with Charles in October 1981, Diana cleverly chose to dress in red and green, the country's national colors—a small, but significant gesture that won her the crowds' acclaim.

Mingling with the Welsh crowds lined up in the rain, she refused an umbrella, putting herself on their level, and literally touched them—an old lady's sleeve, a little girl's hand—and thanked them for coming out to see Charles and her despite the weather. When presented with an award, she spoke Welsh, also roundly applauded. She was a public sensation.

The gestures seem only modestly heroic. Many caregivers embrace AIDS patients every day without attracting the attention of photographers. Every candidate for public office in New York must occasionally speak in a language he or she doesn't know. Diana's hand-holding was not a huge physical gesture in American terms, but her willingness to *engage* a crowd was remarkable in the context of the gestures offered by the royal family of a nation which values personal reserve. She was more physical than others in her culture.

But there were intangibles as well that made Diana remarkable. Princess Helena Moutafian, vice president of one of Diana's favorite charities, Help the Aged, said of Diana: "People like people who vibrate, who carry something in themselves that reflects onto other people. It's a quality great stars have. They attract people like magnets." Diana's step-grandmother, Barbara Cartland, likened her spell over people to the Queen Mother's: "When the Queen Mother is talking to someone, they always feel they are the only person who matters and that she is vitally interested in them as a person. It is this quality that the Princess of Wales has, and which leaves people laughing and smiling long after she has left them."

Anyone who watched the funeral of Gianni Versace on television will remember the comfort she offered the disconsolate Elton John. She and John, who had been friendly once, had not been on speaking terms in the months just prior to the funeral. Diana, characteristically, ignored the disagreement to offer sympathy. It was this way she had of rising to the occasion which endeared Diana to her public.

The public adored her and the media followed her every time she stepped out, even when she shopped. *The Sun* dubbed Diana "Queen of Hearts" and reported on every dress she wore, every step she took, and every gesture she made.

Diana's ongoing duality is what made and kept the Princess famous to the end, contends cultural historian and authority on fame, Leo Braudy. "Today, those who pull together contradictory images attract the most attention," he says.

Complexity captures the imagination and speaks to reality. When reading a novel or play, or viewing a film, the characters with admirable as well as flawed character traits are the most intriguing: Odysseus, Othello, Ibsen's Nora, Puzo's Michael Corleone, Pasternak's Zhivago, Mead's Scarlett O'Hara. In life, estimable people with warts command the public's attention too: John F. Kennedy, Richard Nixon, Winnie Mandela, Fidel Castro, Bill Clinton.

And Diana. Though she was a royal, her trials and tribulations mirrored the struggles of many a commoner, making her one of the most intriguing dramatic personas on the world stage.

During her pregnancy with William, Diana tired of the media. She lost her patience and dispensed with courtesy toward the press because she no longer needed the publicity to capture Charles. This is where the love-hate relationship with the media began, as well as her other highly emotional behaviors.

Despite her initial appearance, Diana was anything but mousy in real life. After the wedding, she dropped the mask of the adoring, obliging girl when she disapproved of Charles's hunting, polo, and other favorite activities, asking that he change. Having been catered to all his life because of his royal birth, Charles was not one to be dominated by a woman whom he had bedded. Privately, he withdrew from Diana, while remaining kind and solicitous when around her, which was as little as possible and preferably in the company of others. Many sources reported the tenseness of the Wales's private relationship, Diana's tantrums, Charles's tendency to seize up when first confronted and then to flee the scene.

Apparently, Charles felt that most of Diana's rantings were squall patterns best ignored. So much for his instincts. The Queen's intuition was better attuned to potential threats to the monarchy. She took note of Diana's sudden violent moods. She aimed to keep Diana as happy as possible to prevent divorce. But she misread the cues. Blaming Diana's stress on media pressures alone, the Queen launched an unprecedented action.

In December of 1981, the Queen called to Buckingham Palace all the editors of the Fleet Street newspapers and pleaded with them to curtail the incessant coverage. She told them that it was unfair of photographers to hide in bushes with telephoto lenses and track the Princess without her knowledge. Then she referred to a picture published the day before of Diana with her arms around her husband's neck, smiling affectionately, as they stood outside Highgrove. In the interview for the PBS *Frontline* documentary "The Princess and the

Press," Lord Deedes, then-editor of the *Daily Telegraph,* found the Queen to be "extremely reasonable, pointing out that it was rough on a girl if she can't walk down the street to buy a bag of sweets without thirty or forty photographers chasing her all the time."

A less contrite *News of the World* editor reminded Her Majesty of the realities of a celebrity's life: freedom of movement will attract attention. "He retorted, 'Why can't she send a footman for the sweets?'" Lord Deedes recalls.

The newspapers backed off on their relentless chase for a while, though not on their coverage of her public appearances, of which there were many, albeit perfunctory for a royal. In a television interview after the meeting, Lloyd Turner of *The Star* indicated that he thought the tabloids would filter out intrusive photographs as a result.

In an incident confirmed by the Princess some years later, Diana, pregnant with her first son, threw herself down a flight of stairs at Sandringham. Prince Charles went riding, as he had planned to do. The fall was reported in the papers.

The cease-fire on invasive pursuits ended in February of 1982, two months after the Queen had spoken to the press. *The Star* sent photographers through the undergrowth of the Bahamas, where Charles and Diana were vacationing, to get a photograph of a pregnant Diana in a bikini. *The Sun's* troops soon followed. Bingo. Recalls Greenslade, "We all knew we were going to publish them, whether or not we said we were doing the right thing. . . ."

The Queen called it "the blackest day in the history of British journalism." Murdoch's men didn't care. Nor did the other tabloids. Throughout the year, headline coverage of the marriage continued: "Loveless Marriage"; "Disco Diana Dumps Charles"; "Old Flame the Prince Won't Forget"; "Fears for Di's Health." Recalls Greenslade: "[Our editor] would adopt, at a conference in the morning, a mock and shocked look and say, 'I'm afraid we've upset the Palace. How can we do it today?'"

As if in a head-to-head battle with Murdoch, the Queen continued to chide editors, demanded and secured injunctions, and finally went to court to prevent her servants from selling secrets. She appealed for press sanctions. She ordered reporters and photographers off Sandringham and banned them from Windsor. She tried to keep them away from all family events, including the royal christenings.

Diana herself was occasionally petulant with the media. During a January 1983 ski vacation in Austria with the Prince and Princess of Liechtenstein, for example, she refused to pose for photographers. Crowding the slopes, shops, and restaurants, throngs of paparazzi shoved aside the crush of tourists, broke down doors, and shattered shop windows as they chased after her. Only the police could restore order. Charles pleaded with Diana to pose for photos. When begging no longer worked, Charles called her behavior stupid.

Photographs of a sulking Diana and a forlorn Charles and the daily commotion appeared in the British press. There were reports of hundred-mile-per-hour car chases, decoys, barricades, roughed-up reporters, and photographers forced off the road.

Reading about the commotion, the Queen dispatched her representatives to calm things down and to remind Diana of the responsibilities of royalty. Rebellious toward courtiers even at this early stage, Diana disregarded the lectures of Francis Cornish, a member of Charles's staff.

However, she warmed to Victor Chapman, a humorous Canadian diplomat who gave her the kind of personal affection denied her by Charles and the royal family. He established such a rapport with Diana that the Queen sent him on the royal tour to Australia with the Prince and Princess of Wales in September of 1983.

Trips to former British colonies such as Australia and Canada, where republican sentiments were strong, were important to bolster the concept of the monarchy. By 1982, the Queen herself had made twelve trips to Canada and nine to Australia. Diana at first refused to visit the land down under but eventually agreed, on the condition that she could bring nine-month-old William. It was a fateful decision; leaving her homeland, Diana began to discover herself.

The Australian tour marked a major turning point for Diana's career. There, her individual star clearly eclipsed the royal family's. This was partly because of the unprecedented global media fascination with her specifically, but also because Diana was now seeming comfortable in her role as Princess of Wales.

Diana's reception abroad was like Beatlemania, and the global media now treated her like the world's Pop Princess. Recalls Ken Lennox, former *Daily Mirror* photographer, in the *Frontline* documentary: "The rules were changing. Instead of seven photographers being there, there were seventy. Before, there had been one from each paper and a couple of freelancers. Now they were coming from France, Germany. Americans were coming to have a look at her. The Japanese were turning up."

Victor Chapman is credited in Kitty Kelley's *The Royals* with teaching the Princess how to rise to the occasion. Chapman genuinely likes women. He flirted with and flattered Diana, encouraging her to be herself, to have fun, to show her style. He encouraged her to go dancing because she loved to do it. And Disco Di was born.

She was, to be sure, in a double bind. She needed and appreciated the crowd's approval but she would apparently cry at night, overwhelmed by all the attention. Moreover, Charles was displeased with being in her shadow. He expected brains to be valued over beauty.

Chapman tried to make peace, advising Charles to approach the situation with a self-deprecating sense of humor, as John Kennedy had when he called himself the man who accompanied Jacqueline

Kennedy to Paris. Charles tried but stumbled, awkwardly saying things like "I'm just a collector of flowers these days." In a frequently aired film clip he says, "I have come to the conclusion that it really would have been easier to have had two wives. Then they could cover both sides of the street and I could walk down the middle, directing the operations."

On purely logical grounds, the royal family could not understand the world's seemingly endless appetite for Diana. Privately, they apparently thought she was spoiled and disagreeable, a moody, unstable girl. Like others, they were unaware of or ignored her bulimia and postpartum depression. But publicly, Diana was a phenomenon. This incongruity underscored the tension that would further tear at the marriage and traditional monarchy.

In an interview for this book, Leo Braudy, an authority on pop-culture, said that Diana was the chosen one because the populace was ready for a new kind of representation. In his book *The Frenzy of Renown,* he writes: "Since the Renaissance, one function of fame has been to attack an entrenched social system by showing how a newly enfranchised audience can create new gods. Famous people are often the weapons we use to attack old values. When they break they are thrown aside like all useless tools."

Diana admitted to being uneasy about the phenomenon, which she didn't understand or feel she deserved. "One minute I was nobody, the next minute I was Princess of Wales, mother, media toy, member of the family. . . ." she told royal biographer Andrew Morton. She described the Australia-New Zealand tour as a turning point. "The whole world was focusing in on me every day. I was in the front of the papers. I thought that this was just so appalling, I hadn't done something specific like climb Everest. . . . When we came back from our six-week tour, I was a different person, more grown up, more mature."

Along with her periodic distaste for the media, Diana's acts of self-mutilation, attempted suicides, raging rows, as well as her bulimia, could have been forms of what Dr. Marion Solomon, in *Narcissism and Intimacy*, terms "acting out" behaviors. These are the defenses—when there is a lack of affirmation and understanding—against the real pain of disappointment that a person with a narcissistic wound had imagined their romantic fantasies would heal. Conscious or subconscious, they could have been attention-getting devices or attempts at control and manipulation of those around her.

Bulimia is a significant indicator of a soul on fire. Eating-disorder experts theorize that the roots of the illness stem from childhood, in family backgrounds where rage and anger were suppressed and hidden. Uncertainty and anxiety in adult life trigger the illness.

Interviewed for this book, bulimia expert Jonathan Rader, Ph.D., CEO of the Rader Institute, said that bulimia can also be used to manipulate the other people in their lives. "A lot of bulimics have borderline personality disorders, between neurotic and psychotic. That type of person thinks everything is about them, the world revolves around them, everything that happens is an indication of them."

Suicide attempts, like Diana's in 1982, are desperate cries for help, but can also be forms of control. Rader explains: "'If I throw myself down the stairs,' Diana might have reasoned, 'can Charles go out of town and be away? No, he has to be there to protect me.' These people understand that acting-out puts them at the center of attention." It is a high-stakes game. If a suicide attempt fails to draw attention, one must do something even more dramatic.

The real duality of Diana was greater than the public knew. The private Di was tortured, empty, unloved, and adrift. Indeed, the very qualities which made her so unhappy propelled her to success with the people and the press. When Diana's real state of mind is understood it makes us question whether the public Di was a pure fiction.

Many Masks

> *"There's no better way to*
> *dismantle a personality*
> *than to isolate it."*
>
> —Diana Princess of Wales
> BBC *Panorama* interview

By the mid-1980s the life of the Princess had become, comparatively speaking, settled. She had embraced the reality of her job as Princess of Wales. Her two sons had been born. She had learned to tolerate her husband's infidelities and the coldness of his family. She had an unstable but basically positive relationship with the media. Many report that she was beginning to luxuriate in her celebrity.

Clearly it wasn't enough. The creative side of Diana's character had always been expressed in her presentation of self. Now, towards the end of the 1980s, she began to experiment, packaging and repackaging herself again and again. Surely she took pleasure in this, but there was nothing capricious or whimsical about her masquerade. In many instances she was responding to opportunities or to challenges from the press or the royal family. Always she was searching to find herself.

And so the world was treated to a tour de force performance as the Princess took up a succession of roles.

Diana had always been wrapped up in her public image and was addicted to the tabloid newspapers. Friends recalled how each morning during breakfast the Princess devoured reports of her activities in the *Sun, Daily Mirror, Daily Mail,* and *Express.* Once those were digested, she'd scan the lesser accounts in the broadsheets.

In *The Spectator,* Mark Honigsbaum recounts one party at which the Princess was looking at a pile of newspapers over his shoulder. He offered to gather them for her. After scanning them, she said: "Not a bad day for me."

Diana gave more than a hundred percent to polishing her public image. At the palace, hairdresser Kevin Shanley styled her naturally flat tresses daily, with the best products money could buy, and also accompanied her when she traveled abroad. Makeup artist Barbara Daly taught her how to expertly apply cosmetics, which were heavily painted on at first, modified later. Fashion editor of British *Vogue,* Anna Harvey, and a British *Vogue* crew worked with Diana's own innate gift for choosing eye-catching clothes and blending colors and accessories, and made her more sophisticated.

"She became obsessed with how she looked," observed a royal family connection. A Spencer cousin concurred: "She started looking at herself the way a director looks at a movie actress."

Estranged from the royal family, Diana tried to be more English than they. As a royal representative for Britain and promoter of its goods, Diana was told by Palace powers that she couldn't wear miniskirts or plunging necklines and that in public she had to wear clothes by British designers. By the time of Prince Harry's birth in 1984, she had metamorphosed from a slightly chubby teenager to a professional world beauty.

Diana did make one break from fashion protocol for royals: no gloves. Says Anna Harvey: "I ordered dozens and dozens of suede gloves in every shade for her because the royal family always wore gloves. Heaven knows where they all went, because she never wore any of them. She made a conscious decision to dispense with formality very early on. She wanted flesh-to-flesh contact."

She told Lord Puttman, "All people want to be touched. You just hold out your hand, let them touch you, the impact is quite extraordinary."

The need for media attention seems to have germinated, and then blossomed, as a response to the lack of affirmation from Charles and the royal family.

Diana herself said in her 1995 *Panorama* interview that since the days right after her honeymoon she was viewed as being low on the totem pole in the royal household, even by her husband. "Charles was in awe of his Mama, intimidated by his father, and I was always the third person in the room."

Nor did the family compliment her in the early days—or ever—for the effort and skill she applied to her job as Princess of Wales, even after that wild success of the Australia-New Zealand tour.

"A lot of public figures who want and crave attention might be responding to the same needs that were not met earlier in life—to be seen, known, and accepted," says Dr. Marion Solomon, author of *Narcissism and Intimacy.* "To have all eyes on you because you are famous, that can fill that need to be affirmed, understood, approved."

Dr. Joyce Brothers, who spoke to me about the Princess, says: "When the bubble of marital bliss burst, Diana built her own life. And the only way to survive in that powerless position [with Charles and the Court] was to draw power to herself. She needed it as a kind of warmth to her soul, the feeling stars get when an audience stands up to applaud."

As her popularity grew, anything Diana did, anything Diana wore, anything Diana attended, and anything Diana promoted became a hot commodity. While she was no innovator herself, whatever she graced seemed to ignite the public's imagination and fire up sales and reputations.

By 1985, according to Kitty Kelley, British opinion polls said Diana was the country's hottest tourist attraction—a bigger draw than Trafalgar Square and the houses of Parliament together. One national survey figured that, between 1983 and 1985 alone, she produced $66.6 million in revenue from magazines, books, and tourism.

Diana loved fashion, and Diana wannabes roamed the country. Women copied her hairstyles whenever a new one was shown in the tabloids, from her early '80s teenage bob to the '90s slicked-back look sported at a New York gala, which led to an upsurge in hair-gel sales. They liked her jewels too. Her $45,600 sapphire-and-diamond engagement ring launched a rage for engagement rings with colored stones, which momentarily eclipsed the traditional diamonds. When she donned a cross as a pendant at a reception at Crown Jewelers Garrard, jewelers reported record demand for crosses. In 1983, when Diana wore her $3.2-million emerald-and-diamond choker as a headband as she danced with Charles during their state visit to Australia, women all over the world copied the style—with less expensive jewelry, of course. Pearls came back into fashion because Diana constantly wore her three-row pearl choker. She made costume jewelry acceptable for daytime wear.

In the early years, she almost single-handedly revived British millinery by consistently wearing hats—from tiny caps to full-sized straw saucers—by such designers as Stephen Jones, Patricia Underwood, and Philip Treacy. In the mid-1980s, when she sported a Robin-Hood-style feathered hat and claret-colored velvet gown, that became the style of the season.

Keen to promote British fashion, Diana became the most important ambassador for British designers. Obligated to buy only British, she tried them all in the early years—Bruce Oldfield, Caroline Charles, Betty Jackson, Jasper Conran, Rifat Ozbek, Bellville Sassoon, Gina Fratini—before narrowing it down to a coterie upon which she relied, including Catherine Walker, Victor Edelstein, Jacques Azagury, and David Sassoon.

"This is where her silhouette changed," *Vanity Fair's* Cathy Horyn says. "Diana understood early on, after a couple of [fashion] mistakes, that she was representing the monarchy. The 'column' became her look, that tall, long, liquid look. A dress might have beading, but it was monochromatic. Or she wore a halter neck. She was regal but in a contemporary way. She went as far as any person had gone in making the monarchy seem current."

In the early 1980s, Britain—then burdened by economic recession—was a poor cousin of the European fashion industry. The French and Italian designers dominated international fashion. Diana "jump-started" an alteration in the balance, says British *Vogue's* Harvey, not only by showcasing British frocks but also by officially attending London's twice-a-year fashion showcase of domestic designs, entitled London Fashion Week, which aims to lure overseas dollars, especially American money, into British fashion-industry coffers. In March 1988, the Princess hosted a Fashion Week reception for one hundred and fifty international retailers and media at Kensington Palace, the first time one had been held in the red-brick, seventeenth-century palace. As an added attraction, Prince William, then five years old, greeted guests.

Such support—direct and indirect—helped London establish itself as a fashion capital today. By 1996, Britain was exporting $430 million worth of designer clothing annually, more than double the amount of a decade earlier, according to the British Knitting and

Clothing Export Council. In September 1997, Fashion Week saw a sixty-five-percent increase in overseas buyers. French design houses began poaching the brightest British stars to take over moribund collections. John Galliano now designs for Christian Dior, Alexander McQueen for Givency, Stella McCartney for Chloe.

In addition to becoming a powerful marketing tool for fashion, Diana sold magazines, memorabilia, and tons of trinkets, as her global identity solidified.

She became a walking billboard for her product and brand choices that were within the wage earner's range. The navy blue Virgin Airlines sweatshirt that she wore to the gym was estimated to be worth $8 million to Virgin. In 1994, when Diana drove an Audi Cabriolet, sales jumped fifty percent. In 1982, Royal Doulton, an upscale English china and collectibles company, charged $395 for its limited-edition Lady Spencer figurine. Soon thereafter, the same figurine was selling for $750, the same price as a Charles counterpart. At the time of her death, the porcelain Diana commanded a minimum of $1500, compared with $1000 for the porcelain Charles. It rose higher afterwards.

In April 1983, *Woman Magazine* named Diana the world's number-one cover girl. Media analysts reported that sales of magazines with Diana on the cover leaped by as much as forty percent. Moreover, her stories were the editorial focus that drew in the advertising, which is how magazines make most of their profits. Naturally, women's magazines found excuses to create a Diana cover story as often as possible.

These are, of course, overlapping roles. But each requires a particular mindset, a particular costume. Diana prepared herself carefully for each role. Her frequent changes of image began to draw negative attention. Around 1984, a media backlash began. Depending on the public mood or sales, the media would rush to their computers or microphones to denounce Diana or Charles. The royal couple became bowling pins in the modern fame game. It comes with the territory of celebrity—be set up, then knocked down.

How can one be loved one day, hated the next? What's the rationale? Profit. A fresh angle sells better. In addition, each approach—positive or negative—is easier to cover than the complete, multidimensional story. And the media can be lazy, which leads to another reason: boredom. Just like their audience, the media aren't exempt from a lack of purpose and meaning in their lives. Moreover, media careers can be made while the media make and break the celebrity.

Another reason is the audience and media's own craving for validation, says author and authority on fame Leo Braudy. Being the first to report or read the latest gossip makes one feel "special, that you can't be fooled, that you understand the heart of things"—indeed that you are top of the heap in your own circle, as the famous person is in theirs.

Once celebrated as a goddess of renewal, Diana now was portrayed as a mindless clotheshorse and a royal shopaholic who spent huge amounts of money. One newspaper estimated that after British *Vogue* became her consultant, she spent $1.4 million in one year—for 373 outfits and corresponding accessories, complete with hats, belts, shoes, and purses. Diana's response was that upon becoming Princess of Wales she had no clothes for tour and had to buy new things—enough to change three or four times a day. Six suites in Kensington Palace were made over into closets for her. One room was set aside for her more than three hundred pairs of shoes. (One fashion concession: She wore low heels while married so as not to tower over Charles.) Kelley says that for a sixteen-day trip to four Arab countries, her clothing bill came to $122,000.

Diana tried to solve the image problem by publicly re-wearing familiar dresses for official duties and limiting herself to dresses by English designers Catherine Walker and Victor Edelstein for special occasions.

Nonetheless, the tide had turned against her. When it did, Prince Charles was the beneficiary. Diana was blamed for the steady stream of royal staff firings, and for forcing Charles to abandon his friends and change his eating habits and his wardrobe.

Realizing that his outward efforts to make light of his wife's greater popularity were not capturing the public's fancy, Charles made further attempts to draw attention to his humanitarian works and his contributions to the public debate. Many of his programs were worthy but his public performances fell flat, were criticized, or were overshadowed by the interest in Diana's style.

Other actions meant to portray Charles as a "man of the people" were brought to the media's attention. Night walks of London streets and visits to homeless shelters were represented as studies of unrest in the inner cities. He toured the slums of Pittsburgh. He preached fuel conservation. He described himself as a "gentleman farmer" dedicated to urban renewal.

For better or worse, he did start one major controversy. In May 1994, Charles addressed the Royal Institute of British Architects. He criticized them as elitists because their designs disregarded the feelings and desires of ordinary people. Pinpointing a modern, glass-and-steel annex proposed for the National Gallery of Art, he described it as "a monstrous carbuncle on the face of a much-loved and elegant friend." The speech made the front pages of British newspapers, and the proposed plan was canceled, which Charles read as a testimony to his influence, despite challenges to his opinion from architects, including Gordon Graham, former president of the Royal Academy of British Architects.

Nevertheless, media ridicule persisted for months. Diana: vapid clotheshorse. Charles: dominated wimp. *Vanity Fair* questioned his manhood. A *Sun* headline screamed "Charles Loses His Trousers to Di." *The Star* asked "Man or Mouse?"

The media's change of heart must have been perplexing and devastating for the young Princess whose relationship with the press had flowered into an agreeable love affair. They courted her and she courted them. They forgave her occasional snits and she learned to put up with their smothering presence.

But to believe that cooperating will silence the media is naïve. The media doesn't give a damn about the feelings of their objects of coverage—they are invested in the bottom line, as Margaret Trudeau Kemper can attest.

Like Diana, the lovely, sexy, ex-wife of former Canadian Prime Minister Pierre Trudeau was in the white-hot media spotlight in the 1970s. Her description of the experience is that it was like having been womanized, loved, then thrown out—essentially betrayed.

"At first, I had a lot of good press and attention. I trusted the people in the media, particularly the British. The Fleet Street boys had a very endearing way about them. On reflection, it was very smarmy, but they were very polite and attentive," Trudeau Kemper recalls. "I got taken in a little bit by it. And that's one of the problems. You start believing your own press and you get carried away. Not until much later did I realize I was being used. It was a business and nobody cared about me at all."

Feeling besieged, Diana was forced into a truce with her husband. They met with members of the press. They arranged an interview on Independent Television. To showcase the image of their choice, they secured editorial control and soft lighting. They were coached by film director Sir Richard Attenborough. Diana sought out professional voice trainers.

By the time of the interview in October of 1985, both members of the Wales family acted his or her role impeccably. During the forty-five-minute inquiry, Charles was a self-confident future king: "I am always conscious . . . of not wanting to let the people down, not wanting to let this country down." Diana, the pretty ingénue always by his side, said that her role was "to support my husband . . . be behind him, encouraging. And also a more important thing, being a wife and mother." Their handsome, young sons could be seen playing in the background. Both parties denied negative rumors. Charles appeared more flexible, more reasonable than he had seemed in the past. The couple played off one another a good deal and smiled often. The interview was shown shortly thereafter in the United States, coinciding with their December 1985 trip to promote a British art exhibit. It was, arguably, the last time the royal couple put up a convincing show of unity.

While Diana seemed capable of controlling her image at home, she had less success when she went abroad. It is an indication of the quiet hostility of the monarchy that, even when Diana was at work in service to her country, she was undermined. To all appearances, this was more than a strategy. As in Austria, where Prince Charles, was recorded putting Diana down in public. The press and public cared not at all what he thought. They adored her.

At the 1985 White House reception, Diana danced with John Travolta, still remembered for his dancing in *Saturday Night Fever* and *Grease*. She looked terrific in the still photos. And Travolta paid her the compliment of his close attention. Like the sun-through-her-skirt snapshot and the wedding pictures, the Travolta-Diana photograph became part of Diana lore.

At a press conference Charles was clearly in a snit. When his wife was asked how she enjoyed the White House dinner, he interrupted to say, "I think, I think you enjoyed it, didn't you? Be an idiot if she didn't enjoy dancing with John Travolta, wouldn't she?"

The list of celebrities whom Charles and Diana met in America is remarkable for its diversity. At the White House they met Mikhail Baryshnikov, Neil Diamond, Tom Selleck, Clint Eastwood, Jacques Cousteau, Mary Lou Retton, David Hockney, Brooke Shields, and Dorothy Hamill. Later, on tour, they encountered Caroline and John F. Kennedy Jr., Bob Hope, Gregory Peck, and Joan Collins. What do these people have in common? All are famous. They are celebrities. They survive by and sustain the media. They are our new aristocrats. Diana belonged with them; Charles was part of the old regime.

Crowds were huge everywhere. Many sources report a recurring phenomenon: The car would stop. Charles and Diana would get out on opposite sides. The side nearest Charles would groan. It had happened in Britain; it was truer in the United States. Charles attributed Diana's success to her clothing. At least it was an acknowledgment of her power.

Diana needed to answer the rebuffs. Whether such overseas adulation encouraged her to come out of her shell or she was simply becoming more confident in expressing herself, Diana boldly unveiled her natural penchant to perform for the first time on her home turf.

As mentioned earlier, Diana had once dreamed of being a dancer. On December 23, 1985, during intermission at a benefit at Covent Garden for London's Royal Opera House, she excused herself from Charles. When the curtain rose, she twirled from the wings to center stage in a slinky, white, satin slip with spaghetti straps, and performed with partner Royal Ballet dancer Wayne Sleep to Billy Joel's pop tune "Uptown Girl." The kick routine brought down the house of twenty-six hundred.

Freeze frame: another picture and story for the Diana lore.

The dance number—which Diana had rehearsed at Kensington Palace—was supposedly a Christmas present to Charles. He publicly stated he was "absolutely amazed" and applauded the turn. His private response was reported to have been less enthusiastic.

Despite the couple's show of togetherness on tour and on television, the rumors and reports of a faltering marriage were true. Diana was increasingly miserable. Charles was deeply involved with another woman: Camilla Parker-Bowles.

The tabloids reported the tensions, recording the number of days spent apart and the separate appearances: Charles returning early and alone from family vacations, the couple arriving separately at the same place. Diana could be seen frequenting London fashion shows and rock concerts with other companions while Charles remained in the countryside, gardening and fishing. Kitty Kelley reports that a Norwegian manufacturer used the Prince and Princess of Wales to sell its food products. Oslo billboards splashed sad faces of Charles and Diana looking at single-serving cans of pasta and beef stew marked *Middag for En*—dinner for one.

Later, in her *Panorama* interview, Diana was eloquent in talking about this period of her life. "I found myself being more and more involved with people who were rejected by society—with, I'd say, drug addicts, alcoholism, battered this, battered that—and I found an affinity there. And I respected very much the honesty I found on that level with people I met, because in hospices, for instance, when people are dying they're much more open and more vulnerable and much more real than other people. And I appreciated that."

Her contacts with ordinary people were not mere altruism. She needed them: "I felt compelled to perform. Well, when I say perform, I was compelled to go out and do my engagements and not let people down, and support them and love them. And, in a way, by being out in public they supported me, although they weren't aware just how much healing they were giving me, and it carried me through."

Her marriage all but gone, Diana more than ever was, in the words of poet Arthur Lamb, "a bird in a gilded cage," trapped but flapping the wings of her emotional spirit for a purpose again. Within the confines of her royal role, she embraced her charity work to fill the spiritual vacuum.

The royal family has shown interest in the paranomal from time to time, even attending seances. Diana went one step further. Through her association with astrologer Penny Thorton, recommended by Prince Andrew, Diana realized that she could turn her suffering into something positive. Making charity appearances was her duty as a royal. Those she cared deeply about numbered two—Birthright and Help the Aged—which went from insignificance to recognition and success because of her name and prestige. Moreover, by throwing herself into work with an eclectic assortment of causes and organizations—Relate, a marriage guidance group; Turning Point, a group for those with addictions and mental problems; the Welsh National Opera—she could keep her mind off the unhappiness of her marriage.

Diana the Beneficent was born.

In 1984, according to Kitty Kelley, Diana attended 177 public engagements. The number rose seventy percent in 1985, to 299—more than half of those in Britain, without Charles. "This was a turning point for Diana," writer-broadcaster Martin Lewis concurs. "Her visits stopped being perfunctory. She was connecting to the inside."

Diana immersed herself in supporting charities that were notoriously difficult and unsympathetic: babies, old people, women, and AIDS. These were the constituents who were essentially abandoned by the conservative Tory government when the "safety net" social programs were dismantled by Prime Minister Margaret Thatcher's market-force strategies which helped the educated and upwardly mobile, especially in London, and widened the gap between the haves and have-nots. Diana's friend Vivienne Parry, interviewed for the A&E *Biography* "Diana, the True Story," says, "The extra thing was she had got it absolutely with ordinary people. She had a way of going directly to the heart in a way I've never come across in any other person."

Her choices threatened Britain's power elite. They feared inflammation of the historical class struggle, for the aristocratic and royal Diana, a member of the haves, was clearly siding with the have-nots. She was always popular with the working classes, but now she could become their symbol, their voice—a motivating force for change. From then on, she would be perceived as sticking her middle finger in the faces of the aristocracy, the government which was insensitive to their needs, and even the monarchy itself. The have-nots would like to flip the gesture themselves, but they didn't have the power. Now there was an ally with stature who could shake things up for them.

Perceived as a rebel and a traitor, Diana took heat from the aristocracy, the government, and the media, who interpreted her passion as narcissism and a need for public approbation rather than as heartfelt. This, along with her troubles with the paparazzi, intensified her love/hate relationship with the media, and is the explanation for her brother Charles's eulogy comment: ". . . I don't think she ever understood why her genuinely good intentions were sneered at by the media. . . . My own . . . explanation is that genuine goodness is threatening to those at the opposite end of the moral spectrum."

Summarizes Martin Lewis: "Diana went to the Live Aid Concert in 1985 [which raised famine relief funds for Ethiopia]. She loved Elton John, Sting, Phil Collins, but she was profoundly moved too. In the midst of this, *The Sun* offered a one-million-pound reward for anyone that would prove [Irish rocker and Live Aid host Bob] Geldof was making money on the side. When Diana gravitated toward Geldof and the AIDS activists, they were also cynical about her and her causes."

The country's mood toward AIDS, in particular, was grim and bigoted. According to Lewis, a government minister said that investing in AIDS research was a waste of money because it only helped homosexual men. In addition, misinformation about the disease was still rampant. People thought that the virus spread through the air, that by being in the same room with an infected person one could get AIDS.

So in April of 1987, when Diana removed the symbolic white glove of royalty to shake hands with an AIDS patient in the Broderip Ward at Middlesex Hospital, Britain's first ward for victims of the deadly disease, she sent perhaps the most potent message of her entire tenure as Princess of Wales. And it was done simply through imagery.

I interviewed Judy Wieder, editor-in-chief of *The Advocate,* the world's most influential gay and lesbian newsmagazine, now in its thirtieth year of publication: "Her photo was more powerful than any word. . . . Here was this sight of someone attractive, someone people wanted to imitate, wanted to be, going out and doing what we are afraid to do—that pulls us across faster than lectures. Diana had said, 'HIV does not make people dangerous to know, so you can shake their hands and give them a hug. Heaven knows, they need it.' But people don't remember that quote. They remember the sight of her."

At first, the action would conjure up a visceral fear in people, a mental picture of Diana's fall from physical grace. "Diseases are terrifying to people. But to imagine a beautiful woman turning into a hag from AIDS . . ." Wieder says. "Let's pretend that [former Prime Minister] Margaret Thatcher or Queen Elizabeth shook the same hand. That part of the message that you won't be aged, you can hold on to your beauty if you mix up with someone unfortunate, would have been lost."

Once over the shock, viewers could begin to comprehend the message that there is nothing to be afraid of because the beautiful Princess herself was fearless. In fact, they should feel sympathy. "Angel-like, Diana made the [sick] person seem more blessed, not a spreader of evil, but a victim, someone suffering," Wieder says.

Her commitment to compassion was perceived as such a threat that even her private vigil for a dying friend was ridiculed by the family and the aristocracy. (A book published by British conservatives in early 1998 blames Diana for an unwholesome rise in sentimentality in modern life. Many others would call that sentimentality compassion.) For months, Diana visited Adrian Ward-Jackson, art dealer and board member of the English National Ballet (of which she was a patron), as he slipped away from AIDS. On one occasion, when she got word that he might die, she left a royal family annual retreat at Balmoral without the Queen's permission, to be with her friend.

According to Lady Colin Campbell, two of her father's titled friends made clear their disapproval of her support of unpopular causes. "All of this jiggery-pokery with buggers just isn't on," said one.

The sheer weight of attention, positive and negative, weighed heavily on the Princess, as it might on anybody. Pressed by photographers at a nursery, Diana sniped, "I don't see why I should do anything for them. They never do anything for me."

The next day, a *Sun* editorial counterpunched. "Princess Diana asks: 'What have the newspapers ever done for me?' *The Sun* can answer Her Loveliness in one word—everything! The newspapers have made her one of the most famous women in the world. They have given her an aura of glamour and romance. Without them, the entire Windsor family would soon become as dull as the rulers of Denmark and Sweden." One has to suspect she knew they were right.

At some point, Diana realized that the tabloids—despite their publication of paparazzi photographs—could be greater allies than the respected dailies. The tabloids reached the masses that adored her. The court of public opinion could be used for the good fight.

That was when her already excellent acumen in press relations turned sharply shrewd. Diana struck a deal with the tabloids about coverage of her charity work. "The quid pro quo was that in return for access to her private office, you would be broadly sympathetic to her charity work," said one tabloid editor. "What Earl Spencer [in his eulogy] doesn't seem to appreciate is that the ones who caused her the greatest distress were the editorializers and sneerers of the broadsheets."

Diana soldiered on in her missions through the years. The Establishment press kept hammering away. In the early 1990s, London's *Evening Standard* accused Diana of being a "disaster groupie."

Nevertheless, her social advocacy is exactly what endeared her to the common people—and it also excited the media, according to Dick Morris, the political consultant who masterminded President Clinton's second-term victory. "There are two ways to deal with the media—do their agenda, or do your agenda. When you take on a role like the Princess of Wales, which came with a thousand years of expectations, it is normal to conform to the modus operandi of predecessors."

But Diana cleverly broke the mold, thus drawing attention and becoming newsworthy, for better or for worse. "Diana was able to create a new genre, spun off from the existing job," Morris continues. "She transcended the normal range of ribbon-cuttings and safe charities and segued into making an important social statement. She transcended what was essentially a nonpolitical process to a process of social advocacy. She was good as a political consultant."

Morris imagined her thinking: "'Okay, I have to support charities and attend state functions. If I must visit the sick, okay, then let's make it AIDS patients. If I must visit another country, then let it be the poorest.'"

Then he adds, "It was brilliant. She took a genre that was systematically bleached with meaning—a monarchy that developed impotence to an art form, which was the goal of English democracy—and invested it with a political importance in a social way. It was extraordinary, and extraordinary that she thought out and understood it."

Indeed, Diana's own comments to British-born Tina Brown, now editor of *The New Yorker*, attest that she shrewdly understood and applied modern-day, public relations techniques. Brown recalls that, during lunch with the Princess in June of 1997 in New York, Diana discussed in marketing terms that the Windsors were a dying breed, one that required repositioning by a media genius—perhaps someone like Peter Mandelson, the political strategist who helped get Tony Blair elected.

In *The New Yorker*, Brown quoted Diana: "I tried again and again to get them to hire someone like him to give them proper advice, but they didn't want to hear it. They kept saying I was manipulative. But what's the alternative? To just sit there and have them make your image for you?"

Diana preferred to suffer through bad press rather than little or no press. When the media threw Sarah Ferguson into the spotlight, beginning with her wedding to Prince Andrew in 1986, Diana became resentful.

This is not surprising or unusual among actors or celebrities. Narcissism can be significantly exacerbated by career choice, such as the alcoholic who decides to become a bar owner. The more attention they get, the more they need, and when the attention is diverted to someone else, they panic.

When Sarah Ferguson began to court with Prince Andrew, Diana tried to embrace her and her boisterous ways. She may have envied the approval Fergie received from Charles and the rest of the royal family.

Bursting on the scene, Sarah Ferguson was a very different sort of person from the Princess—a fireball of jovial energy. She rode with the Queen, went carriage driving with Prince Philip, and visited with the Queen Mother. Charles told Diana, "I wish you would be like Fergie—all jolly. Why are you always so miserable?" Recalled Diana to Morton: "Suddenly, everybody said: 'Oh, isn't she marvelous, a breath of fresh air, thank God she's more fun than Diana.'"

There were numerous reports of the two being silly, dressed absurdly, cutting up in public—at a Spider concert, Royal Ascot, a London bar. They improvised a can-can at the Windsor Castle Christmas party. During a ski holiday, in front of photographers, Diana and Fergie staged a wrestling match on ice.

The newspapers blasted them. "Far too much frivolity," puffed the *Daily Express.* Interestingly, though both behaved outside of royal decorum, Sarah was the main target of ridicule, while Diana was handled with kid gloves. "The Princess of Wales escapes such censure because she is prettier," wrote *Sunday Times* columnist Craig Brown, "and less, well, obvious than the Duchess of York. It is the peculiar capacity of the Duchess to mirror modern Britain, its gaudiness, its bounciness, its rumbustious lack of mystery."

Diana obviously had found her role and didn't succeed at Fergie's game. But she envied the Duchess's freedom to be frivolous.

By 1987, Diana and Charles had little in common, except for their children. They were leading separate lives. They both had regular confidants and companions. When the media got wind of one of Diana's new confidants, merchant banker Philip Dunn, they supposed the marriage's disintegration. Both Diana and Charles felt this was an unwarranted intrusion into their private lives.

The irony is that while the royal family cried "invasion of privacy," they unwittingly set themselves up for even more intense scrutiny in June of that same year when they appeared on the television show *It's a Royal Knockout.*

Based on an old slapstick game-show series, the mock Tudor knockabout showed the younger royals—Princess Anne, Princes Edward and Andrew, and Fergie—in Elizabethan garb and letting loose, in an attempt to win over the public with a show of camaraderie after years of press about mounting tensions.

At this point, nothing was held off-limits. Photographers showed up at holidays, a no-no before, arguing for shots with humorous hats or with the children. On ski holidays, paparazzi ignored the staged photo opportunities, following the family up and down the slopes for days until they got unique shots that sold better.

Diana tried to expand her audience. Across the Atlantic, the media was out to ring up the sales any way it could too. At *People,* James R. Gaines confesses that Diana was called "our gift from heaven. . . . I wish I could say we meant that in the theological sense, but in fact it just meant that putting her picture on the cover made the magazine seem to fly off newsstands. . . . We knew she was a great story, even without being able to say quite why. . . . I must confess, the why of it didn't really matter much to me."

If the reason wasn't clear then, he and the rest of the media would know why by 1991. That's when the life of the Princess publicly began to follow a soap-opera story line, with each development presenting another episode for serialization and monetary gain. This story—an open war between Diana and the royal family—continued for the next four years. It ended in divorce and the emergence of a different Diana—a new image that the media could again cash in on.

The Princess Speaks

*". . . I'm a great believer that
you should always confuse
the enemy."*

—Diana' Princess of Wales
Panorama interview

When we review media historically, whenever there have been a number of small outlets competing for market share attention, each becomes more sensational out of necessity. So, for example, in 1910, when there might have been five or six newspapers vying for sales in any major city, each outlet had to become more lurid; the market demanded it. That's how yellow journalism was born.

What do we have going on today? Lots of outlets vying for attention. A little over a generation ago there was radio, three TV networks, a few independent channels, and a few theatres downtown, each screening one film. Today there are seventy channels, home entertainment centers, multiplex cinemas, the Net: lots of small outlets. Lots of opportunity for sensationalism. In this context, Rupert Murdoch, Robert Maxwell, and the other purveyors of tabloid news were not so much innovators as opportunists hanging on tight to an ever more out of control historical/techno-logical force.

There is an interesting parallel between the growth of yellow journalism and the present explosion of media. When competing for market, media outlets rely on pictures. Newspapers that used lots of photos had an advantage in the early part of the century. Today, the press and broadcast outlets compete for advantage with one another using instant, up-close pictures. Color photos—now used even in papers of record, like the *New York Times*—show us the importance of the image.

Diana understood this. She made sure that she was photographed often. The record of her first ten years in the public eye could be fairly represented in a coffee table book. Little would be missing.

By the beginning of the 1990s the press became increasingly unpredictable with Diana. The public appetite for her was as strong as ever and there was fierce competition for stories and photos. It is a testimony to her skills that, most of the time, the Princess was able to exert some control over the press. Even more impressive, in an era when the average person is overwhelmed by verbiage, in an era when a sound bite can change the results of an election, Diana, for years, managed her successful campaign with images only. As she came of age, she was like a good director of silent films moving into the era of talkies.

She was forced by the difficulty of her situation to learn and to grow. The famous personal reserve of the British upper classes makes it easy to underestimate the intense passions and the fierce hostilities that underlie the conflicts among the members of the royal family. In the early 1990s, Diana's struggles with Charles resembled a chess game, as I've said, because, despite the interference of the royal family and the gross intrusions of the press, it seemed to be a fairly even series of tit-for-tat maneuvers to gain advantage with the media and the public. When it became clear to Diana that she could not win, she changed the rules.

To carry the story forward, I must revisit some of the events described briefly in the first chapter's chess game, but this time in more detail and with an eye to their subtleties and nuances and to the motives and strategies of the Princess.

In 1990 or 1991, goaded by the Prince's indifference, losing control of her relationship with the press, sensing she was in danger—or perhaps sensing an opportunity—Diana allowed the simmering animosity she felt toward Prince Charles to escalate into a campaign.

Approaching her thirtieth birthday, Charles offered to stage a ball to celebrate the event. Diana turned him down, saying that a festive event would look frivolous at a time when British troops were fighting in the Gulf War. It's been reported that she had plans to spend the night with a lover. She had become involved, in the late '80s, in a series of romantic liaisons. One assumes that she sought in her lovers the same redefinition of self that she looked for in assuming a sequence of public roles.

When the tenth anniversary of the marriage was celebrated in 1991, the media acknowledged the rift between the royal couple and generally blamed Diana.

A small PR campaign was undertaken by the royal family to repair the damage. An official photo shows the family on a picnic. A suited Charles stands tall in the center—as any future king should—with Diana seated on a wrought-iron bench in front of him. One hand rests on her shoulder and the other on Prince Harry, who stands next to his father holding the reins of a horse. Prince William is seated on the ground by his mother's feet.

Now that we have a better understanding of the tensions within the family, we can better read the picture. "Rather than look unified, they clearly seem divided," notes Dr. Alan Entin, a Richmond, Virginia, family psychologist known for analysis of family issues through photo albums. "The bench is a dividing mark between the two. Charles has his hands on Harry and Diana in a controlling way. William looks sullen and his only connection to the family is at his mother's knee. And what's Diana doing in this picture dressed in riding gear when she is known to have a fear of riding horses?"

Diana knew she could clarify the situation with another photo. She found an opportunity during a four-day tour of India with Charles in early 1992. They arrived on separate planes, not on speaking terms. While Charles addressed a business meeting, Diana staged a photo session in which she sat—alone—in front of the Taj Mahal, the seventeenth-century monument to romantic love. The image spoke for itself.

The year 1992 was a dreadful one for the entire royal family. Diana's father, John Spencer, died in March. The following month saw the release of Lady Colin Campbell's book *Diana in Private* —a history of Diana's relationships with four men: King Juan Carlos of Spain; Philip Dunne, a banker; James Hewitt of the Life Guards; and Sgt. Barry Mannakee, one of her detectives. The book was serialized in the *Mirror.* Rumors of the impending separation and divorce had been circulating for months. Unconvincing denials had been issued all around.

The Princess fought all the harder to promote herself, continuing to use photographers to her advantage. During the next few months, several contrasting images appeared in the newspapers: Diana, on official tour, standing in front of the Egyptian pyramids, alone, while Charles vacationed in Turkey with his mistress, Camilla. Diana visiting leper colonies, while Charles played polo. Diana consoling cancer patients in Liverpool, while Charles shot birds at Sandringham. Diana conferring with Mother Teresa, while Charles partied with the Sultan of Brunei, the world's richest man.

Despite potentially damaging stories about her personal life, Diana was winning the campaign.

But clearly she was concerned about the possibility that news—which had become ever more personal as the marriage faltered—could be used against her. In 1992, the Princess made her boldest move yet. She spoke out publicly, by proxy. In 1991 she had given permission for her best friend, her lover, her masseuse, her brother, and her father to cooperate with Andrew Morton in the writing of his book *Diana: Her True Story.* Her father turned over to the publisher the rights to eighty photographs from the Spencer family album. Diana herself secretly collaborated by sending audiotapes to Morton through an intermediary—an action she denied to the Palace. The book represented the Prince and his family as cold and unsupportive. She mentioned Charles's affair with Camilla Parker-Bowles. It described her own personal crises—bulimia, suicide attempts—with considerable candor. She was depicted by Morton as a woman on the modern path to self-discovery through astrology, hypnotherapy, aromatherapy, ballet, music, and spiritual reading. This very contemporary woman with contemporary problems made the royal family look as though they came from another era, if not from another planet.

With the publication of the book, the foundation of the monarchy was struck with a sledgehammer. Among the populace, polls showed that seventy-five percent of Britons believed the House of Windsor was disintegrating. Half believed that by the end of the twenty-first century the monarchy would be gone entirely, without consequence for Britain.

Republicans were given ammunition. In the House of Commons, Labour MP Dennis Skinner called for dissolution of the monarchy: "It is high time we stopped this charade of swearing allegiance to the Queen and her heirs and successors because we don't know from time to time who they are. . . . Labour MP Anthony Benn sponsored a bill to replace the Queen with an elected president, separate church and state, and give Wales and Scotland their own parliaments. (Note that an independent parliament was approved for Scotland in early 1998.) Charles's position was jeopardized. Divorce wouldn't prevent him from ascending the throne. Remarriage would.

Recalled Max Hastings, editor of the *Daily Telegraph* at the time, in the PBS *Frontline* segment "The Princess and the Press": ". . . when [the book] came out, I was inclined to believe two things which, actually, responsible journalists shouldn't let themselves believe. One is, 'It's not true,' and the second is, 'Well, if it is, they shouldn't say so.'"

This first experiment in the use of the written word had worked for the Princess. "The Morton book was cataclysmic for the royal family," said Richard Stott, former editor of the *Daily Mirror,* "because it virtually confirmed ten years of reporting. . . . [I]t vindicated what had been going on in terms of the tabloid papers."

"My resentment sprang from the fact that we are damaging something which is very precious," recalled Sir Peregrine Worsthorne, *Sunday Telegraph* columnist. "And to the older generation—still a hell of a lot of people over fifty in this country—that, I think, was their reaction, a feeling of sadness, profound sadness. It obviously sells papers, but it damages the national interest. . . . [I] wrote a vicious article, which I would do again."

Harrods declined to sell the book, which seems ironic now, given that Mohammed al Fayed, the father of Diana's last lover, owns the store. It became, nonetheless, a bestseller. In the view of many, including avid Diana-watcher and television producer Jay Mulvaney, Morton's remains the definitive book on the life of the Princess.

The tide had begun to turn against the House of Windsor. Stories, editorials, and television commentaries questioned the need for the monarchy and the royal family.

The troubles of the royals intensified. Sarah Ferguson, Andrew's wife, had a fling with Steve Wyatt in Morocco. She and the Prince separated a couple of months later (ending an occasionally valuable family connection for Diana). Sarah stayed in the news—a royal embarrassment—photographed topless in the south of France. Princess Anne was divorced and a paternity suit was filed against her husband, Captain Mark Phillips. Anne remarried before the year was out. And there was continuing controversy about the sexual orientation of Prince Edward.

Kitty Kelley reports in *The Royals* that Charles had reached his breaking point. He began to discuss with his mother the possibility of a divorce. The Queen was opposed. She felt concern about what a divorce might do to her grandchildren, to Prince Charles's public image, and to the monarchy in general.

The Court was unable to force action from the Press Complaints Commission, a self-regulating body made up of representatives from various media outlets. PCC head Lord McGregor stated: "I had heard of a number of rumors that the Princess had been in regular touch with editors about her own situation and her own relationships. Now, if this is the case, I was not going to issue a statement."

It had not been able to prevent the publication of Morton's book. The Court's only strategy now was to make Diana recant. As mentioned in the first chapter of this book, she did so in a tepid statement: "I cannot be held responsible for what my friends say." It was an excellent caption.

Once he'd seen the denial, Lord McGregor reversed himself. Believing this to be "an honorable and direct denial" that Diana had communicated with the press, Lord McGregor publicly described press coverage of Charles and Diana's marriage as "intrusive and speculative" and "an odious exhibition of journalists dabbling their fingers in the stuff of other people's souls. . . ."

The tabloid writers and editors were astonished. "So I said to him, 'Well, look, Lord McGregor, if you don't believe me,'" recalled Andrew Knight, then-chairman of Murdoch's News Corp., "'just look at tomorrow's newspapers.'"

Diana had made a terrifically clever plan. She felt that the favorable results, for her, of the book's publication must not be undone. But she couldn't endorse it officially. She had to find a way to signal that she stood behind the Morton book without coming out and saying so.

She would do it through a staged photo op.

Daily Mirror photographer Ken Lennox was one of several photographers who were tipped off by a well-spoken woman who did not request payment.

"I got a phone call at home in Chelsea inviting me to go to Carolyn Bartholomew's home," Lennox said. ". . . Almost on the button at nine o'clock, Carolyn, her husband, and her baby all appeared in the doorway. Diana kissed Carolyn's husband, kissed the baby, and kissed Carolyn. I phoned the office and said, 'Diana just vindicated everything Andrew Morton has said in the book.'"

Though Morton would later claim that Diana's visit was a casual one to an old friend, most of the media believed that Diana had surreptitiously staged the photo opportunity to signal her approval of the book. Her very public closeness with Carolyn could only mean that Diana was aware of and endorsed her friends' contributions.

The photos of this apparently innocent social visit ran even in *Life* magazine, where royal biographer Robert Lacey, in describing Diana's bold offensive, labeled Diana a latter-day Eleanor of Aquitaine, "once shy and Machiavellian, now tough and Machiavellian, taking on all comers. . . . Eleven years ago, 'Lady Di' won her husband, in no small part, through her ability to handle the press. Now she is deploying that same skill to enlist the press against him."

After comparing all the stories, which were similar in nature, Lord McGregor now realized there was a common source and concluded that Diana had invaded her own privacy through her participation—albeit thought to be indirect at the time—in the Morton book. Commented Max Hastings, then of the *Daily Telegraph*: ". . . it did seem amazing, first of all, that she should want to talk at all, but secondly that she should engage the Murdoch press in this process . . . it suggested a degree of will for self-destructiveness."

Members of the Princess's class and those close to the royal family were immensely disappointed. "For a royal figure to put their own desire to get their marriage case understood by the public against their husband, this was an irresponsible thing for a royal princess to do," said Sir Peregrine Worsthorne. "By the old rules of the game, if you marry into the monarchy, you take the rough with the smooth and you are sort of morally obliged to play by the rules, which she didn't do."

Hastings and Worsthorne couldn't know, as became clear later, that Diana was not self-destructive and probably not, in her own mind, a traitor. She was taking risks because she had a longer-range goal—a public life free from the royal family, with power based directly on popularity with her mass audience.

That the Princess was in a state of despair soon became apparent. Her first official engagement after *Diana: Her True Story* hit the headlines was at a hospice in Merseyside. There, a sympathetic old lady stroked Diana's face, and her tears streamed. Morton wrote that a friend was not surprised, saying, "She is a brilliant actress who has disguised her public sorrow." She was better than that: a brilliant actress who *showed* herself hiding her sorrow.

Paradoxically, the royal family needed Diana now more than she needed them. She was more popular than they and she gave them luster. Moreover, she was the master of an art form that utterly baffled them. The Queen and Prince Philip continued to reject the idea of a public separation. The Queen demanded a show of unity. Charles and Diana were told to resolve their differences during a trial period of three to six months.

During that time, according to Morton, Charles's courtiers and friends went to work with several newspaper editors on positive stories about Charles as a contributor to national life and an unassuming but doting father whose attempts to see his sons were being thwarted by Diana.

Characteristically, the royal family kept faith in the power of written and spoken propaganda. It would appear that their models of persuasion came from the previous generation—men like Churchill, Roosevelt, even Hitler and Mussolini—all masters of the spoken word, all out-of-date in the modern electronic age.

Diana diffused the criticism with a self-deprecating remark at a charity appearance: "I'm supposed to be dragged off any minute with men in white coats, so if it's all right with you, I thought I might postpone my nervous breakdown to a more appropriate moment." It seemed a supremely self-confident thing to say. Her words, however, may have been less important than the fact that she looked good.

We know for sure now that she suffered from post-partum depression, bulimia, and mood swings during these years. She felt that no one in the royal family sympathized or understood. But her dark moods didn't prevent her from appearing publicly with her children.

The public liked the image of Diana as a hard-working mother. Though the dull, bourgeois style of the royal family, cultivated for more than a century, no longer interested or convinced many Britons, they liked the solid qualities—devotion to family, personal responsibility—the royals theoretically stand for. They liked them especially when found in such an elegant package as Diana. A Tiffany package. Among tabloid readers, Prince Charles was seen as an erratic parent. So long as the Princess was a great-looking, devoted mother to the future king, Robert Lacey wrote in *Life,* divorce would not remove her royal or public status.

But a story could—the *Sun's* publication of a pirated conversation between Diana and good friend James Gilbey of the gin family. The relationship was said to be platonic, but sex wasn't the issue. Both parties on the tape sounded silly. Gilbey's pet name for Diana was "Squidgy." The affair became known as Squidgygate.

Rupert Murdoch had acquired the illegally-recorded tape eighteen months earlier, but held off publishing it. Some speculate he might have been fearful of precipitating the introduction of a privacy law that would limit coverage of the monarchy.

In the tape, Diana slammed Charles and the royal family for deception, for suppressing her ambitions, and for ingratitude for what she had done to reinvigorate the monarchy. She voiced a desire to break loose.

In response to a strange, intrigued look of pity that the Queen Mother had directed toward her during one lunch, Diana rambled to Gilbey, "I just felt really sad and empty, and thought 'Bloody hell, after all I've done for this f***ing family . . . always being innuendo, the fact that I'm going to do something dramatic because I can't stand the confines of this marriage." Then, she dreamed of dumping Charles: "I'll go out and conquer the world . . . do my bit in the way I know how and leave him behind. . . . It's so difficult, so complicated. He makes my life real, real torture, I've decided."

Diana's previous attempts to mold an image as a serious social advocate were damaged by this scandal. *People* characterized her as a "dim-bulb Sloane Ranger surrounded by sycophants" because of her "giggly chatter about shopping, spending, and horoscopes." The *Evening Standard* quoted Cambridge fellow John Casey: "The Princess comes across as a bird-brained egomaniac."

According to *Times* editor Simon Jenkins, the "completely tasteless" and "totally intrusive" tape should never have been published. The incident could have been grounds for an invasion of privacy lawsuit. However, because Diana had collaborated with Andrew Morton, the royals may have thought their chances of curbing press intrusion into their lives were lost.

The media was, of course, divided. A steady rain of pro-Charles stories appeared in the press, including an announcement that broadcaster Jonathan Dimbleby had been invited to write Charles's biography. Diana, on her own, began making direct contact with editors and even newspaper owners.

After a long, bitter, and increasingly public battle involving the Prince and Princess, the Queen and Court, the Church of England and the leaders of Parliament, an official separation was declared on December 9, 1992. The separation was said to be amicable. There were no plans for divorce and no change in Diana's constitutional position.

With all of the parties to the campaign—Diana, Prince Charles, the media, and the Court—drawn into well-defined positions, there was an impasse. Charles continued to be weakened by stories of his infidelity.

And then there was the fire that nearly destroyed one wing of the beautiful Windsor Castle—named for the royal family which changed its name to Windsor during World War I. A significant collection of old-master paintings was destroyed. Nothing was insured. The fire could be seen as a metaphor for the state of the monarchy: it was aflame, it had lost many of its assets, and it seemed in danger of collapse.

In her annual Christmas address, the Queen—a remote but sympathetic figure—appealed to other members of dysfunctional families to shore up support for the monarchy: "The past year is not one I shall look back on with undiluted pleasure. In the words of one of my more sympathetic correspondents, it has turned out to be an *annus horribilis*. . . . Like many other families, we have lived through some difficult days this year. . . . It has touched me deeply that so much [support] has come from those of you with troubles of your own. If we can somehow lift our eyes from our own problems, and focus on those of others, it will be at least a step in the right direction."

Reporting on the speech, *The Times* wrote: "What matters is the national sense that something is wrong with the state of the Royal Family, that, while the Monarch remains high in her subjects' esteem, the rest of 'the firm' is variously at fault and failing to live and work as it should."

Whatever she might have planned in response to the Christmas speech, Diana had no need to act. In January of 1993, the "Camillagate" scandal erupted. *The Sun* and *Today* printed extracts from the Charles-Camilla taped conversation—a story picked up on the front pages in fifty-three countries. Supposedly recorded in December of 1989, the interchange was intimate and highly salacious.

CHARLES: "Your great achievement is to love me. . . . You suffer all these indignities and tortures and calumnies."

CAMILLA: "I'd suffer anything for you. That's love. It's the strength of love."

CHARLES: "I want to feel my way along you, all over you, and up and down you, and in and out . . . particularly in and out. . . . I'll just live inside your trousers or something. It would be much easier."

He wishes he were a tampon, the ultimate in closeness. Delighted with the joke, Camilla cries that she wants him day and night, "desperately, desperately, desperately."

Before hanging up, Charles says he'll "press the tit," referring to the phone button. Camilla: "I wish you were pressing mine."

Neither Charles nor Camilla denied then or today that the tape was genuine; to do so would have been folly, for they were easily identifiable. ". . . this chap walked in with the tape and it was unbelievable what we were listening to," recalled then *Daily Mirror* photographer Ken Lennox in the *Frontline* documentary. "It was Charles and it was Camilla. You didn't need to be an expert to listen to it."

The *Mirror* refused to publish the tampon segments, and yet, "that's the bit that everyone knows about, 'I would like to be a Tampax,'" Lennox said. "And I think in Italy he's still known as 'Il Tampanini.'"

Diana bided her time. The tape vindicated what she had purported in *Diana: Her True Story,* but what many had passed off as the delusional jealousy of a madwoman—that Charles was unfaithful with Camilla.

Men on the street derided him. "[Tabloid editor] Richard Stott said, at the time, every time Prince Charles walks past a building site, he would get a face-full from the blokes up the scaffolding," said Lennox. At an official engagement, a man in the crowd shouted: "Have you no shame?" Opinion polls showed that only one in three Britons felt Charles was entitled to be king, despite the constitutional realities that guarantee his hereditary right, barring abdication or an act of Parliament.

Through 1993, Charles struggled to redeem his image. Giving up polo entirely, he autographed soccer balls at a London recreation center, cut ribbons, laid wreaths, inspected factories, visited an inner-city housing project, called on troops in Bosnia, stopped in at a former concentration camp in Poland. Despite the effort, his appearances seemed ceremonial and removed.

Diana, meanwhile, increased her highly publicized visits to shelters, hospices, and care facilities. She went to India and Nepal in March of 1993, continuing her good works. She continued to win the media contest. A media research firm reported that during the first six days of March alone, press coverage of Diana totaled 3,603 inches of newsprint while Charles's press coverage totaled 275 inches.

The Palace and Charles accelerated a campaign to pull Diana out of public life and out of the newspapers by treating her as a second-class royal and sabotaging her charity work. She was not invited to royal family functions. The royals refused to give her a platform from which to speak.

Though constitutionally Diana would always remain the mother of the future king, her public role after the separation was uncertain. As Diana herself remarked in Andrew Morton's book, "People's agendas changed overnight. I was now the separated wife of the Prince of Wales, I was a problem, I was a liability. 'How are we going to deal with her? This hasn't happened before.'"

Diana might have her way with the media, but the Palace, led by Prince Charles, was the ringmaster, the director in the staging of events. Diana was forbidden to become head of the British Red Cross. When she traveled her tickets were downgraded to business class. The band greeting her in Nepal was forbidden to play the national anthem.

She was deprived of staff—ladies-in-waiting, courtiers, aides. While Charles retained nine officials working directly or indirectly to publicize his interests, Diana had one part-time press officer, paid from the Prince's estate of the Duchy of Cornwall. Wrote Andrew Morton: "For a Princess used to an adoring media, this change in fortune undermined still further her precarious self-esteem and fed her existing anxieties."

Diana was driven to the media for support. The royal family tried to restrict her access. As she continued to behave as if she were a member of the royal family, the Queen and her circle rebuffed her. Diana requested permission to attend the memorial service for two children killed by an Irish Republican Army bomb in Cheshire, Warrington. Prince Philip was sent. In September 1993, the Palace forbade her private visit to Dublin to meet with Irish president Mary Robinson, for "security reasons," though two months later she did attend the Remembrance Day service in Enniskillen, Northern Ireland.

As the struggle continued, the royal family began to show a pattern of misunderstanding that seriously undermined their position. They believed that if they could muzzle the Princess, prevent her from speaking out (as she apparently had done for the Morton book), they could lessen her effectiveness. They did not understand that the power of a good picture was far greater than speeches from the Queen or from MPs.

The Queen is rightly credited with understanding the power of the new media. At her insistence, her coronation in 1953 was televised around the world. But the Queen, some of whose charm lies in her plainness, was no match for Diana, a beautiful woman with a strong personal sense of style. Moreover, Diana, born in 1961, had grown up in the television age. Even Prince Charles, fourteen years her senior, was of a generation that did not understand television in the way that she did.

Diana liked the company of her boys, and found more and more occasions to be photographed with them. Realizing that it was Diana's game to look motherly, Charles adopted her methods and took the boys on vacations. Boldly reaching across the Atlantic for an audience, Diana took the Princes to Disney World in Florida.

Attracting an ever-wider audience through the media, Diana must have felt that she was winning the match. Throughout the separation, she stepped up her courting of the media, including *The Sun* and others with the highest circulation, to elicit more sympathetic coverage than Charles was getting. But the temptation to speak out, to find another tool to gain an advantage, was stronger all the time.

She entertained writers who wrote about her tours, sent them notes when she liked their stories about her, and kept track of their birthdays. She invited Oprah Winfrey and Barbara Walters to lunch at Kensington Palace. She attended parties sponsored by *People, Harper's Bazaar,* and *Vanity Fair,* and posed for *Vogue.*

And when she took a fall, it was images that hurt her. Almost a year after the separation announcement, Diana discovered that the game she was playing was more dangerous than she had realized.

On November 7 and 8, 1993, the *Sunday Mirror* published full-body shots of Diana working out at a gym. According to Kelley's *The Royals,* the *Mirror* had paid $250,000 to fitness-gym owner Bryce Taylor for the photos taken through a hole cut in a ceiling panel. Once the photos were printed, Taylor contracted with a photo agency to syndicate the eighty-two pictures.

After publication of the photos, there were days of public controversy about the invasion of privacy and the wisdom of legal press curbs from the Palace, Parliament, and publishers. The Mirror Group withdrew from the Press Complaints Commission. Taylor called what he did "a legal scam." With the backing of the Queen and Prince Philip, Diana sued the newspaper and photographer. An injunction froze the money due Taylor. Kelley reports that, in a sealed court document, Diana stated: "I was unaware that any such photographs had been taken and had at no time given my consent to being photographed by the club in any circumstances."

Determined to assist in the creation of a privacy law, Diana was prepared to testify in court. Bryce Taylor was assigned Geoffrey Robertson, an expert counsel under Britain's legal-aid system. Robertson, an Australian republican, began a personal attack. He constructed a case that caricatured Diana as a pickup begging for attention by flirting with men, wearing skintight clothes to show off her body, and working out in front of the window for public view.

More than nine hundred reporters, anxious to cover the trial, had applied for credentials in a courtroom that could seat only seventy-five.

Clearly no longer able to manage media coverage, Diana appeared shaken. She could only temporarily count on the support of the royal family. When her detective was scheduled as a defense witness, he was transferred from her service. She did her best to keep up a brave front but the media smelled blood. There was widespread speculation about the Princess's state of mind.

Uncertain whether Diana could withstand rigorous cross-examination, it is alleged that the Queen authorized counsel to make an offer to Taylor, who at first refused. After further negotiation, however, a deal was cut and the suit was settled out of court. The Mirror Group issued a public apology and paid $40,000 in damages to a charity in Diana's name. They didn't write about the case. Taylor also gave a public apology, and relinquished the photos and negatives, agreeing never to discuss the case. It was reported by Kelley that he was paid off in secret monthly payments totaling $450,000—from a blind trust. All parties signed confidentiality agreements to not reveal details.

Diana appeared to have won. Newspapers exclaimed "Di's Smashing Victory." Though the settlement meant that newspapers could avoid regulation, the media became more guarded. Their fear of tighter regulations may have played a part in their newfound restraint. Media managers may also have sensed that when they turned on Di they lost touch with their readership.

Although Diana had become accustomed to thinking of herself as a commodity—she had once said, ". . . you see yourself as a good product that sits on a shelf and sells well, and people make a lot of money out of you"—she must still have felt betrayed by the media over the publication of the gym photos. After all, loyalty was a quality Diana prized, and she had generally been loyal.

The betrayals of the media, however, were predictable. Even if a celebrity has made friends with the press, they still won't spare him or her the bullet. But the bullet will be softer. Nevertheless, if a public figure does something obviously stupid, the media will not save him or her regardless of a congenial relationship having been established. However, in a gray area, where the ball is right on the line and could fall either way, the press is more likely to give a friend the benefit of the doubt.

Diana began to understand the danger of using only images. She began to speak out at greater length. Her new tactic was to present her "true" self, to package herself in such a way that she would seem to be more genuine than she had ever seemed before.

On December 3, 1993, at a charity luncheon, the Princess appealed for time and space after more than a decade of scrutiny:

"When I started my public life . . . I was not aware of how over-whelming [media] attention would become, nor the extent to which it would affect both my public duties and my personal life. . . ."

She announced that she would continue to back a small num-ber of charities—about 120—and devote more attention to her chil-dren. A few months later, at a gallery reception, according to Morton, she conversed with actor Jeremy Irons, who mentioned, "I'm taking a year off acting." Diana replied: "So have I."

The tabloids shouted "Ab-Di-Cation." Admirers dubbed her withdrawal a tragedy. Detractors called her a cunning actress looking for public solace. Both were correct

Instead of finding the anonymity she sought, she created even more interest in herself, especially among the paparazzi. The media tactic was to startle her by suddenly appearing in front of her, face to face, anticipating that she would lose her composure. The ambush "stalkerazzi" tactics produced photos that sold for even more money. Did Diana anticipate this? Had she simply used a piece of reverse psy-chology to gain attention?

Her friend Sam McKnight, appearing in the A&E *Biography* "Diana, the True Story," gave an example. He met Diana one day when she'd been driving. A photographer on a motorcycle had repeatedly pulled even with her car. "The guy on the bike screamed abuse to make her cry. . . . And the picture is in the paper next day. . . . She felt as if she had been raped daily. No wonder she had black moments."

"I had just lost her in a crowd," recalled freelance photographer Glenn Harvey, "but all of a sudden I saw this flash of blonde hair fly-ing left to right toward this other photographer on my right, and she was about an inch away from his nose. She just screamed at the top of her voice, 'You make my life hell!' . . . and then she sort of went off with her hand on her head and realized what she'd done. It was the first 'loon attack' that we'd seen."

These stalkerazzi techniques have been lambasted by numerous celebrities and lawmakers. But the media maintained that Diana's attitude smacked of a double standard. When she wanted attention, she made sure she was seen—in top form—at public events or on private outings with her children. To expect she could switch the media off and on at will was surely unrealistic.

The *Daily Telegraph*'s Max Hastings offered perspective on the situation: "I think she would have withered on the vine if she'd been left alone."

Diana was in hiding, but she was fair game. She removed herself further and further from the royal family, allowing more layers of protocol to be stripped away. The media began to take more potshots, confronting her physically, criticizing her appearance and behavior.

Diana persisted. During her hiatus from public life, she worked to perfect her public image. She planned to experiment further with speaking to the press. Morton says that for advice she looked again to director Sir Richard Attenborough and to actor Terence Stamp, as well as to voice coach Peter Settelen, who describes his input as helping her make an emotional commitment to her speeches. She was never a great public speaker, but the idea of the Princess being a person as opposed to an institution was innovative for a member of the royal family.

In the fall of 1993 the television documentary *Prince of Wales* aired in Britain. It showed the Prince at work and at play and with his sons. As an attempt to ingratiate Charles with the public it was a crashing failure. Particularly damaging was the Prince's candid confession that he'd been having an affair with Camilla Parker-Bowles. Palace insiders viewed the admission as a reckless move that showed a secret agenda to make an honest woman of Camilla, paving the way for their mutual divorces and preparing the public for an eventual marriage—and possibly a new queen.

The response of the papers was worse than critical. In headlines and articles the Prince was made to look foolish. *People,* however, published a remarkably even-handed review: "Charles comes across as a complex man plagued by self-doubt, an introspective altruist who often dislikes his job but who does his best to find meaning in a role that, to outsiders, often seems absurd."

People felt, nevertheless, that Charles gave the impression that he was unsuited to be king, a private person not good at "being a performing monkey," who described following a schedule set months in advance as "a horror." Diana could learn from the example of the Prince that interviews may backfire.

Diana knew about the airing of the interview in advance. She had time to prepare. Her friend Lord Puttman told her to lie low. Whatever she said, he felt, would look like tit-for-tat, cheap public bickering. Any statement, moreover, might someday somehow be used as a weapon against her.

But Diana couldn't let the event pass without a response. As the interview was being broadcast, she attended a *Vanity Fair*-sponsored gallery benefit. Wearing a low-cut, black cocktail dress, she looked stunning. Diana continued to upstage Charles at every opportunity. Her reasoning seemed to be that the more desirable she appeared to others, the more ridiculous Charles might seem for having given her up.

I've often done crisis management for clients. My company has been a pioneer in rapid response. We understand that we live in a world in which, if you respond to a crisis with humility, speed, and responsibility, you will do well, generally. And if you don't, you won't. One of the impressive things about Diana at this phase in her career was that she seized the initiative. Apparently working mostly from intuition, she seemed to know exactly the right thing to do.

But in this highly charged, highly competitive atmosphere, the press couldn't make permanent alliances. Loyalty was not a factor. Having just drawn blood from Charles, they found a way to go after Diana. In late August 1994, *News of the World* broke the story that, beginning in September 1992, a lonely and obsessive Diana had anonymously called platonic confidant Oliver Hoare three hundred times in an eighteen-month period. The harassment story suggested that her life alone and in exile was prompting a nervous breakdown.

Diana did her own damage control. On August 21, before the story broke, but realizing that it was about to, Diana summoned Richard Kay of the *Daily Mail*. Kay was a correspondent who had befriended her on a 1993 Nepal visit. It was rumored that after he had turned down an offer to be her press secretary, they'd made an agreement that Kay would give Diana advice in exchange for news scoops. During a three-hour conversation in Kay's Volvo near Talbot Square, she told her side of the story. Diana insisted there was no truth to the Hoare story—she was the victim of a plot.

The *Evening Standard* responded on August 22: "High-level conspiracy against the royal family—or one woman's descent into madness?" The claim was made later that the calls had been faked by a schoolboy.

The tabloid press wasn't buying her stories. They showed little sympathy. Rumors began to circulate about her wild overspending. One source close to Charles said that she'd spent $250,000 on personal items alone during the previous year. Charles sensed an opportunity. He derided her as shallow and materialistic. It was an unwise move.

Diana revealed that Charles had spent $650,000 during that same year. She itemized the list. It included manicures and polo ponies.

Diana could no longer count on the support of the press. After years of being jealous of Fergie, she joined forces with her sister-in-law to curb the press, according to Kitty Kelley's *The Royals*. No longer royal family members on the public payroll, they felt entitled to their privacy. They filed a criminal complaint and sought an injunction against photographers who trespassed on private property. They drew up a list of sympathetic journalists. The list grew shorter and shorter.

On October 3, 1994, Anna Pasternak's book *Princess in Love* was released. It told the story of the affair between Diana and former Life Guards officer James Hewitt. After paying a reported $4.5 million for the manuscript, Bloomsbury rushed it into print to capitalize on Charles's confessions of adultery and to preempt author Andrew Morton's new book *Diana: Her New Life,* scheduled for release that November. Hewitt described Diana as an emotionally wounded and hungry woman who was both like a child (her Kensington Palace bedroom was chock-full of stuffed animals) and a mature female who "let her passion rip."

The public ate it up. By midday, the first run of 75,000 had sold out. Now being viewed as a duplicitous adulterer who had her own part in destroying the marriage, the betrayed Diana was apparently in tears. Some feared this was the straw that would make her crack; Bloomsbury editors were counseled on how to conduct themselves should Diana commit suicide. Others were more sanguine. One veteran Diana-watcher told *People*: "She is a supreme actress, and as a friend of hers told me, 'She is going to hold her head up high.'"

Diana tried to repair her connections with the press. She invited Rupert Murdoch, *News of the World*'s Stuart Kuttner, and Landon Jones, then managing editor of *People,* along with *People*'s London bureau chief Fred Hauptfuhrer, to meet with her.

Her goal was to change the image of a volatile, unbalanced woman that had been sold in the press.

It was a smart strategy. Diana may not have known what her next move would be, but she wanted it reported favorably. At the end of the twentieth century there is enormous value in having a well-established connection with the media. Howard Kurtz, in his book *Spin Cycle,* says that at the end of President Clinton's first term, several of his advisers lobbied Clinton to extend a portion of his charm to the media. He was reluctant at first, but when he finally did it his press coverage improved immeasurably.

Landon Jones, interviewed for this book, recalls Diana as a woman who thought personal rapport with the media might turn the tide. "She decided to take charge," says Jones of their meeting, his first personal encounter with Diana though he had edited more stories on the Princess than any other *People* managing editor. He asked her how she was coping with the onslaught of publicity. "She said that she tried to ignore it but was concerned about 'its impact on William and Harry.'"

Jones wrote about the encounter in the *Princeton Alumni Weekly.* He quotes Diana saying that her solution "is just to laugh at it. For instance, the boys joked with me about the idea I would make all those telephone calls [to Oliver Hoare]. They said, 'Mummy, you are too busy to make all those calls they said you did!'

"The Princess then said that she concluded that one way to deal with her problems with the press was to get to know it better, so she was having small meetings with editors. She said she had recently met with 'Mr. Murdoch.'"

Jones wrote that he told the Princess that President Clinton was pursuing the same end through small dinners with the press. "'Did it help?' she asked intently. I said that perhaps it did, but the expectations could be raised too high on both sides by such meetings, and she would be wrong to expect instant results."

If Landon Jones's impressions of the Princess were any indication, the meeting was a success in terms of damage control and image reversal. "If it was possible to be both professional and flirtatious, she was. Her visual appearance was of girlishness and shyness, but her personality was outgoing and confident. She had this image of being a dim bulb, but she came across as intelligent, brighter, and more involved than I had thought," Jones wrote.

The Prince of Wales, the long-promised authorized biography of Charles by his supporter Jonathan Dimbleby, was released in October of 1994 and excerpted in London's *Sunday Times.* Charles had handed over his diaries and ten thousand letters to Dimbleby, who also interviewed family members, including Prince Philip and the Queen Mother, as well as friends. Dimbleby was given carte blanche on commentary, with Charles reading only for factual accuracy. The Prince did not have final approval.

Dimbleby put forth that having never loved Diana, Charles proposed to her because of the pressures from the media and Prince Philip, who told Charles his only honorable alternative was to marry Diana or end the relationship. Dimbleby says that Charles "felt ill-used but impotent" and "interpreted his father's attitude as an ultimatum." Furthermore, Dimbleby paints Charles as an emotionally-deprived pawn, abandoned by his mother, bullied by his father, and tortured by a paranoid wife intoxicated with publicity, whom he had tried to help by arranging for her to see a psychiatrist in 1982.

Charles's long-planned, calculated attempt to reinstate himself was another disaster. The newspaper *Today* blasted him as "a self-obsessed, self-indulgent and selfish man constantly turning molehills of problems into insurmountable mountains. . . . There must now be serious doubt about his fitness to wear the Crown." Royal-watchers had said that divorce negotiations were already in progress, but were held up by issues of who would be the initiator, guarantees for Diana to continue her charity work, and retention of her royal title.

Diana gained in sympathy from Charles's faux pas, which overshadowed the Hewitt debacle and corroborated Morton's story that Diana had felt like "a lamb to the slaughter" on the eve of her wedding, having just realized that Charles was still seeing Camilla Parker-Bowles. In an October 17 telephone poll of thirty-seven thousand viewers of a morning television show, fifty-four percent sided with Diana, while forty-six percent said their hearts went out to Charles.

One can feel some sympathy for the Prince. He was brought up to believe in the virtues of another age. He takes seriously, perhaps too seriously, the responsibilities of his position and clearly doesn't always know how to manage them. In his A&E *Biography* there is an extraordinary moment. His young son Harry is balanced on his knee as the two look through the viewfinder of a large, old camera. Half to himself Charles says, "There are people in there. Look at them. Trapped."

By the middle of the decade it was clear that neither Diana nor Charles was going to win the favor of the media or of the public by presenting themselves as virtuous human beings. This worked to Diana's advantage. She could continue to play the woman scorned, blaming her own infidelities on her husband's philandering. Though now in her mid-thirties, she could still get away with a claim that she was discovering herself. Diana had still working for her the fact that she was more attractive, a more alluring package than the Prince. Glamour was her not-so-secret defensive weapon. Charles, on the other hand, had the entire cultural and political Establishment on his side.

In 1996 stories began to be heard about a long flirtation between Diana and Will Carling, the twenty-nine-year-old captain of England's national rugby team, whose wife, Julia, worked in fashion, PR, and the media. Julia was a match for Diana (and was even said to look like her). By mid-month, Julia had stated in an interview for the *Mail* that her husband was naïve and was one of a number of attached men who had made liaisons with the Princess, a pathetically grasping "other woman."

The tabloid press loved the story.

Diana called Richard Kay and assured him that her friendship with Carling was innocent. Then she asked the *News of the World*'s managing editor to back off. She called the *Daily Mirror* and insisted the friendship was platonic. They quoted her as saying "I don't need a lover." Seven months later, Julia Carling filed for divorce from Will.

Though she had experimented with speechmaking to win support, Diana had never taken her case directly to the people. This mysterious silence made the few words she did say all the more powerful. In our interview, Richard Greene, who became one of Diana's speech advisers in 1996, told me: "If you are of interest to the media and you give interviews every other week, the value of the thoughts and message goes down. The fewer words spoken in public, the more rare they are. Diamonds are more valuable than nickel or lead."

Diana the actress now prepared for the greatest role of her life. Having gradually crept back into public life, she sat down for an unprecedented, one-on-one, television interview that aired on the BBC—and then throughout the world—in November of 1995.

Confessor

> *"What we're dealing with is a modern woman, a post-feminist woman of the '90s who feels she's got rights."*
>
> —Helena Kennedy, barrister
> *The Times* of London

Diana had moved beyond conventional guidelines; it may be that she was forced to. She felt that she was too often losing her prestige in press exposés. Her marriage had failed and she was fearful of losing personal influence altogether. She'd had considerably more than the fifteen minutes of fame guaranteed by Andy Warhol, and she wasn't sure she could count on attracting the spotlight forever. She was a unique figure, on her own in unknown territory. Instinctively she understood that to win back the favor of the public she had to make a bold stroke.

Barbara Hower, a best-selling writer and former correspondent for *Entertainment Tonight,* who put together a two-hour, prime-time, syndicated special on the royal family in the late 1980s, was interviewed for this book. She felt that the Princess needed better advice: "How could she have been so stupid and so lacking in historical information as to think that she was going to live happily ever after with Prince Charles? She was ill-equipped in any direction. Where the f*** was her mother? Now they talk about her mother this, her mother that. I never saw a picture of her mother. I wouldn't know her mother in a police lineup. Her father was a geek beyond the geeks. I knew him, and married to that . . . Diana was like Romulus and Remus. She brought herself up."

Her mother, Frances, was, I suspect, very much in Diana's mind as she made her next move in her war with the royal family. She wanted to avoid losing her position and the custody of her children as her mother had.

In 1994, Diana was in detailed, secret discussions for an ITV documentary on her life. She decided against cooperation, wanting not to compete with Charles's interview with Jonathan Dimbleby and hoping to avoid the courtiers' antagonism. She saw how badly Charles's confessions had been received. She hoped to learn from his mistakes.

That year she began to assiduously search her soul about the next career to pursue. I spoke about this period in her life with American motivation guru Anthony Robbins, a counselor to Diana, who said: "In a [royal] world in which pretense was the basis of operation, Diana was unbelievably real. She was trying to deal with expectations [of her status] and be true to herself. She wanted a role that respected the monarchy but also allowed her to have her own identity."

Throughout 1995, Diana aggressively sought specific career advice from PR chiefs, former cabinet ministers, Parliament members, newspaper and television executives, captains of industry, and marketing executives, according to Nicholas Davies in *Diana: The People's Princess.*

She invited these VIPs to a series of lunches at Kensington Palace. Davies was asked, along with two others, to script a scenario—a vision statement—for her new vocation. They proposed that Diana preside over a new charity entitled The Princess of Wales Foundation, which would have offices and a small, full-time staff, including a director general.

Diana decided on a role as worldwide royal ambassador. She envisioned jetting around the globe visiting charitable organizations, raising money for her causes, directly communicating with and helping society's victims and disadvantaged. To prepare herself, she began a new series of luncheons and meetings, calling upon therapists, image groomers, and media consultants. Among them: mother-figure Annabel Goldsmith, wife of multimillionaire Sir James Goldsmith; Angela Serota, wife of Tate Gallery director Nicholas Serota; ITV chat show host Clive James; and her closest confidante, her psychotherapist, Susie Orbach.

Author of *Fat Is a Feminist Issue,* Orbach points to men controlling women in unequal partnerships as the root of Western women's obsession with weight, shape, and food. Brought up in a patriarchal aristocracy, married to a man who didn't love her, expected to quietly withdraw after she completed her duty of producing heirs, Diana took to Susie and devoured her theories.

Having decided her direction, and knowing that the Court would never support her goals, especially since divorce negotiations were in the works, Diana decided that the only way to bypass the Establishment was to rally public support, according to Davies.

A television interview would be the vehicle. Keeping the project secret would be vital. And she would require that questions be submitted beforehand so that she could carefully script her answers.

It would answer a number of the questions this book poses if we could know to what extent Diana was advised in her course of action. Did she, as she said herself, "lead from the heart," knowing what moves to make, what positions to take, by intuition? Or was she coached? Though it has been reported that Diana consulted with a number of advisers and experts, none has taken credit for what she did.

Her friend Vivienne Parry, in the A&E *Biography* "Diana, the True Story," remarked, "I can't think of anybody who was a friend [who wasn't] 'out' at one stage or another." Diana picked up and dropped friends often. Aside from her children, only one person, Paul Burrell, seems to have kept her confidence throughout the period of her greatest trials. Certainly Burrell offered companionship, comfort, and serenity. During her turbulent relations with the Windsors and the media, in good times and in bad, he stood by her. He was her protector, which may have made him more important to her development than any of her intellectual or spiritual advisers.

Officially Burrell was Diana's butler, acting as her personal assistant, press secretary, and chauffeur. He was about her same age, and a married man with two children. Richard Greene, a speech coach to Diana, told me, "[Burrell] advised her on virtually everything, and she almost always took his advice." (Greene is working with Burrell on an oral history of Diana.)

Burrell was so loyal they were said to stick together like melted candy in a coat pocket.

"He helped her decide where to go, whether Angola or Bosnia. How to approach the press. How to stand, what to wear. What to say, what not to say. He was very involved in the BBC interview. He'd be there when she called and was insecure. She was desperate to keep him near. If he went away, she'd say, 'What would I do without him?'"

Because of her mercurial moods, Diana hired and fired some thirty employees through the years. Burrell was the only one left. Diana called him "My Rock." Greene says, "She was getting better advice from one person than from all of them. He had great wisdom. He saw the whole picture."

He was her alter ego, Greene says, the true side that she could-n't always show but needed to keep alive in order to remain sane. "He knew her as well as he knew himself."

Though never romantically involved, they connected often with-out words. "I first noticed the bond when I went to lunch at Kensington Palace," Greene recalls. "He and Diana shared playful but knowing nods to exchange information." On trips, he instinctively knew if she would want water or a pear or a granola bar. His family even accom-panied Diana and her sons on outings to theme parks and movies.

They met in 1980, when Charles brought Diana to Balmoral for the first time. Her Majesty's footman at the time, he stumbled upon a young girl lost in a corridor and helped her to her room. Later, he taught her how to curtsy and how to address the Queen. She could talk to him easily. In 1988, Diana requested he become butler at Highgrove, Charles's country residence. When Charles and Diana split, the first two words she wrote when listing the things she wanted to take from Highgrove were "Paul Burrell." He moved to Kensington Palace, occupying a three-bedroom apartment one hun-dred yards from Diana. When she was stripped of her HRH title, Burrell continued to bow and address her as Your Royal Highness.

Why did Diana gravitate to Burrell? "He emanates instant trustworthiness," Greene says. "He has an almost Buddha-like pres-ence about him. That is comfortable to those who are child-like, to have someone that stable and centered and calming. And Diana was like a little kid in many ways. She'd burst with tremendous joy, then suddenly become quiet and sullen. During one conversation, she was very playful, until the talk turned to how she had just let go one of her aides. She became very serious, like a child betrayed by a friend who might say, 'I'm never going to play with him again.'"

Like Diana, Burrell had a great sense of humor. And he was pro-tective. Says Richard Greene, "When I first went to Kensington

Palace, he was completely checking me out. His eyes were warm and glistening, but you could tell he was seeing everything. He had an elegant but sophisticated knowingness."

"There's the possibility that Diana felt a deeper love, a pure love, for Paul than she had ever experienced with men she was intimate with," Greene says. "He was in some ways sent to her."

It can be argued that what made Diana so remarkable a world figure was visible, tangible authenticity—charisma in its original sense. If so, we may look past the press lords, coaches, gurus, and counselors, to Paul Burrell who gave her a strong enough self-confidence that she was able to take on a host of persons and institutions who seemed to have every advantage over her.

Diana prepared to take her case to the people. To make ready, she picked the brains of many more invitees to another series of lunches during the summer and fall of 1995. She never told them specifically that their input was helping her craft her position. Rather, she explained her predicament and asked advice on how she could break out of the constraints of her official position to lead a more worthwhile life. Playing the beleaguered, trapped princess who just wanted to help people—a lass misunderstood, lonely, aggrieved—she charmed them into believing that they, too, were on a mission.

In due time, a select few became privy to her specific plan to conduct a television interview. They helped her refine her thoughts, rehearse answers to possible questions, and fine-tune her physical and verbal presentation, which to that point had been hesitant, flustered, and flushed. Among them were her old friend Sir Richard Attenborough; film producer Sir David (now Lord) Puttman; Sir Gordon Reece, who had worked with former Prime Minister Margaret Thatcher on her television technique; Susie Orbach; and the motivation teacher Anthony Robbins. "I helped her clarify what she felt, thought, and wanted to get across, so she could walk into the interview and be herself," Robbins told me.

For years, Diana had been courted for interviews by broadcasters, including ITV's Clive James (taking her to dinner twice and even escorting her into the studio), Oprah Winfrey (over a private lunch), Barbara Walters, David Frost, CBS (which, it has been alleged, offered Sarah Ferguson a lucrative job hosting celebrity interviews, provided she could deliver Diana), and Martin Bashir, the quiet *Panorama* reporter. "While every other member of the royal family, most notoriously her husband, had used television to promote their causes and latterly to talk about their private lives, Diana knew that she would never be allowed that freedom by the Palace," Morton wrote.

By fall 1995 she could no longer delay. Diana had decided to talk to Martin Bashir for *Panorama,* BBC's flagship current affairs program. Bashir was considered thorough, but not in the league of evisceraters David Frost or Jeremy Paxman. Like Morton, Bashir also got the Princess to agree to an interview, after several requests, by agreeing to secrecy. BBC executives, fearing censorship, kept the corporation's governors in the dark.

According to newspaper reports, Bashir had the freedom to ask what he wanted, forewarning Diana about topics but not specific questions. But Nicholas Davies says that Bashir not only submitted questions in advance, but he also went over them, one at a time, line by line, for three days with Diana until she was happy with them and could concentrate on her answers. Diana demanded no questions be posed about her relationship with Will Carling.

The filming at Kensington Palace was done in absolute secrecy. Bashir and crew used special compact cameras for filming, on Sunday, November 5. To prevent leaks, Diana dismissed her staff for the day.

The interview was shot in five hours, with many breaks so Diana could check each question and prepare her answers, which were deliberately brief, to the point, and exact. To enhance the visual appearance of seriousness and maturity, she wore a low-key, dark suit with a simple white top and dark makeup around her eyes.

Diana watched the video three times before granting permission to show it. According to Davies, her reaction was "Brilliant!" She repeated this word time and again. Then she congratulated Bashir and editor Steve Hewlett on "an excellent documentary."

On Tuesday, November 14, 1995, Diana phoned Sir Robert Fellowes, the Queen's private secretary and husband of Diana's sister Jane. Before leaving for an official visit to Broadmoor, the top-security jail for the criminally insane, she had wanted to tell Her Majesty that she was going to be on BBC's *Panorama* the following Monday, November 20. Just herself. An interview in which she would discuss marriage, life with the royal family, the tabloids, Camilla, and Charles.

The Queen, of course, had been unaware of the plan, and was impotent to quash the airing. Diana had proceeded without permission, thereby defying royal precedent. This was the first time in the reign of Queen Elizabeth that anyone in the royal family had ever had the audacity to go over her head. Without exception, all members cleared television, radio, and print interviews with senior Palace aides, who gave permission only after consulting with the Queen.

Furthermore, the interview was in the can and out of the reach of royal hands, even at the BBC, which operates under a royal charter. Chairman Sir Marmaduke Hussey was married to the Queen's chief lady-in-waiting, her friend and adviser for twenty years. The BBC's agreement with Diana to keep the interview secret, given the Queen's connections, was another blow to the charter protocol that gave special deference to the monarchy.

The Queen really had few options. Quite aside from the constitutional protection against censorship, the royal family was up against Diana's primal, anti-authoritarian impulses. She was determined to have her say.

Diana was unequivocally her own best manager of her message. Though he first began to work with her shortly after the *Panorama* interview aired, speech adviser Richard Greene said in an interview for this book that he became privy to the strategic choices made by Diana and her aides when preparing for the interview. He says that she saw herself as "David in a David and Goliath situation. She was the underdog fighting against the paparazzi, the press, the royal family, and [a segment of the] public who did not believe in her sincerity. She was carrying a huge burden because everything she did was scrutinized, dissected, and criticized."

The timing of the interview was perfect. November 14 was Charles's forty-seventh birthday. When the Queen called the Prince in Berlin, where he was on an official tour, he and the Queen were reportedly "spitting tacks" over the coup. At 8:00 A.M. the BBC had broadcast the national anthem in honor of Charles's birthday, but by noon, after the BBC released the news of Diana's first solo and world-exclusive interview, Charles and his recently publicized (and newly more public) love affair with Camilla Parker-Bowles was dumped from the BBC news agenda.

Now Diana was in the spotlight. Or more like under klieg lights from around the globe.

Every major broadcaster worldwide rushed to buy the program. Within two hours of the announcement, the BBC had signed deals with America, Australia, Canada, and all of Europe. Asia began phoning as soon as the news hit its time zone.

The night of airing, Diana attended a London gala dinner. She'd played one role for the BBC. She didn't have to live that role.

Any media professional could tell that the interview was premeditated and crafted. Here was a woman who had spent millions to look glamorous, yet during that hour was so obviously dreary and doleful that no man who had first met her would ask for her phone number. That's not to say her emotion was insincere. Diana came across as genuinely hurt, devastated, and humiliated over her husband's adultery and coldness. She clearly was a troubled soul. In that respect, the *Panorama* interview was a remarkably successful effort to gain public sympathy.

As a member of the British ruling class, Diana had, like members of the royal family, been raised by nannies and sent off to boarding schools. But in this interview she spoke—truthfully, it seems—about her concern for the moral education of their children. She could have been a conscientious soccer mom:

QUESTION: What are you doing to try and effect some kind of change?

DIANA: Well, with William and Harry, for instance, I take them round homelessness projects. I've taken William and Harry to people dying of AIDS—albeit I told them it was cancer. I've taken the children to all sorts of areas where I'm not sure anyone of that age in this family has been before. . . . I want them to have an understanding of people's emotions, people's insecurities, people's distress, and people's hopes and dreams.

She spoke very explicitly about her hopes for her own future:

DIANA: I'd like to be an ambassador for this country. I'd like to represent this country abroad. . . .

When I go abroad we've got sixty to ninety photographers, just from this country, coming with me, so let's use it in a productive way, to help this country. . . . I've been in a privileged position for fifteen years. I've got tremendous knowledge about people and how to communicate. I've learnt that, I've got it, and I want to use it.

And when I look at people in public life, I'm not a political animal but I think the biggest disease this world suffers from in this day and age is the disease of people feeling unloved, and I know that I can give love for a minute, for half an hour, for a day, for a month, but I can give—I'm very happy to do that and I want to do that.

QUESTION: Do you think that the British people are happy with you in your role?

DIANA: I think the British people need someone in public life to give affection, to make them feel important, to support them, to give them light in their dark tunnels.

She faced, head-on (and certainly well-prepared), the most serious criticisms that could be leveled against her:

QUESTION: Up until you came into this family, the monarchy seemed to enjoy an unquestioned position at the heart of British life. Do you feel that you're at all to blame for the fact that survival of the monarchy is now a question that people are asking?

DIANA: No, I don't feel blame. I mean, once or twice I've heard people say to me that, you know, "Diana's out to destroy the monarchy," which has bewildered me, because why would I want to destroy something that is my children's future?

And, in a sentimental finale, the Princess hearkened back to the nickname given her by the press a decade earlier:

QUESTION: Do you think you will ever be queen?

DIANA: No, I don't, no. . . . I'd like to be a queen of people's hearts, in people's hearts, but I don't see myself being queen of this country. I don't think many people will want me to be queen . . . because I do things differently, because I don't go by a rule book, because I lead from the heart, not the head, and albeit that's got me into trouble in my work, I understand that. But someone's got to go out there and love people and show it.

"Diana had a very keen sense—Diana and her aides—of how to maximize their situation," says Richard Greene. "The interview was brilliant. It accomplished exactly what she wanted to accomplish. It was PR at its best, a brilliant move to have everything controlled, from keeping the interview to one hour to picking who would ask the questions."

In *The Guardian,* showbusiness PR man Max Clifford—with whom Diana had struck up a recently much-publicized friendship—concurred with Greene about Diana's adroitness: "Oh, her timing is brilliant. . . . Up until two years ago, her image was perfect. But it's become a bit tarnished."

But it was the tone as much as the content of the interview that was so remarkable. The idea permeates our culture that the world operates at several levels of reality. Certain truths are acceptable at one level of reality and not at another. We know, for example, that our parents had sexual relations with one another. But we don't want to know any specific details about our parents' sexual lives in the past or present. We know that men in power, including many of our political leaders, have had active extra-marital sexual lives. But so long as these stories only come to us secondhand, we don't much care. There were well-publicized rumors about President Clinton's infidelities from the beginning of his national career, but his administration was seriously shaken only when we saw live young women interviewed on television ready to allege specifics.

Similarly, there had been stories for years about an affair conducted by Diana with James Hewitt. Anna Pasternak's *The Princess in Love* told the tale in passages like the following, which describes Diana on her honeymoon:

"As he was her first lover, she was still swathed in the chiffon of her romantic imagination. She had envisaged that afterwards they would lie together as one, physically and spiritually. She had believed that every day, as their love grew, they would deepen their union as they extended the bounds of their physical discovery.

"If she had known the truth then, she would have known that that was impossible, that she would always lie desperate and alone next to her husband, just as he would lie alone next to her.

"For he had found his ultimate passion with another woman, and he too had to face the savage truth, the realization that his married physical life would never be truly fulfilling, however hard he tried."

Diana's affair, expressed in such fervent, overwrought prose, indeed seemed like a fairy tale. It could be acknowledged and dismissed as irrelevant to more important affairs. But when a dark-eyed, distraught young woman appeared in a television interview acknowledging that she was unhappy in her marriage and had taken up with another man, the effect undermined the very foundation of the monarchy.

QUESTION: Were you unfaithful [with Hewitt]?

DIANA: Yes, I adored him. Yes, I was in love with him.

Capped with . . .

QUESTION: Do you think the Prince of Wales will ever be king?

DIANA: Who knows, who knows what fate will produce? Who knows what circumstances will provoke? . . . Being king would be a little bit more suffocating . . . and I don't know whether he could adapt to that.

Within the Commonwealth, 23.2 million British saw the interview, almost double the audience for Charles's documentary in July. Grid engineers had installed an extra power station to handle the expected national surge in electricity from those who tuned in.

In Australia, sixty-six percent of viewers tuned in. Worldwide, two hundred million people from one hundred countries had watched Diana express her most intimate personal feelings.

Most importantly, the world witnessed her take command of her image, lay down terms with Charles, and declare her wish to assume the role of British ambassador for the first time. Says writer-broadcaster Martin Lewis: "In political terms, whoever defines the debate, wins. Diana stopped reacting, and started creating. She was in the lead."

The revelations were so shocking that the process of reporting the event, for some of the media, was as melodramatic as Diana's soap-opera life. "I was editing," recalled *Sun* editor Stuart Higgins in the *Frontline* documentary, "and the paper was changing by the second . . . every fifteen words, there was a new splash, a new page, and we were going back into the paper, taking more and more pages to get every word in."

"You could almost hear the country's collective gasp," said one television commentator on the late news about Diana's suggestion that the crown pass directly to Prince William when he comes of age. Media worldwide swirled with reviews, many of which interpreted the interview as calculated—from the words to the makeup to the gestures.

From the London *Times:* "The Princess of Wales had been primed and polished and at 9:00 P.M. last Monday the world's most powerful blonde bombshell went off. It was a brilliant performance. . . . "

Kitty Kelley quotes royal biographer Penny Junor, who usually sides with the Establishment point of view: "A brilliant performance—totally plausible. Charming, demure, vulnerable . . . but a performance—an acting job."

From *Newsweek:* "She had almost certainly been coached in what to say and how to say it."

From *People,* quoting royal author Brian Hoey: "[Diana probably] . . . rehearsed with a media professional. Never again will anyone accuse her of being thick as a plank."

Some critics dismissed her performance by immediately chastising her for using what they termed "psychobabble." The fruits of her psychotherapy were clear throughout, from self-mutilation (". . . you have so much pain inside yourself that you try to hurt yourself on the outside because you want help, but it's the wrong help. . . ."), to bulimia (". . . a secret disease. You inflict it upon yourself because your self-esteem is at a low ebb. . . ."), to the Court's plots to drive her into a mental hospital (". . . there's no better way to dismantle a personality than to isolate it . . ."").

Even savvy media insiders appreciated her performance. Former Clinton political consultant Dick Morris, interviewed for this book, took the long view: "For years, the Western image of a hero was Clint Eastwood and John Wayne, omnipotent supermen. But the modern movie hero is Everyman, the ordinary citizen who develops skills and talents he never realized he had until he desperately needs them to overcome adversity, like Robert Redford in *Three Days of the Condor.*"

Writer-broadcaster Martin Lewis concurs: "Out of tragedy and adversity, one draws on depth of character, and like a lizard, she shed her skin. The part that emerged struck a chord. The British saw that she had balls. She took on the royal family and called a spade a spade: 'Charles had an affair. I had an affair.' The people's response was, 'This is a woman of courage.' It was the ultimate underdog action and the British public loved it—she was open and honest, warts and all."

Of course, not all were taken in by Diana's unguarded disclosures. Some saw her as vain and selfish. The aristocracy felt she had disregarded the feelings and welfare of her children. They were contemptuous.

The Times of London anonymously quoted several members of the ruling class: "I have to question a program of that sort when you have two very sensitive children who are going through all the problems of a separated marriage. . . . Even those who think she did a jolly good job would agree that the children's interests were paramount. She said they were, but they couldn't have been. . . . In years to come, they will despise their mother for it [giving the interview]."

Cable Neuhaus, Los Angeles bureau chief for *Entertainment Weekly* and former *People* staffer, was dismayed that Charles, with the Jonathan Dimbleby documentaries, and then Diana, with the *Panorama* interview, betrayed the dignity of their positions and thus let people down. In our interview he said: "Despite all the little exposés along the way, they surprised me because [the interviews] made them something less than we had hoped they were. On the one hand, they were royalty and the world's most admired couple. On the other hand, he's acknowledging affairs, she's acknowledging affairs. It was not a pretty sight."

But it was exactly this candid demeanor that made Diana a victor in the eyes of the masses, particularly in England and America. Wrote Cathy Horyn in *Vanity Fair:* ". . . she was a visible wreck. Nervous and weepy, she looked miles beyond frazzled; her angst hung around her like Spanish moss. . . . On the one hand, you were sympathetic. Poor dear! On the other, you just wanted to change the channel."

Speaking to me for this book, American syndicated television and film critic Michael Medved added: "It was well-handled because she was able to project victimhood. I believe that is her sense of herself. She projected passivity. She is just an object. Hewitt, Charles treated her badly. Even with a divorce, she projects that it isn't her idea when she says, 'There were three of us in this marriage.'"

Minutes after the broadcast, damage control began by Charles's camp. The theme: We told you she was crazy. On BBC's *Newsnight*, government minister Nicholas Soames, for whom Charles was once best man, declared that Diana showed "the advanced stages of paranoia" in a performance that was sometimes "toe-curlingly dreadful." Ironically, the statement seemed to confirm Diana's contention that an enemy within the palace walls did indeed exist.

Whether Diana's sentiment was postured or pure, her revelations were in perfect sync with the mass mood of our media culture: the electronic confessional. In this country we associate the public TV confessional at its best with Oprah Winfrey, and Diana had met and spoken with Oprah. Oprah's approach has been to say, in effect, "I feel your pain." She has tried to approach her subject matter with empathy. If asked why this approach strikes a chord with the public, Oprah herself likely wouldn't have a definitive answer. She might have said, "I don't know. People seem to want to talk. When I cry, I see other people cry." But Diana didn't know about confessional from Oprah. The two—perhaps out of a genuine sense of compassion— picked up on the same cultural currents. They had an intuitive sense of the value of confession. Diana, needing the approval of the crowds she met, learned what moved them. The interview for her was the verbal equivalent of physical contact.

A Gallup poll in Britain showed that seventy-four percent of respondents thought Diana was right to bare her soul on television. That's because, British-born writer-broadcaster Martin Lewis explains, "The recovery movement and the twelve-step programs—

which were peaking in the United States—were just beginning in England, and *The Oprah Winfrey Show,* which had more of these kinds of programs, had been airing [in Britain] since the early '90s."

People's Landon Jones documented the history of this media genre: "In the early 1970s, the intimate details of a celebrity's life became a valid topic of journalism when [First Lady] Betty Ford admitted to breast cancer, and then alcoholism. It accelerated when Rock Hudson had AIDS. Today, to be rehabilitated, the confession is the way out. Diana caught that wave [in the *Panorama* interview]. Her instincts were good. She sounded like a woman who had been through a lot of therapy with a feminist therapist. She talked about issues that affect women."

Expressing one's misery is entertainment, says John Leo, contributing editor for *U.S. News & World Report.* "You can't go on a show if you have a happy life because no one wants to hear about it. Today, it makes you really attractive if you start talking about your defective ovary or your boss that smacked you around, because Oprah and others have opened the door to sympathy, empathy, and congratulations when you are abused or have a horrible life."

In Martin Lewis's opinion, the *Panorama* interview rocketed Diana's global celebrity into the stratosphere—as defined by the all-powerful American media, the inventor of the electronic confessional. "America is forgiving if you admit your faults and resolve to do better. To be cleansed—especially if you're a celebrity—you go to the Betty Ford Center. Before the interview, Diana was a star, but this moved her into the superstar category. The interview was her right of passage, her Betty Ford Center."

But revelation alone isn't enough for success, John Leo adds. Ingenuousness of storytelling is essential for the audience to believe and accept the confessor. "You have to be sincere, direct, as well as confessional. You have to not look like you are putting on any airs or that you're holding anything back."

Cathy Horyn believes this genre defines the modern concept of fame, which began in the late 1960s when stars began to write their confession-filled autobiographies. It continued into the 1970s with the talk shows. "They try to be more human so the audience must think [they] are part of them," she says. "The BBC interview is the most symbolic of modern celebrity. Here was a modern royal figure who said publicly 'I failed, this marriage failed.' The drama of their marriage and divorce exists as something special. It's not like going to the Betty Ford Center. It is unprecedented."

Or was it? Kelley quotes journalist and historian Paul Johnson proclaiming her a heroine. Her sexual indiscretions were forgivable, Johnson said, because "she was chaste when the Prince began the adultery game." He quotes novelist Jane Austen's defense of Queen Caroline, the estranged wife of George IV. "She was bad, but she would not have become as bad as she was if he had not been infinitely worse."

Cultural historian and author Leo Braudy, interviewed for this book, somewhat facetiously refers to the genre as "telepathology," defined as the healing of oneself by performing on television. This domain is not reserved for celebrities; indeed, previously unknowns who appear on sensationalist shows—and now even on the more mainstream nighttime newsmagazine shows—to tell of their personal trials and triumphs become famous too, if only for the time they are on the screen. "Among the hopeful, the desire for media attention . . . drifts easily into the belief that it will be healing. . . . Only by performing, by being seen, can the pain be distanced."

Braudy writes in *The Frenzy of Renown: Fame and Its History:* "This vision of fame as therapy is the complement to the pervasive sense of victimization that fuels so much popular psychology and political discussion. [Fame] has evolved over the centuries into the desire for fame in one's own lifetime, fame not as the crown of earthly achievement but as psychic medicine for a pervasive sense of loss and personal failure. Behind all this obsession with immediacy and satisfaction now is the spreading urge for fame as compensation for whatever faults and fissures there are in the sense of self."

Diana's message also endeared her to the audience. "She made a bond with the audience through self-exposure," Braudy says. Cleansing herself of her burden of silent suffering, she conveyed 'I feel just like you.'" Audience acceptance of the celebrity as one of them is a key element of modern fame, Braudy contends. Fame today is democratic in nature; anyone can earn it through accomplishments or simply by attracting attention to oneself. But for fame to sustain itself, the audience must be able to relate to the famous person.

Was Diana's merely an effective performance? The *Panorama* interview has proven to be unforgettable for viewers and was pivotal to Diana's life. To this day, *People* creator Richard Stolley remembers an actress at her best: "The way she focused on the interviewer. There were no annoying or distracting gestures, no irrelevant movements, nothing to distract you from that face, with the occasional bite of the lip. That is true star power. That is one-take Diana."

Prominent syndicated entertainment columnist Liz Smith said to me, "It was one of the most brilliant things I have ever seen. I don't know if she was coached for it, but her poise and sincerity was unbelievable," meaning, of course that it was extremely believable.

Writer and producer Barbara Hower recalls, "I found it quite genuine, but I wanted to say, 'Sweetheart, get a grip on yourself.' Where Diana lost me was that she had no touch with reality."

Vanity Fair correspondent Cathy Horyn thought the interview rang true as well. "She had the capacity for empathy," says Horyn, who met Diana at a couple of functions and has written articles about her. "She could openly discuss her problems on the BBC and people could understand."

Like many, Horyn sees the interview as the most extraordinary and damaging royal statement since the abdication of King Edward VIII in 1937. Granted, an abdication is more shocking than a divorce, but the lead-up to the abdication was kept silent and private lives were kept private back then, she recalls. "Diana's story was different because so much leaked out . . . and the fact that she went public."

The morning following the interview, Diana scanned all the national newspapers—the four quality papers and five tabloids—most of which highlighted her confession of adultery with Hewitt. Had she succeeded? Morton believes the interview was a failure because the papers emphasized the affair and her comments about Camilla, overshadowing her plea to become an ambassador and thus postponing the realization of that ambition. Nicholas Davies writes another scenario of that day: With each reading of another article offering applause for her "gut-wrenching honesty" and determination to "not go quietly," Diana became more ecstatic. Clenching her fist and punching the air, she said, "Done it. Done it. Done it."

What exactly had Diana accomplished? She immediately regained public sympathy. In a MORI poll, seventy-two percent said Diana had been treated badly by the royal family, and seventy-four percent of *Daily Mirror* readers who responded said that they still wanted Diana to be queen.

A Gallup poll taken the following day logged that forty-six percent thought more of Diana after the interview than before, seventy-four percent believed she was right in giving the interview, and twenty percent believed she should have remained silent. More specifically, fourteen percent thought she gave the interview to avenge

Charles and the royal family, seventeen percent believed it was a cry for help—and seventy-seven percent thought Diana simply wanted to get her side of the story on record. Those consulted believed Diana to be strong, sincere, loving, intelligent, and a good mother.

Some negatives surfaced. Of those who questioned the wisdom of the interview, thirty percent believed Diana had revealed herself to be self-centered, manipulative, and vengeful.

For the most part, the public lined up overwhelmingly behind her, the demarcation lines being class, income, sex, age, and temperament. Most of the working class supported her. The middle class—representing sixty-five percent of the British people—were divided: Older citizens tend to back monarchy through thick and thin, while the younger people could understand Diana's demand for more freedom. Like every Gen-Xer in the world, she wanted, figuratively, to move out of her parents' house.

She did seem to have dispelled myths that she was emotionally unstable and stupid, an image that had been haunting her for a decade and a half. *Newsweek*'s Michael Elliott and Daniel Pedersen concluded: ". . . it's hard not to think there is another agenda at work, one which, fifteen years ago, few would have been expected to be in the head of a girl who was portrayed as a rather dim baby doll. . . . Well, don't worry: now we know you're not." Helena Kennedy, one of Britain's leading barristers, was quoted in *The Times* of London with the bottom-line truth: "What we're dealing with is a modern woman, a post-feminist woman of the '90s who feels she's got rights."

As for her role as ambassador, the Palace's senior aides announced, less than twenty-four hours after the interview, that they wished to "see how we can help her define her future role and continue to support her as a member of the royal family." A typical headline: "Diana: Palace Peace Offer."

But as time passed, the interview, while memorable and significant, seemed to have returned less than the Princess had hoped for. After the fallout from the *Panorama* bomb had settled, the Establishment press revisited the interview. These commentaries were much less glowing and reprised the theory that Diana was unstable. *Country Life,* a magazine for the landed gentry, called the interview "deplorable" and characterized as "ludicrous" and "tragic" her suggestion that Charles might not be king. Other media pointed out that her discussion certified the Court's portrait of her as distressed, unhappy, impulsive, and self-obsessed. They also portrayed her as Machiavellian, determined to achieve her ends regardless of consequences for others, especially her own sons. Establishment newspapers and magazines were beginning to put Diana's good works in perspective by also reporting on the substantial charity work carried out by other royals, especially Princess Anne. The implication was that Diana wasn't more generous, she just knew how to get attention.

There were constitutional repercussions as well. As recently as October of 1995, Diana had attended a private dinner party hosted by Sir Gordon Reece, image consultant and Diana's informal adviser. On that occasion, Lord Wakeman, chairman of the Press Complaints Commission, urged the press to leave Prince William alone. Diana thanked him, saying that "the family is in favor of a privacy bill."

If her 1992 collusion with Andrew Morton didn't kill the possibility of a right to privacy, then her BBC appearance hammered the nails in its coffin. "If we court publicity or reveal matters that should remain private," Wakeman clarified, "we run the risk of finding ourselves in a spotlight which may prove harsh and intrusive. Those who do that may place themselves beyond the PCC's protection and must bear the consequences of their actions."

The longstanding conflict was heightened as a direct result of the *Panorama* interview. Without the cachet of her royal title, Diana needed the media more than ever to build her role as humanitarian and ambassador. She began to lay the groundwork for a television career. BBC sources told the London *Times* that they'd heard film producer Sir David Puttman was helping Diana decide how to front documentaries for her charities.

Palace aides indicated they would meet with Diana, upon her return from a goodwill trip to Argentina, to discuss establishing her as a kind of Minister of Good Works. An actual ambassadorship seemed increasingly out of the question. The Queen wanted to limit Diana to charity work because an ambassadorship would have made her a rival to the Court. The Queen, Prince Philip, and Prince Charles are all cleared by the Foreign Office. Diana couldn't be presumed to understand or represent British policy. Charity visits were deemed acceptable because they were viewed as personal.

Diana had planned a South American trip on her own. A BBC simulcast was scheduled. Diana's goal was to show the public the new role she wanted to carve out for herself. She confided to a businessman: "I thought I would arrange things like this so the Establishment will be able to judge for themselves how successful or otherwise the trip will have been. If it's successful, then maybe they will agree to let me carry out more such visits."

With a diplomat's instinctive flair, Diana demonstrated her uncanny power to metamorphose a negative mood into a positive one in Argentina. Upon arrival, sailors screamed "Puta!" (whore) and the Buenos Aires press mocked her with headlines like "Husbands beware, adulteress Di is coming." These reactions to the *Panorama* interview validated the Court's belief that Diana was a risky representative for Britain.

Once she was shown practicing charity, however, Diana turned everything around. In three days, she visited seven hospitals and clinics, including Garrahan Pediatric Hospital, run by the Association for the Prevention of Infant Paralysis, and Casa Cuna Hospital, where she talked to battered wives and children, and teenage drug-users in rehabilitation.

Suddenly, the Argentine media that had earlier dubbed her "confessed adulteress" and "unfaithful princess" began to use such words of adulation as "radiant visitor."

All in all, ninety press photographers had followed her; only the week before, just one photographer had accompanied Charles on his official visit to Germany.

Diana deliberately steered clear of anything smacking of politics. Other than lunch with President Menem—with whom she could empathize, given his recent estrangement from his wife—she stayed away from the capital's central plaza, where she had been invited to a meeting with the mothers of those who had "disappeared" during the Dirty Wars of the military regimes of the 1970s. The 1982 war between Britain and Argentina over the neighboring Falkland Islands didn't come up, nor did she bring it up. The daily *La Nacion* called her "the mute princess."

To one of the photographers on the trip, Diana said: "I believe that through my TV interview, I have finally won my independence."

Three weeks later, Diana flew to Manhattan to accept Humanitarian of the Year honors from the United Cerebral Palsy of New York Foundation. Introduced by the Nobel Prize-winning diplomat and king of diplomacy, former U.S. Secretary of State Henry Kissinger, Diana spoke about compassion. She mingled with Donald and Marla Trump, Randolph Hearst, Rupert Murdoch, and General Colin Powell. Her association with the rich and powerful of America signified acceptance of her as a royal ambassador.

But her dream was not to be. Prime Minister Major—who at one time openly supported Diana, even after her television interview—discussed a possible ambassadorial role with the Queen at their weekly meetings. The Queen remained opposed. One minister said: "We could not trust her with a political brief." (Morton reports, however, that Tony Blair, soon to become prime minister of a Labour government, was very interested in finding an official position for Diana.)

"Make her a duchess and let her go to California. If you take the job, you have to take the package." That was the cry of a source close to the Conservative Party leadership, as expressed in *The Independent* the day after the *Panorama* interview.

Dump her. And that's what Diana had been implying in the interview. But by deferring to Charles, she forced him to make the decision so that he would once again be seen in a bad light. After two years of legal separation she could file for divorce, but she didn't want to look like the aggressor. "No mileage in it," said Diana.

In fact, London papers had been rife with reports that negotiations had been going on for months, and her *Panorama* statement "[I] won't go quietly . . . I'll fight to the end. . . ." directly communicated that the Prince better take her demands seriously, among them the financial settlement.

Charles asked her to marry him, he must ask for the divorce. Unhappy as she was with the marriage, she knew that much of her good work of the past dozen years would be undermined when she left the royal family. She felt frustrated and unappreciated.

Furthermore, as long as she held on to her position she could be effective in promoting her causes. A divorce would mean she was no longer royal, reducing her power on the world stage—or so she had believed before the BBC interview. No doubt, visions of Wallis Simpson's ostracism flashed through Diana's mind.

On December 17, 1995, Queen Elizabeth wrote to Charles and Diana expressing her concern for her grandchildren and urging them to agree to divorce "amicably and with civility" as soon as possible. The Queen even went public with her request. She sent the letters by messenger, authorizing the Palace to confirm their delivery two days later.

Charles agreed provisionally, insisting that Diana agree as well. He also declared he would not remarry. Diana did not respond for more than two months. A private meeting was arranged for February 28, 1996, in his office at St. James's Palace.

On February 28, at 6:15 P.M., Diana's PR woman Jane Atkinson issued a statement through the British Royal Press Association: "The Princess of Wales has agreed to Prince Charles's request for a divorce. The Princess will continue to be involved in all decisions relating to the children and will remain at Kensington Palace with offices in St. James's Palace. The Princess of Wales will retain the title and be known as Diana Princess of Wales."

The Palace did not anticipate the press release. Diana had, once again, shown herself in the best light by beating the Palace to the press. Said royal biographer Brian Hoey in *People*: "The first [the Palace] knew of the announcement was when they heard the news reports. . . . They were upstaged again. And Diana managed to make it look as if Charles is starting the proceedings when he's really responding to the Queen's request that they divorce." *The Guardian* reported the following day that courtiers described the announcement as a negotiating ploy, not a definitive picture of the settlement, for which negotiations would take months. "She has stated what she wants to achieve . . . but it may not be what is finally agreed," said a Palace source.

Diana may have hoped that, divorced from the royal family, she would be a free agent who could do what she wished without clearance—including, even, the pursuit of an ambassadorship. The timing of her meeting with Charles, and the subsequent announcement, may even have been calculated. The announcement came on the eve of her appearance at an International Red Cross event on February 29. The Palace had previously nixed offers of a presidency of the British Red Cross.

The Archbishop of Canterbury said: "[I] hope and believe this is in the best interests of all concerned." *The Times* declared: "The Princess of Wales's agreement to her husband's request to a divorce promises to draw a welcome line under what had become a protracted and painful parting of the royal ways. . . . Now the country can rest at ease. And so can the Princess. . . . [She] can now start a new life . . . can still perform a useful role in charitable work. If she wants to enlarge upon that role overseas, as a humanitarian ambassador, so much the better . . . liberated from many of the constraints of royal protocol. . . . She will always, after all, be the mother of the future king. In that capacity, she deserves to lead a dignified and useful life."

In the United States, *People*'s cover shouted in celebration: "DI–VORCE! Her Future Begins."

The settlement, like most divorces, left both sides unhappy. In mid-July 1996, the terms were announced. Diana retained equal access and custody; the couple would share the responsibility of raising their sons. She was to live at Kensington Palace until she moved or remarried.

Another thorny issue was her royal title. Charles's lawyers proposed that she trade in HRH the Princess of Wales for Duchess of Cornwall. Diana turned to her media fans, who begged the Queen to retain Diana's status and keep her within the royal family. Prince Philip objected to the fact that any future children she might have could inherit the title. The Queen agreed.

Diana was spared the shame of the physical exile imposed on the Duke and Duchess of Windsor. An inserted clause in the final agreement said that she would be "considered on occasion as a member of the royal family." But for all matters of protocol, she was ostracized. The Queen directed the souvenir shops of Balmoral, Windsor Castle, and Buckingham Palace to cart away all memorabilia with Diana's likeness—ashtrays, mugs, postcards. Her name was stricken from the official prayers said for the royal family in Parliament.

Diana was now socially inferior to her children. She resigned her patronage of more than one hundred charities. In his book *Diana: Her True Story*, Andrew Morton contends that at this point Diana didn't care about the title. "She didn't resent it at all because she wasn't somebody who stood on ceremony," said her friend Rosa Monckton. Staff would no longer be required to bow or curtsy; the public could use their judgment.

The public thought the demands of the Palace were spiteful. Even members of the aristocracy worried. Wrote historian Paul Johnson at the time: "I fear for her. One society matron said to me yesterday: 'If I was publicly castoff like that, I really think I'd be tempted to do away with myself.'"

The media slanted it as a defeat. "Di KO'd in Palace Rigged Title Fight" was one headline. Even anti-royalists acknowledged that she had been felled. "She has lost something," wrote Stephen Glover in the *Daily Telegraph*, "which, according to the standards by which she lives, was infinitely precious."

In another era, if not beheaded for treason against the Crown, Diana would have been exiled or sequestered. Even the *Daily Mirror*, in a story headlined "Has She Gone Mad?", suggested treason for undertaking the interview without the Queen's permission. But this was John Major's England of the 1990s not Henry VI's of the 1530s. In a parliamentary society with a titular monarchy, the public rules. And they form their opinions that determine their votes based on information conveyed primarily through the media.

Constitutional experts said that doing the interview on the sly brought the monarchy several steps closer to demise. *Time* magazine called it "as penetrating kick to the Crown jewels as any woman in history." Dr. John Barnes at the London School of Economics suggested in *The Independent* that the way in which the authority of the Queen was ignored brought the prospect of a republican United Kingdom nearer.

Through her BBC performance, Diana won the PR battle against Charles by confessing her faults with dignity. Charles also had been candid in his documentary and biography, but he appeared beaten and self-pitying. Diana had bested the Prince once again because she had style. She declared that her trials had made her stronger and able to give. She married bravery to vulnerability. In so doing, whether conscious or unconscious, she tapped into the *Zeitgeist* and came across as a contemporary heroine.

But without her royal connection, Diana was treated with less respect and pursued more hotly than ever. Bad manners and unflattering photographs became the norm, as the media began to approach her more as they would a pop diva or rockstar, à la Madonna, Michael Jackson, or Mick Jagger.

Aware of the media's change of attitude, Diana responded by wooing them even more fervently, especially the tabloids, wrote Mark Honigsbaum in *The Spectator*. At the start of 1996, she invited the editors of the *Mirror, Sun, Daily Mail,* and *Express* to lunch at Kensington Palace. In one case, Prince William was present. Her agenda, she told one editor, was to develop a rapport and instruct the future king. "I just want to talk to you about a few things, get to know you. And I think it would be quite useful for William to meet an editor," Diana had said. Her technique then as before was to ingratiate herself with the media by making herself accessible as an anonymous source.

To an extent, Diana was cynical in her manipulation of leaked stories, followed by phony denials and feigned outrage, all cleverly calculated to advance her agenda. Honigsbaum reports that one editor called Kensington Palace to alert the Princess to a story his paper was about to run. It covered a speech she had given at a private visit to an eating-disorder clinic. Diana picked up the phone herself and briefed the editor for forty minutes about what she had said and what she hoped to achieve, as well as about her own problems with bulimia. The understanding was that the quotes would be reported as being from her speech, not directly from her.

The next morning, Diana issued a statement, via the Press Association, deploring the report. "I rang her immediately and congratulated her on a brilliant operation," the editor said. "It amused me that the way it had been communicated to the rest of the media was that she knew nothing about the story until it appeared in the paper. [In fact] she was the one who had told me."

Honigsbaum reports another example of Diana's collusion with the press which occurred when she was photographed by *News of the World* as she came out of a London hospital where she had been secretly visiting late at night with her then-boyfriend, heart surgeon Hasnat Khan. Furious, she struck a deal to stop the story by giving them a world exclusive about her secret, late-night visits to hospital patients.

Her aim was to paint a positive picture of herself, even if it meant making others look bad. Honigsbaum records *Daily Express* columnist Ross Benson saying, "She didn't distinguish between the tabloids and the broadsheets as much as between those journalists who were sympathetic to her and those who were not," summarized Benson, who met often with Diana. "Of course, she resented the intrusions by the paparazzi, but she got on with the tabloid staff photographers very well. . . . If she was pleased with something you had written, she would let you know. But you learned a lot quicker if she was unhappy. . . . Diana was a media brat."

She was also a long-range planner. She understood that if you expect to need editors as friends you must cultivate them before they know you have to have them on your side. The press doesn't like to feel it is bought or influenced. It likes to maintain at least the illusion of its own impartiality. But now, as in the time prior to the *Panorama* interview, Diana understood that the media could be seduced and, as she began the next new phase of her life, she wanted to be sure she had them on her side.

CHAPTER 11

Liberation

> *Fame is a bee.*
> *It has a song—*
> *It has a sting—*
> *Ah, too, it has a wing.*
>
> —Emily Dickinson

So wrote poet Emily Dickinson about the double-edged nature of celebrity. Had she lived in the late twentieth century, she might well have been writing about Diana—especially after the divorce.

Released from Charles, freer than ever before to explore her own interests, Diana flew out of semi-seclusion and soared into high-profile campaigns and appearances for her causes. Now more than ever, she had to show the substance beneath the image. She realized that she needed more polish before she could face the ever-increasing scrutiny to which she would be subject as a non-royal public figure.

I have represented a number of athletes, several of them at the ends of their careers. Usually financially secure, well-connected, comfortable in the public eye, athletes about to leave competition have a variety of opportunities. In the choices they make of second careers we often find clues to who they really were while on the field or on the court. My client Kareem abdul-Jabbar, for example, was a solid, sober athlete who, on retirement, decided to explore business interests. The great running back Walter Payton, also a good citizen, explored business too, working hard for years to put together a deal to bring a new football team to St. Louis. But Payton craved the kind of excitement he'd felt in competition and so he also drove racing cars. Some, like Joe Namath, go into show business. Others, like Larry Byrd or Phil Jackson, move into the ranks of coaches. Many who were team leaders go into broadcasting. Some just feel lost. They fed on the excitement of the game and on the instant-recognition factor. Now in civilian life, they don't know what to do or even, sometimes, how to enjoy themselves.

Diana, like an athlete at the end of one career and the beginning of another, had to assess not only her opportunities but also her real interests. Her whole life had been lived in reaction to the wishes of others. Now, she could pretty much do what she wanted to do. And so she began a period in which she explored possibilities and tried to shore up those strengths to which she wanted to commit.

She had learned to perform public service as a member of the royal family, but clearly she truly enjoyed charity work. Though she had fewer opportunities and possibilities, she wanted to continue in that endeavor.

She felt that she wasn't a good public speaker and looked to speech adviser Richard Greene, among others, for ways to improve. Greene, who was generous with his time and his insights, spoke to me at length about Diana at this stage of her life: "Diana was wonderfully confident and charming one-on-one, but she was not comfortable standing up and giving a message to a group of people," Greene says. "Diana enjoyed her celebrity. Although she was awed by the attention showered on her at first, she grew to like it. She knew she had the ability to pick up the phone, make an appearance, and create headlines. She was neither power hungry nor egotistical in the use of her power. She never boasted from her ego about the things she could do. But she was aware of the power of the position. It gave her the ability to do many things that she could not do otherwise.

"[Diana also needed that power] to overcome her deep insecurity—an insecurity that would always be there no matter how powerful she became, that would make her question, 'Hold on, maybe I'm not that powerful or good looking.' It's a black hole when someone is that deeply insecure. There's not ever a time when that is gone. That is true of presidents and prime ministers too. Everyone fights that demon."

Giving a speech was daunting to Diana. "Like every beautiful woman, she wanted to be taken seriously for the content as well as the package," Greene says. "She was not the most academically-educated and was insecure [about] how she came across. . . . She wanted credibility. She believed in the message that she was sharing. It wasn't just a public relations ploy. She was a very warm, compassionate human being."

Diana envied how comfortable Charles was when he extemporaneously made a joke during a speech. Greene reassured her that she could be an effective communicator by being more herself. "Charles was left-brain, Diana right-brain. He was auditory digital, expressing himself through words, concepts, and rational logic. Diana's strength was in the visual. She was childlike, creative, kinesthetic. She could zap people into a quasi-hypnotic state through [the use of] her eyes. She was perfect for our visual age."

Moreover, Greene advised, she should allow her sense of humor to bubble to the surface; it was her humor that had captured his attention when he first met Diana at the Harbour Club Gym in London. "We were both working out and she mentioned that she wanted constructive feedback on her speech style. Then, after looking at her trainer, she batted her eyes and said, 'She's been beating up my body, you may as well beat up my mind.'"

Critiquing a number of her previous speeches, Greene counseled her to be conversational, human, and warm. He complimented her on a personal reference and on a comeback to an agitator during her December 1995 speech for the United Cerebral Palsy of New York Foundation, which was also attended by General Colin Powell, ABC's Barbara Walters, former U.S. Secretary of State Henry Kissinger, and other dignitaries.

Powell is a very distant cousin of Diana's, which she found out only during Powell's introduction. When Diana began, she said, "Good evening, Mr. Chairman, Mr. Kissinger, Barbara . . . and cousin Colin." "It was cute and everyone roared," Greene says. (It was a politically savvy aside. In racially diverse New York it can only have seemed very cool for a blonde aristocratic European woman to acknowledge kinship with an African American.) As Diana spoke about education and children, a heckler caustically interrupted with "Where are your children, Diana?" Says Greene, "She paused, looked at the woman, calmly said, 'They're in school,' and went on with her speech."

It's ironic that Diana, who so effectively won over the masses and anyone she mixed with personally or professionally, would question her own abilities. Yet, her insecurities about her verbal communication skills are understandable given the potshots fired at her beginning in the mid-1980s. "She had street smarts," Greene says. That gave him something to work with.

Martin Lewis, who has wide experience in both English and American television, makes her personal evolution seem almost heroic: "I can't stress how much [the Establishment] was threatened by an independent woman. Her actions were not in the job description, which was to be cute and have two kids," Lewis says. "They thought they got a Princess Barbie. What they got was a woman who took baby-steps to become an empowered woman."

Greene agreed. "She became a role model for millions of women. This transcended discussions in the media about smarts or manipulation. . . . If people like you on a human and emotional level, you can do almost anything. You can be shallow, manipulative, vulgar. This is the Teflon effect. It is achieved by establishing a human connection. Reagan did it. Clinton does it. Since the BBC interview, women of the world looked beyond any criticism [of Diana]. They were touched by her authentic and vulnerable femininity."

Greene continued, "On the heart level, even critics were touched. A head person probably did not give sway to the emotional impact, and still criticized her for being manipulative."

Diana was smart without being intellectual. "She had no capacity for pretentious words or concepts, no intellectual stamina to discuss abstract, intelligent things for hours. She was fascinated with philosophy, especially Eastern philosophy, but she was more day-to-day oriented, more practical, about them. If she read esoteric philosophy, she didn't care about philosophical trends in literature, but how she could use it in her life," Greene concludes.

Her friend Rosa Monckton had described Diana as an "intuitive genius," referring to her psychic ability and uncanny empathy. Morton reports that Diana herself spoke of her own ability to "see inside someone's soul" when she first met them.

Indeed, Diana seems to have possessed what has come to be called "emotional intelligence"—a concept that was introduced in the international bestseller *Emotional Intelligence: Why It Can Matter More than IQ* by Dr. Daniel Goleman, former senior editor for *Psychology Today* and current behavioral and brain-sciences writer for the *New York Times*.

Drawing on groundbreaking research, Goleman explains how factors such as self-awareness, self-discipline, and empathy are the kind of intelligence that often allow people with modest IQs to flourish. When it comes to predicting people's success, Goleman asserts, brain power as measured by IQ and standardized achievement tests might actually matter less than the qualities of mind once thought of as character.

As she got her bulimia under control, matured, and understood herself better, Diana was better able to listen to and act on her gut feelings. Her instincts were excellent at identifying golden opportunities—everything from how to play the media to her advantage, to choosing charities and causes that resonated with the masses.

Her instincts were less acute, however, with individuals and didn't protect her from insincere, opportunistic lovers. Nor was she consistent in dealing with friends, with the people she employed, or with the paparazzi who followed her. She was, nonetheless, loved and perceived to be loving.

Empathy builds on self-awareness. Writes Goleman: "That capacity—the ability to know how another feels—comes into play in a vast array of life arenas, from sales and management to romance and parenting, to compassion and political action."

Self-control and empathy help to improve social skills. In the corporate world, Goleman asserts, IQ might get one hired, but EQ—the acronym for emotional quotient (emotional intelligence)—gets one promoted. Rising stars can fade out because of interpersonal flaws, despite technical ability. He recalls a manager at AT&T Bell Labs, a think tank for brilliant engineers, who ranked top performers not as the ones with the highest IQs, but the ones whose e-mails got answered, who collaborated and networked well, and who were popular. These were the traits that allowed them to reach goals.

Managing with heart, Goleman says, is a form of leadership not by domination, "but the art of persuading people to work toward a common goal . . . [and] recognizing our deepest feelings about what we do—and what changes might make us more truly satisfied with our work."

Diana recognized that she needed to focus her gifts. She had been accused of backing causes that would attract attention to herself. She disliked being attached to too many charity committees and events only as a figurehead to help generate donations. After the BBC interview, Diana targeted the causes she most cared about and those most in need of attention.

Beginning in 1996, according to Morton, she dropped more than a hundred charities from her portfolio. She retained the Leprosy Mission, Centrepoint (a charity for the homeless), the National AIDS Trust, the Royal Marsden NHS Trust (a cancer hospital), and the Great Ormond Street Children's Hospital—charities devoted to helping those on the margins of society and life. For personal reasons, she also maintained her association with England's National Ballet.

As a private citizen, Diana traveled around the world on behalf of the poor and the ill. As a humanitarian ambassador, the Princess began to earn the respect of those who believed notoriety must be earned through one's own accomplishments and contributions to society.

Now Diana was truly worthy of serious news coverage as she went into service as teacher, healer, and minister. She attracted an increasing amount of mainstream media attention because her efforts went beyond her previous social advocacy and took on a controversial political tone. Was she looking over her shoulder at the Establishment that had not accepted her? This aristocratic mother of the future king had carved out a job that bucked tradition; in modern times, the royal family as figureheads had assiduously avoided taking a stand on political issues.

A hard-hitting BBC documentary featured shots of Diana taken during her January 1997 visit to Angola. The Princess pleaded for an immediate worldwide ban on antipersonnel landmines. The British Red Cross estimated that each month two thousand people, mostly civilians, many of them children, were killed or maimed by the many millions of active landmines scattered worldwide. Undergoing an armed civil war for thirty-five years, Angola had at that time logged seventy thousand landmine victims from the millions of mines that have been spread across the countryside. The country has one amputee for every 334 citizens; Luanada is the world's amputee capital. Yet there were only five artificial-limb facilities in Angola.

Diana visited and comforted children in hospitals, where she was shown artificial-limb fittings. One vigil made the print media but was kept out of camera range because of its particularly grisly nature. Tears welling as she took the hand of seven-year-old Helena Ussova—whose intestines had been blown out as she was on her way to fetch water and was now being kept alive through saline solution—Diana asked her about her treatment. Afterward, her wound suppurating, flies buzzing around her head, Helena asked: "Is she an angel?"

Donning a blast-proof face shield and flak jacket, Diana walked into a minefield and blew up a mine by remote control. "One down, ten million to go," she said.

Diana made the front pages the next morning and became swept into a political storm. She had termed her journey a "private visit," meaning that taxpayers didn't foot the bill and she was not officially representing Britain. Nevertheless, she was attacked by the Tory junior defense minister, Earl Howe, who called Diana a "loose cannon" because her remarks were out of line with British policy. Her position coincided with calls for immediate, unilateral action on landmines from Labour and Liberal Democrat MPs. Another Parliament member, Peter Viggers, huffed that Diana was "not up to understanding an important, sophisticated argument." Reluctant to press for a total ban, especially in strategic war zones, the Conservatives supported the banning of exports as well as the destruction of obsolete mines as soon as practical.

In Angola, Diana deftly and calmly responded to the "loose cannon" charge in a statement to the assembled press: "It's an unnecessary distraction which we don't need; I think it is sad. I'm a humanitarian, not a politician."

Afterward, Diana's campaign won the support of Gulf War commanders General Norman Schwarzkopf and Sir Peter de la Billiere, as well as that of the International Red Cross, making the British Establishment look foolish for their disapproval of her efforts.

Diana stayed her course. In the BBC documentary, she calmly spoke to viewers' emotions: "Before I came to Angola, I knew the facts, but the reality was a shock. . . . It was moving and encouraging to see the confidence shown by those learning to walk again. But the millions of unexploded landmines in their country will go on shattering lives for decades to come. . . . If these children are to have a future, we must end the use of these evil weapons. The only way forward is for a total, worldwide ban on antipersonnel landmines."

By May, foreign secretary Robin Cook said that the Labour government would work with Germany and France to secure a worldwide ban on use, production, and transfer of antipersonnel landmines. In June, Diana shared a platform with Clare Short, Labour's international development secretary, at a conference calling for a ban on landmine use.

This action constituted a new and the most boldly powerful defiance of protocol for Diana. "A royal 'seal of approval'—in public—for a government policy is almost unprecedented," said Greg Neale of the *Telegraph*. "The Princess's attendance at the conference [created] a startling new alliance of the outspoken: two high-profile women who have never shrunk from taking on the Establishment and [who] won widespread public acclaim in the process."

In August, she flew to Sarajevo for a three-day visit with families of some landmine victims in Bosnia, also ripped apart by civil war. She was accompanied by Lord W. F. Deedes, a distinguished journalist and a Tory, who reported in the *Daily Telegraph* that Diana did not seem to be upset by what he found to be harrowing stories. "She was very stoical . . . like a very good-natured nurse. . . . Through an almost impassable language barrier she can convey . . . depth of feeling she holds for them."

Earlier, in June, Diana had traveled to the United States. She paid a forty-five-minute visit to an ailing Mother Teresa at her Missionaries of Charity residence in the Bronx, where the eighty-six-year-old nun had been staying for several weeks. While Diana's two-hour-late arrival brought oohs and aahs from little children, it was Mother Teresa who warmed the hearts of the crowd more as the two emerged holding hands. Diana uncharacteristically held back while Mother Teresa mixed with children and adults alike. New York's *Daily News* headline: "Two Stars Glow in BX, but Saint Outshines the Princess." A surprising flip-flop of attention from the media and public would occur in less than three months, when the two would die within days of one another.

That same month, in her triumphant visit to Chicago, Diana was featured at a fund-raiser expected to raise $1.4 million for cancer charities. While there, she also visited a number of hospital wards and hospice units.

Though the city is home to Chicago Bulls basketball great Michael Jordan and showbusiness maven Oprah Winfrey—two superstars of great substance and accomplishment—the people and press were still awed. "Di Wows Chicago" exclaimed the cover of *People*, reporting on her three-day debut visit that was covered by five hundred journalists who had been issued security tags with Diana's likeness. Traffic was snarled. Puddles were mopped up to ensure the royal foot would be kept dry. More than a thousand people packed the lobby of Cook County Hospital, awaiting her arrival. The *Chicago Sun-Times* hailed the reception a "Lovefest," the *Chicago Tribune* headlined it "A Royal Flush." Interrupting regular programming, the television channels showered such adjectives as "charming," "warm," "gracious," "dazzling," "stunning," and "awesome."

Some more practical-minded media and residents didn't understand the hoopla. Chicago is thought of as a town that cares more about the punctuality of garbage trucks, trains, and snowplows than it does about glitter and glamour. "Media Have Made Diana What She Is: Princess of Hype" wrote the late Pulitzer Prize-winning columnist Mike Royko in his column in the *Chicago Tribune*.

But it was exactly Diana's aura of lightness and her royalty, some observed, that captured hearts. "Princess Di is a relief from Hillary Clinton," rationalized Joan Beck of the *Chicago Tribune*. "Stories about her don't require us to decide whom to vote for, make us feel guilty or worry about new taxes or the state of the world. . . . It's fun to see her jewels . . . check out her wardrobe . . . see how very, very good Diana is at what she calls her 'work'. . . ."

Leslie Baldacci of the *Chicago Sun-Times* said, "She gave the people what they wanted . . . then she gave them even more."

Could she have sustained a career as a humanitarian without a power base?

One senses that she was more aware of what she was leaving behind than of what she was heading towards. Later that month, at son William's suggestion, at a Christie's auction in New York City Diana sold off seventy-nine gowns worn between 1981 and 1996. The collection included fifty designed by Catherine Walker and ten by Victor Edelstein. The offerings raised nearly $3.26 million for five British and U.S. cancer and AIDS charities. Another $2.5 million was raised from the sale of the auction's catalogs and associated fund-raising events.

As always, Dianamania erupted. Bidders from all over the country paid in excess of $25,000 for a gown that might or might not be wearable. The Franklin Mint—which bought Jackie O's faux pearls in order to create reproductions at $200 a necklace—paid $151,250 for a strapless gown and cropped jacket, studded with faux pearls and sequins (said to be "Elvis-style" because its stand-up collar was reminiscent of the king's Vegas costumes).

The Christie's auction showed that anything pertaining to Diana was as valuable a commodity as ever. Selling the frocks of the past, her costumes in the Windsor drama, Diana suggested that she was ready to give up earlier roles—Pop Princess, Queen-in-Waiting, Diana the Good—in order to move on to a new career.

Simply by pursuing her own agenda at her own pace and in her own way—sans the bitter, soap-opera, tit-for-tat public relations battles against Charles—Diana was successfully carving out a new role that was upstaging the monarchy. As a result of her 1997 efforts, *The Independent* characterized her as "the protagonist of a new drama: that of patron saint of the very good cause." Referring to the July 1997 *Vanity Fair* photo spread publicizing the auction, it called her "the newly casual and modern magazine cover."

In the same time period, the coverage of the royal family's activities was less than flattering, highlighting privileged self-involvement rather than concern for the people. The biggest story about the Queen in early 1997 was the government's decision—with her blessing—to purchase a new royal yacht. The highest-profile coverage of Charles was a trip to a fancy Swiss ski resort.

While Diana was discovering herself, the climate and topography of the world she lived in was changing. On her own, she was fast becoming "a kind of alternative monarchy," observed London-based Fred Barbash of the *Washington Post* Foreign Service. Former editor of *Majesty* and current editor of *London* magazine Nigel Evans concurred: "At the moment, she is winning." A MORI public opinion poll in early 1997 had already reported disillusionment with the monarchy; sixty-two percent said "privilege" characterized the House of Windsor and fifty-two percent said that Britain doesn't get good value for the money spent on the royal family.

By June, as he was finishing an article for the September *Vanity Fair,* contributor Christopher Hitchens—an English republican and royal expert—felt the ground was about to open up under the monarchy as an institution, as a number of challenges erupted at once.

First, the Labour Party's Tony Blair was elected prime minister. The party's agenda is toward greater democracy, in particular the granting of autonomy to Scotland and Wales and firm determination to settle the tensions in Northern Ireland. "[This] makes the whole definition of Britain as a monarchy or 'United Kingdom' rather iffy," wrote Hitchens. Furthermore, the Labourites want to abolish the right of hereditary peers to vote in the House of Lords, which would make the Windsors the only family to enjoy political privilege as a right of birth. "If heredity is an obviously absurd way to pick lawmakers, how can it be justified in the case of a single person (the Queen or King) as Head of State, Head of Church, and Commander-in-Chief of the armed forces?"

Scandals continued to be unveiled about the royal family. Kitty Kelley's book *The Royals* was about to be published, alleging a range of improprieties and embarrassments for the royal family.

Hitchens believed that Diana and her continued visibility in charitable work was a third challenge to the monarchy. "She has done more, even if only by accident, to undermine the idea of 'the succession'. . . . Indeed, by her devotion to her children, she has put the whole idea of 'the succession' into doubt."

Hitchens says Diana could have headed a rival court, in spirit though not in body, that would have been extremely threatening. "As the Princess of Wales and mother of the future King, she could give instructions or make waves to contradict the existing monarchy's positions."

Hitchens strongly believed then that the monarchy could survive scandals, constitutional impasse, and succession crisis, one at a time—but not two crises, let alone three, at once. With the republican movement gaining adherents, the monarchy now must "prove their case. . . . What happens when the Queen drops off the twig? Prince Charles, who has gone stale well before his time . . . would be King of about ten percent of the population and of nobody who was his own age."

The emerging Diana had completed her experimentation with roles and now felt a "sense of inner continuity," as eminent psychologist Erik Erikson termed the completion of the discovery of ego identity that marks adulthood. There was no more need to act because her previously diffused identity had finally fused, as she wrangled with life's real problems and exerted discipline—the key, as Dr. M. Scott Peck purports in his book *The Road Less Traveled,* to solving problems in ways that honor the true self.

Nowhere was that authenticity more evident than in the series of photographs by Mario Testino that accompanied the story in the

July 1997 issue of *Vanity Fair*, a story to promote the Christie's auction and also the grown-up Diana.

A month earlier, Diana had sat for the royal photographer, Lord Snowden. (Some of these appeared in an American *Vogue* piece also about the Christie's auction.) In the Snowden photos, Diana—then just shy of thirty-six and known to be physically buff from disciplined exercise—looks matronly, posing erect in a strapless gown with full skirt.

The Testino images for *Vanity Fair* have an entirely different spirit. The bold, black-lettered headline on the piece screams "Diana Reborn." The pictures justify the assertion. Diana was playing without inhibitions as Testino's camera clicked away. She pranced about to the music of Dalida, about a French dance diva gyrating toward destruction. She strutted like a runway model as she learned to catwalk.

She seemed to be uncharacteristically self-confident. She agreed to work with Testino, though she had never done so before. She requested new hair and new makeup. Interspersed between the sultry poses in black velvet, sequined, or silk crepe gowns were candid shots that captured the moment—Diana cutting up, arms poised as if she were teasing a toddler. Her mask had dropped. She seemed happy to be herself. She was, as poet Percy Bysshe Shelley rejoiced in "The Witches of Atlas": "A lovely lady, garmented in light/From her own beauty."

"No one is beautiful when they are tense," said Nancy Friday, interviewed for this book. "When Diana was married, she looked more like a mannequin, a Barbie doll. Here, she's given in, she's having fun, she's being herself. And her life had changed. She must have felt the warmth of the world, her children were no longer dependent, and she was becoming a grown woman. She looked in the mirror and saw someone she could like. No more downcast eyes. She must have known how eyes were drawn to her, as she reached the height of her womanly powers."

A power that finally emanated sexuality. "Diana's beauty always lacked the movie-star sexuality of, say, an Elizabeth Taylor," Friday continued. "Her kind of beauty was such a pool of serenity, one could dive in and not be threatened. There was no hard, erotic edge. But once on her own, she began to have a sexual life."

For the first time, men and women began to comment that Diana looked sexy, recalls Cathy Horyn, who wrote the *Vanity Fair* text accompanying the Testino photos. "That is not a word that had really applied to Diana."

In fact, it was this sense of freedom, this erotic unleashing, that convinced the *Vanity Fair* editors to feature the story on the cover. The original story was a five-hundred-word, inside piece pegged to the auction, along with photos. "But I remember looking at these pictures with [editor in chief] Graydon [Carter], the art director, and other editors," Horyn recounts, "and we all thought they were phenomenal. She looked like a woman liberated from the tower."

Despite the apparent freedom of the shoot, Diana wouldn't let go enough to speak extemporaneously in an interview with either *Vanity Fair* or American *Vogue*. To expand the piece, Horyn faxed a dozen questions to the Princess for her written response. She answered all but three, but her answers dealt only with the dresses and her charity work. She held tightly as ever to the reigns that controlled her image.

So Horyn wrote around the subject by interviewing those at the shoot as well as friends. And everyone attested to knowing or seeing a woman who had, as Gustave Flaubert characterized Madame Bovary, "an indefinable beauty that comes from happiness, enthusiasm, success—beauty that is nothing more or less than a harmony of temperament and circumstances." Said friend and designer Gianni

Versace, just months before his tragic death: "It is a moment in her life, I think, when she's found herself—the way she wants to live."

Could she have continued to charm ordinary people with her peculiar combination of glamour and compassion as she approached middle age? Everything we know about Diana suggests she didn't look ahead; she was happy to be of service in the here and now.

Could she simply have acquiesced to being a private person? Like many athletes and even some political figures, she might have become the spokesperson for a company. She might have gone into early retirement. Or she might have left the scene altogether.

The image of Diana has become fixed in the public perception as inextricably linked to her charity work. Diana has become myth: an almost saintly humanitarian, and innocent victim of the media. Both characterizations are too pat to stand up to close scrutiny. Would this image have stuck if she had not died as she did? Would mourners still have lined the streets and tuned in around the world if she had died from a heart attack at age fifty-six? Probably not.

More to the point, if she had continued to pursue the style of life she was leading, even five years later, it is doubtful that the networks would have sent their prime anchors to cover her funeral. I suspect that in five years Diana would have been viewed as just another celebrity who did some good works.

To see how quickly the mighty can fall from public favor, one need only go back ten years before Diana's wedding to be struck by the similarities between Diana's situation and that of Margaret Trudeau, another young woman whose marriage, as mentioned earlier, thrust her into the spotlight.

Margaret Sinclair was the daughter of an industrialist and past minister of fisheries in the Canadian government. In 1971 Pierre Elliot Trudeau was the dashing, bachelor prime minister of Canada, often compared to John Kennedy. Not quite a daughter of the nobility matched with a future king, but for North America, a close approximation.

Like Diana, Margaret had grown up a daddy's-girl with a head full of romantic notions. Coming of age in the '60s, she got involved in campus politics, and when she went to Europe on her graduation-present holiday she immersed herself into the student-hippie lifestyle. Before the year was out, she was back home in Vancouver with no idea of what to do with her life. One day she got a call from a man she had met briefly during a recent family vacation in Tahiti—Pierre Trudeau.

After one casual date, Margaret decided that it was she who must become the wife of the prime minister. Like Diana, she set her sights and went about capturing her heart's desire by using her family connections to be near him. She got a job in Ottawa and, to please and flatter Pierre, she studied French, learned to ski, and converted to Catholicism. Though, like Charles, Pierre was reluctant, she finally got him to propose. Margaret was twenty-two and Pierre was fifty-one when they married.

Although the media was a little more civilized in 1971, they went crazy for the couple. Like Diana, Margaret was unprepared for the glare of the world spotlight or the demands of being the wife of a national leader. Like Prince Charles, Pierre Trudeau was aloof and serious-minded. Like Diana, Margaret was young and somewhat flighty. Although not a royal court, the uptight Ottawa Establishment was the next best thing, and young, romantic Margaret did not fit in. The press had a field day reporting on every dress she wore, every naïve thing she said, and every social gaffe she made.

Just as with Diana, Margaret's marriage grew cold and distant, there were rumors of affairs, she was ridiculed and shunned by the Establishment, and hounded by the media to the point of a nervous breakdown. Within six years it was over and, like Diana, Margaret remained married in name only while she and Pierre negotiated a divorce that would allow her access to their three children.

Free of a stifling, high-visibility marriage, Margaret, like Diana, cast herself in the role of the independent woman struggling to define herself. But she, too, had become addicted to the spotlight, which she kept focused on herself by being the most outrageous of the Andy Warhol–Studio 54–drug-and-jet-set. She engaged in scandalous affairs with movie stars and international playboys, and partied harder and later than anyone, while constantly playing to the cameras.

As with so many who are raised high by the media and then long for their invaded privacy, Margaret, when her star began to lose its luster, became a part of the very media which had created her. She made two ill-fated attempts as a movie actress, tried photojournalism and failed, wrote a tell-all autobiography, and chased stardom until she ended up back in Ottawa co-hosting a local television show. Margaret's fifteen minutes of fame were over.

Diana had started down that same well-worn path at the time of her death. She was running with the international set, dating a notorious playboy, talking to Hollywood producers about movie offers, and having serious discussions about appearing as a television hostess. Diana may have protested the media attention, but like Margaret, she couldn't bring herself to leave the stage.

In all likelihood, Diana would have had no more success at it than Margaret Trudeau or the dozens of beauty queens and other instant-celebrities who try to parlay their moment into a second significant career. (Consider the number of beauty-contest winners who become anchors of local TV news shows.) Chances are that the spotlight would have panned away to a fresh face.

Margaret Trudeau tried to stay on stage too long after the audience got bored and started to leave. Finally she realized what she was becoming and, by all accounts, bowed out gracefully. She has since maintained a low level of celebrity, which she uses occasionally to draw attention to some of the charitable causes she supports. (However, her successful return to ordinary life was more presumed than real. In the spring of 1998 several newpapers in the U. S. and Canada reported that Kemper was being treated in a psychiatric ward. In a recent interview in *Maclean's,* commenting on the depression she has suffered since early menopause, she said "I thought my usefulness was finished. . . . I believed my job on Earth was to procreate and be a pleasant sexual diversion for successful, hard-working men.")

Diana, for her part, never showed any sign of wanting to be out of the spotlight. In fact, she continued to play cat-and-mouse with the media, keeping high the value of her photo. If she were easy to shoot, the paparazzi would have looked elsewhere. As the conflict between Diana and the royal family quieted, as it inevitably would have, her charitable activities would have become less of a personal public relations tool. Diana would have probably ended up leading the usual life of the privileged and wealthy, where charities and causes are a large part but not the whole of their lives. Elizabeth Taylor and the late Audrey Hepburn come to mind.

However, Diana didn't have the opportunity to become a garden-variety celebrity do-gooder. Her sudden death—like the deaths of celebrities from JFK to Marilyn Monroe to James Dean—caught her in a freeze-frame before the public had the chance to see her good works in their true perspective, and then to take her for granted.

It was one last flirtation with danger that killed the Princess, saving her from or denying her the opportunity of an ordinary life.

Dalliance or destiny? That was the question posed by *People* about Diana's love affair with Dodi al Fayed, international playboy, sometime Hollywood producer, and son and heir to the fortune of Mohammed al Fayed, owner of London's famed Harrods department store.

Dodi al Fayed was a rather good-looking, charming, insecure, superficial, B-grade playboy. His father was a larger-than-life figure. An Egyptian who had married money, then made millions more, Mohammed al Fayed tried to buy his way into British society. He had been denied citizenship following questions about his financing of the Harrods purchase and had admitted paying Tory MPs for political favors, a move often credited with speeding the demise of John Major's government.

Dodi had been raised by nannies and collateral relatives. In a well-researched piece by Sally Bedell Smith for *Vanity Fair,* it appears that there were whole years of Dodi's childhood that no family member can now account for. He attended private schools in various parts of Europe and took a short course at Sandhurst. He rarely made trouble. With a generous allowance from his father, Dodi didn't have to work and chose not to. He settled nowhere. He lived high, often spending much more money than he had and having to go to his father for help. He hung out at the best spots. During my brief professional relationship with him, I saw clearly that Dodi wanted to be in the film business, though it wasn't always clear that he had the necessary talents or the work ethic. He invested in feature films and had marginal roles in production, though he seems to have bypassed opportunities to learn the business. He also sold foreign rights to films he did not own. He pursued beautiful women, fell madly in love, and ran up huge debts courting them.

He was polite, generous, fun. A good diversion. Friends close to Diana say she couldn't have taken him seriously. For one thing, says Richard Greene, "their basic core values were not enough aligned." Celebrity biographer Donald Spoto, who has authored books on Elizabeth Taylor and Marilyn Monroe, among others, concurs. In his

November 1997 book *The Decline and Fall of the House of Windsor,* Spoto contends that the relationship was a summer romance based on strong, mutual attraction, but that Diana at this point in her life would have wanted a substantial relationship. Rings and earrings would not have won her, because she had material wealth.

As evidence, he recounts one night when Diana began telling Dodi about her charities and causes. He listened for a short time, then cut her off, saying, "But, Diana, we're due at dinner in Paris." Spoto doubts if Diana could have spent her life with someone so shallow.

One of Diana's friends had told *People* that Diana would steer clear if there was definitive evidence of Dodi's alleged financial problems. "She'll wake up to it. She'll be sensible." There are many reasons to think that this relationship would not have become serious. The two had been involved only a short time—five weeks. Dodi was a womanizer. He had no relationship to speak of with Diana's children, and they were dear to her.

Nevertheless, Diana was still an emotionally bereaved woman. Her divorce had only recently been finalized. And Dodi may have been just what the doctor ordered for what poet W. E. Aytoun termed "the grief that fame can never heal." According to various profiles of Dodi, he was attentive. That would have been quite a lure for a woman like Diana, who had been neglected, abandoned, and betrayed by men all of her life.

At a certain level, too, there may have been chemistry between them. He was, as an Egyptian, a Muslim in name, an outsider, someone utterly unacceptable to the royal family. That could have been a plus. And yet, he also had qualities that must have reminded Diana of her husband and her friends. Like Prince Charles, and like Diana herself, he was a man overshadowed by his parents and his heritage, ill-equipped for life and sheltered by wealth.

But rumors persisted through August that the affair was serious. Many speculated that Diana would be leaving Britain for a life of leisure with a new, wealthy husband. They made an analogy between Dodi and Diana, and Jacqueline Kennedy and Aristotle Onassis. There were reports that Mohammed had visited and was about to purchase the Duke of Windsor's Paris house. In June of 1997, Dodi had bought the Malibu compound of producer Blake Edwards and his actress/singer wife, Julie Andrews. That California retreat was perceived as another possible long-term love nest.

Beginning in mid-July of 1997, Diana and her sons were photographed—without resistance—with Dodi and his family on vacation at the elder al Fayed's St. Tropez villa. She was also photographed with Mohammed's arm around her as they stood on the deck of one of his yachts. Nothing could have pleased him more than a match between his son and the Princess.

Morton reports that Diana was bothered by media commentary that she had chosen an inappropriate holiday host, and one day motored over to a boatload of British journalists to complain about their meanness. Al Fayed was a longtime Spencer-family friend, she explained.

The next weekend, she was photographed jetting to Paris for dinner with Dodi at the Hotel Ritz, owned by al Fayed, and then boarding a helicopter on her way to a five-day Mediterranean cruise with Dodi.

It was during this trip that the famous series of photos of Diana and Dodi, hugging, kissing, and playing in the water, were shot. They were predicted to ultimately earn $3 million worldwide for paparazzo Mario Brenna. Mark Honigsbaum reports in *The Spectator* that the *Sunday Mirror* bought the first rights to "the kiss." The *Daily Mail* acquired the second rights and days later also bought and published other paparazzi pictures of the holiday. Diana was close to the *Daily*

Mail's royal correspondent Richard Kay. She must have known about the photos and approved their publication. Those who asked her Kensington Palace private office were told she was "very relaxed" about the pictures.

Dodi reportedly enjoyed the tabloid coverage as well. Always in the shadow of his powerful father, Dodi at about forty was still looking to make a mark for himself.

In mid-August, the *News of the World* and *The Sun* ran a story about Dodi's fiancée, thirty-one-year-old model Kelly Fisher of Los Angeles, who was suing Dodi after he jilted her to take up with Diana. She claimed that he failed to pay her a promised $440,000 in premarital support in exchange for giving up her modeling career. The check that Dodi had written to her in the amount of $200,000 had bounced. Fisher also alleged that Dodi was a two-timer, saying that while Diana was vacationing on the elder al Fayed's yacht in St. Tropez, she and Dodi were on a nearby boat making love.

Regardless, Diana continued to pursue her relationship with Dodi. Back in London, she was photographed visiting Dodi's Park Lane apartment, where she stayed until 1:00 A.M. When she flew to Bosnia to campaign against landmines, she was followed by some forty cameramen and journalists more concerned about the status of her romantic relationship than about her humanitarian views.

The media, characteristically, was making a big story out of the romance for their own profit. The *Sunday Mirror*'s overheated prose made it sound as though Dodi was the love of Diana's life: "You only have to look at the sensual body language to know that they have found physical and spiritual fulfillment in each other."

After Diana's interminable, fractured-fairy-tale saga, a Diana "at long last love" story provided a more dramatic arc than a Diana "hot summer fling" story. And the better the story, the better the sales.

Diana's uncharacteristic openness about this romance at face value suggested she enjoyed Dodi's company and his attention. Did she take pleasure in knowing the discomfort she was causing the royals? In the light of her recent successes in Africa, Chicago, and New York, it seems unlikely. But old habits, like the habits of hatred and resentment, die hard.

The tabloids had just shown Charles celebrating Camilla's fiftieth birthday. In response, knowing that cameras were following her during the cruise, Diana often dived off the yacht into the water and struck playful poses that accented her great legs to show that she remained eminently desirable and sexy. In *The New Yorker,* editor Tina Brown read the action as a relapse: ". . . a wounded and wounding gesture, triggered by the galling emergence of Camilla Parker-Bowles as the no-longer-unthinkable wife-in-waiting. The frantic Diana lurked beneath the surface after all." Dodi was the pill for the aching humiliation of the youthful, beautiful Diana—the most photographed woman in the world—who was dumped for a Plain Jane older woman.

"My feeling is that this relationship was a great opportunity for Diana to assert herself," Greene says. "Dodi wasn't English. He wasn't white. England is an island culture, and all island cultures have a harder time accepting foreigners. But she liked being with someone who was ethnic and of a different culture. She was a seeker and loved learning about different people. I think she was saying, 'I'm just going to have fun. I'm going to do what I want to do. To hell with you.'"

During the yacht's tour through Grecian waters, Diana reportedly told Rosa Monckton, who had accompanied her on this leg of the tour, that she was dismayed by Dodi's lavish gifts and had made no plans for the future. She also implied to *The Spectator*'s society columnist, Taki Theodoracopulos, that marriage was not on her mind. "It took her a long time to get out of a loveless marriage, and she's not about to get into another."

Five days before her death, however, Diana had suggested in an interview with the newspaper *Le Monde* that she was considering a dramatic change, that if not for her sons, she would gladly leave behind Britain and the "ferocious" press and go abroad, where she is "received with kindness."

Six hours before her death, Diana had telephoned the *Daily Mail*'s Richard Kay. She told him that she planned to complete her obligations to her charities and the landmines cause, and then completely withdraw from formal public life. Though she had often stated this dream, Kay believed her this time. She loved Dodi, and she believed he loved her. She would continue her good works, but more behind the scenes. Mohammed al Fayed had agreed to help finance a charity for victims of landmines. Diana had also sketched out a plan to open hospices all over the world. Perhaps she intended to take steps toward a quieter life with Dodi, a more ordinary life.

But the circumstances of her last hours suggest that Diana was still a thrill-seeker, a risk-taker who was a long way from giving up the excitement of public life.

Paris

> *"I would like to end by thanking God for the small mercies he has shown. . . . For taking Diana at her most beautiful and radiant and when she had joy in her private life."*
>
> —Charles, Earl of Spencer
> Eulogy for his sister Diana

The Princess's last hours perfectly reflected the melodramatic quality of her life. Until the real story was told, her death seemed as predictable as if it had been the last moment of a screenplay. Diana Spencer had worked since childhood to design and inhabit the package in which she presented herself, and she offered that package to the media, and through the media, to the world. For many years it was impossible to distinguish the Princess from the package.

And then, following her divorce, Diana had begun to make moves to escape the package. Arguably, that was what killed her.

Diana and her lover, Dodi al Fayed, had arrived in Paris that morning, the last day of August, 1997, followed by photographers. They spent the day together, at one point exchanging gifts. He gave her a ring. She gave him a silver plate.

In the evening, they had driven to the Ritz in a black Range Rover often used by Diana. In late August there is little breaking news in Paris; the city is on holiday. In the hope or expectation that Dodi and Diana might announce an engagement, two hundred photographers massed in front of the hotel. Dodi's security guard came out to talk to them, reassuring them that they would get a picture. But an intimate photo of the two could command a high price, and so there was fierce competition for position. The circumstances were right for any number of invasions of privacy, including a chase.

An ordinary person accustomed to privacy would obviously have been a victim in such a situation. But Diana had long since surrendered the anonymity of ordinary people and she had done so consciously and with enthusiasm. Press attention gratified her vanity and publicized her causes. Moreover, she may have wanted to be photographed with Dodi al Fayed. Photos would shock the royal family. And if she were in love, as some claimed, she may have liked the press attention for sentimental reasons. Her ambivalence is clear in the way that she, Dodi, and the people who worked for them behaved that night.

In his own way Dodi, like Diana, had made a deal with the devil. In *Vanity Fair,* his friend Jack Martin noted that Dodi was not bothered by the tabloid coverage of his romance with Diana. He was drawn to Diana's notoriety. "As an adult, he had to prove himself and make himself seem bigger than he was," Martin says, "Dodi wanted to be famous, God knows."

Diana and Dodi shared a private dinner that evening at the Ritz's Espadon Restaurant. Just before midnight they decided to leave for Dodi's apartment on the avenue des Champs-Elysées near the Arc de Triomphe. To avoid the photographers who congregated outside the front entrance, they exited by the back door and got into a Mercedes belonging to the hotel. They were accompanied by Henri Paul, a driver employed by the Ritz, and British bodyguard Trevor Rees-Jones. The Range Rover that the couple had originally arrived in and Dodi's Mercedes were dispatched from the front of the hotel as a decoy.

The escape plan apparently was Dodi's, concocted "amid some confusion and a tense atmosphere," according to an Agence France Presse report. Dodi had used decoys similarly during the July 25–27 weekend he had spent with Diana in Paris. (On that occasion, his regular chauffeur was driving.) This night Dodi spoke over the phone to his father and said that he planned to use one or more decoy cars again to escape attention. Mohammed al Fayed thought the plan was dangerous and urged them to sleep at the hotel.

Diana had used personal decoys from the early days of her marriage, but this plan to send out several cars may not have been familiar to her. Once separated from Charles, Diana had chosen to give up the twenty-four-hour British security required when she was a full member of royal family. Scotland Yard opposed her choice, but she still used official bodyguards only at public events or when out with her children. The night of the accident, she was under al Fayed's protection.

Much later, Rees-Jones recalled disagreeing with Dodi's decision to send a vehicle ahead as a decoy.

While Diana and Dodi were in the restaurant, Henri Paul waited at the bar drinking anisette. Paul held his liquor well. When al Fayed family representatives screened a twenty-six-minute videotape, edited from two hours taken by hotel security, Paul did not appear drunk. Photographers, however, described his behavior as "bizarre" and "chattier than usual" when he conversed with them in front of the hotel. Two cameramen suspected he had been drinking. Later, results of lab tests on Paul's blood and hair revealed that he had been in a state of "moderate chronic alcoholism" for eight days, and that for months he had also been ingesting a combination of drugs prescribed for the treatment of alcoholism. When he slid behind the wheel of the Mercedes his blood alcohol level was at 1.75 grams of alcohol per liter, or 3.5 times the legal limit. The National Association for the Prevention of Alcoholism declared that a person at that level would have had to drink the equivalent of nine shots of whiskey in rapid succession. French television claimed that such a level increased the likelihood of a crash by thirty-five times.

But when his memory returned, Rees-Jones remembered nothing to indicate that Paul was drunk, though he had seen the driver consuming anisette at the bar.

Paul was sure he could drive. A lawyer for one of the photographers claimed that Paul allegedly taunted cameramen outside the hotel with the remark, "You won't be able to catch me."

Hotel photos show, and eyewitnesses confirm, that Paul accelerated at a moderate rate when pulling away from the hotel. Friends of Dodi's have pointed out that he was a cautious man, particularly known for his dislike of high-speed driving. Though he collected race cars in England, Dodi drove them slowly, even in open country.

Some of the paparazzi were not fooled by the decoys. As the Mercedes left the hotel, two motorcycles, one scooter, and one or two cars driven by photographers followed it west on the rue de Rivoli, along the Jardin des Tuileries.

At the Place de la Concorde, the Mercedes stopped for a red light. But before the light turned green, the car "took off with a roar." It would appear that someone inside—Paul or Diana most likely— decided to speed up the game. The decision, whoever made it, may have been prompted by the popping of a flashbulb near the car at the red light. (A photo exists showing the two in the car, Dodi's hand on Diana's knee. No one has claimed having taken it.) The car turned right onto the cours la Reine (the street name in English would be "Queen's Way") speeding toward the Pont de l'Alma underpass.

Who can forget that Diana used similar evasive techniques during her courtship, timing her driving so that photographers would be stuck at red lights? Speech adviser Richard Greene believes this to be a highly likely scenario. ". . . Diana was very childlike and impulsive. It's very possible she could have authorized the speeding, 'Come on, let's go, let's get away from them.' It's possible that it became a game because of her playful personality and her capability of being angry about it."

Many members of the press later suggested that Diana and Dodi set themselves up to be pursued. Cindy Adams, the gossip columnist for the *New York Post,* told me, "Someone tipped off the paparazzi originally to this romance. It had to have been either Dodi or Diana. It could not have been anyone else during the early days of the romance itself." The reasons? "They wanted to stick it to the Queen. Diana wanted to show how valuable a human being she was, that she was sought-after by someone she knew the Queen would hate. They used the press as much as the press used them. Unfortunately, sometimes you unleash a tiger."

Don Hewitt, creator and executive producer of *60 Minutes,* agrees. The 'beautiful people' don't mind paparazzi for their own purposes," he says. "Diana was fairly friendly with the editors. When she participated in her good works, all the British tabloids went after her. She loved it. She loved those guys. If Diana and Dodi had walked out of the hotel and no paparazzi were there, they'd have wondered, 'Have we lost our cachet?'"

Did someone in the car think they could shake the paparazzi? Hewitt believes Diana's party expected to be pursued. "If you are being chased with machines guns, you drive a hundred and twenty miles an hour. Like a madman. If you are chased by cameras, big deal." The full number giving chase will never be known. Motorcycle paparazzi had been speeding in front of the car. A white car also pursued the Mercedes. Some of the motorcycles apparently fell behind, unable to keep up the pace.

There is a dip in the pavement near the entrance to the tunnel and the Mercedes was going much too fast—sixty to a hundred miles an hour in a thirty-mile-per-hour zone. A car or motorcycle may have been moving in from the right, forcing the car to the left. One witness said on television that he had been passed by the speeding Mercedes as it entered the tunnel but had seen no motorcycles behind it. Police would later theorize that the Mercedes came up behind a white Fiat Uno, made between 1983 and 1989. They believed that Paul braked suddenly when overtaking the slow-moving car, then sped up to pass on the left, sideswiping it. Trying to recover, Paul again stepped on the gas and lost control. Pieces of debris from a Fiat were found at the scene, though they could have come from a previous accident.

Whatever the cause, at eleven minutes past midnight at the tunnel entrance the Mercedes went out of control. It swerved left into a center median's thirteenth concrete support pillar. Some reports indicate it bounced against the right wall, then hit a second pillar on the left. The flattened roof suggested that the car overturned and righted itself, its left side careening against the wall, facing against traffic as it came to a halt.

Henri Paul died instantly. Some reports say Dodi al Fayed also died immediately, others that he passed away minutes after the ambulance arrived. Only Diana's bodyguard, Trevor Rees-Jones, was protected by a seat belt and an airbag. Personal security officers usually leave the belt off so that their movements won't be restricted in case they must act, and it is unclear why Rees-Jones was the only passenger wearing one. Nevertheless, he suffered horrifying wounds to his head and face. For many months afterwards he retained no memory of the accident.

According to a *Newsweek* story published in mid-October, paparazzi appeared on the scene two minutes after the collision. There were reportedly twelve photographers at the site. One phoned for help. Then, according to witnesses, they began snapping pictures furiously.

Six months later, *Dateline NBC* featured a man who claimed to be a motorcyclist close to the accident. Eric Petel told Victoria Corderi that the first thing he saw of the accident was a car bounce back from the wall and face him. He did not see a second car that the Mercedes could have sideswiped. He stopped, recognized the Princess, then headed out. Moments later, he called the police from a nearby pay phone, relaying that Diana had been in an accident. When the police didn't believe him, he drove to a precinct and then was escorted to headquarters to give a statement. The statement, however, was not forwarded to investigators until months later. Those familiar with the deliberate pace of French bureaucracy might find the story believable.

By most accounts, police response was slow and medical assistance slower. By the time the police arrived, five of the photographers had fled; the police detained seven for interrogation and impounded their film: Nikola Arsov of Sipa Agency, Jacques Langevin of Sygma, freelancer Laslo Veres, Stepane Darmon of Gamma, and Serge Arnal of Stills. The other two, Christian Martinez of Angeli and Romuald Rat of Gamma, were released on $16,000 bail and forbidden to work as journalists while the case was pending. Martinez and Rat had allegedly obstructed the emergency services. The photographers were charged with involuntary homicide and violation of France's Good Samaritan law. Arsov's lawyer called the probe a "show trial" to please public opinion. Rat's lawyer argued that his client merely took Diana's pulse to see if she were alive, while also taking photos of the wreckage as the first officers arrived on the scene. That was not obstruction, he insisted.

According to police reports, Martinez told an officer, "You're pissing me off. Let me do my work. At least at Sarajevo the cops let us work." For the paparazzi, the whole world is in a perpetual state of war.

There has been, of course, much speculation about the causes of the accident. Pictures confiscated from paparazzi showed that six cars passed the wreck before traffic was stopped. Rumors about the white Fiat persisted for months. The underlying issue—legal and moral— was: Did the paparazzi cause the crash?

Diana was pulled out of the car by an ambulance rescue crew and paramedics began working on her at about 12:40 A.M. Under the immediate care of the Paris SAMU (Urgent Medical Aid Service) ambulance, she underwent initial resuscitation efforts. The French system mandates "field stabilization" while the American method is "scoop and run." Paramedics worked on Diana for about forty-five minutes. Fifty-two minutes after arriving, seeing how grave her condition was, they decided to drive her to the hospital that had twenty-four-hour emergency medical services. Hôpital La Pitié-Salpêtrière was four miles away. The drive would normally take five to ten minutes, but traffic was still relatively heavy. The ambulance left the tunnel at 1:25 A.M. and arrived at 2:05 A.M., almost two hours after the crash. At about 2:00 A.M., Diana's heart had stopped beating. Doctors in the ambulance injected her with adrenaline.

Arriving at La Pitié-Salpêtrière, Diana experienced a "grave hemorrhagic shock" in her chest. Cardiac arrest swiftly followed. An emergency thoracotomy showed a critical wound in the left pulmonary vein. The wound was closed and heart massage was administered for more than two hours. Despite the efforts, no circulation resumed. Diana was pronounced dead at 4:00 A.M. The official news was read by Dr. Bruno Riou, an anesthesiologist and duty physician, and co-signed by Dr. Alain Pavie, one of France's foremost cardiovascular surgeons, with other key officials present: Jean-Pierre Chevenement, the French interior minister; Britain's ambassador, Michael Jay; and Paris police prefect Philippe Massoni.

At 5:30 A.M., more details were revealed at the Paris hospital where Diana had been taken and treated. Dr. Riou summarized the Princess's condition and treatment after the accident, and reaffirmed her death.

Fifty journalists were present.

It had been a good marriage, Diana's to the media. It was a volatile relationship but the two, most of the time, were good companions and worthy adversaries. It was not unfair to claim that Diana had been a victim, as her brother did at her memorial service, but it was inaccurate. Diana was not outmatched by the media, she was only outnumbered, which may also have contributed to her death.

Diana had, through a kind of naïve intuition and a willingness to learn, been as successful as any modern figure who has used the media to personal advantage. But the story was not over when she died. No reader of this book will forget the extraordinary response of the media to the Princess's tragedy. At first, without her as a partner, the media fed on itself for material—a phenomenon that I mentioned in the introduction to this book. Within hours, the story of Diana's death became the story of the immense sense of loss felt by ordinary people.

Not until the late months of 1997 had there been such an extraordinary opportunity to see at work the rules and formulas which govern the media in its packaging of public figures. Nor had it ever been so clear how celebrities and those who report on them can direct and manage the public's sense of truth and reality.

PART II

The Package

CHAPTER 13

The Audience of Mourners

"People everywhere, not just here in Britain, kept faith with Princess Diana. They liked her, they loved her, they regarded her as one of the people. She was the People's Princess."

—England's Prime Minister Tony Blair

Diana's funeral was full of poignant images and sounds, from the exquisitely staged ritual to the mourners, family, and admirers. It was comparable to the unforgettable pageantry of her wedding.

There were the bereaved faces of ordinary Britons, more than a million strong, watching the casket as it wound through the streets of London toward Westminster. There was the casket itself, draped in the royal standard, borne on a cart flanked by red-coated Welsh Guards, followed on foot by the men in her life—Prince Charles, sons William and Harry, brother Charles, and Prince Philip, plus representatives from her charities. There was Prince Harry's note, addressed "Mummy," tucked into the bowl of roses atop the casket.

Big Ben tolled 11:00 A.M. as eight Welsh Guards bore the casket inside the abbey, its soaring Gothic arches bathed in sunlight through the stained-glass windows. There was the impassioned performance of "Candle in the Wind," originally written by Elton John and Bernie Taupin to celebrate Marilyn Monroe, rewritten and movingly performed by Diana's friend John: "Goodbye, England's Rose . . ." Outside, in the streets and in Hyde Park and Regent's Park, loudspeakers and three mammoth television screens showed the service, mourners holding candles, their flames flickering in the wind. Diana's sisters, Sarah and Jane, read poetry. Brother Charles gave an eloquent and angry eulogy that eviscerated the royal family as he described Diana as "someone with a natural nobility who was classless, who proved in the last year that she needed no royal title to continue to generate her particular brand of magic." Applause began outside the abbey and swept forward toward Diana's coffin. The boys' choir sang traditional English airs.

Diana's funeral was the biggest television event ever in the United Kingdom. On the day of the funeral, Saturday, September 6, the BBC used one hundred forty-one live cameras to capture the moments along the funeral procession, at the funeral itself, and of the motorcade escorting Diana's body from London. Four of the cameras provided feeds to international broadcasters. In addition, the signal was carried on the BBC World satellite service.

At the funeral site alone, Westminster Abbey in London, ten BBC cameras covered the outside while twelve BBC cameras and ten ITV cameras were stationed inside. Sky News, the third United Kingdom broadcaster, took a BBC camera-feed of the indoor funeral ceremony. The three broadcasters pooled coverage of the motorcade from the abbey; forty cameras followed the hearse to the main motorway link that would lead to Diana's final resting place at Althorp.

If I had been an investigative reporter on the scene, trying to understand the significance of this young woman's remarkable life and tragic death, I'd have tried to follow Paul Burrell. He had remained closer to her than anyone over the years. He counseled, teased, and comforted her. Their children played together. He knew the public Diana and the private one as well.

Burrell was there for her even in death. Upon hearing of the fatal accident, he reportedly was "knocked sidewards," but flew to Paris, where he clothed her in a dress from her closet, tidied her hair, and held her hand, while awaiting the arrival of Charles and Diana's sisters. He prayed by Diana's coffin at St. James's Palace through one night, and was intimately involved in all aspects of her funeral, assisting with invitations and selecting Diana's favorite music. He was the only non-family member among the ten mourners at Diana's private burial at Althorp.

In subsequent weeks, as we shall see, it became ever more difficult to hold on to the real Diana in the sea of tributes, counter-tributes, and controversy. Burrell knew what was important. He began taking inventory of Diana's belongings. In mid-December, he accompanied Princes William and Harry around their mother's rooms to collect personal items. In a final farewell to the apartment that had been home to them since birth, the boys wandered through the rooms for an hour, escorted only by Burrell. Nothing had been removed or touched since the day their mother left for her final holiday.

(Paul Burrell remains a semi-official custodian of her memory. In early November of 1997, he received the Royal Victorian Medal for service to the Crown. He has been asked to sit on the Diana Princess of Wales Memorial Committee. In March of 1998, the Spencer family revealed that their sister's will was altered to leave him fifty thousand pounds. He has turned down many lucrative film and book contracts for his version of Diana's life, though he is taping an oral history with Richard Greene.)

Burrell spoke openly about Diana only once, in January of 1998, when he objected to the Spencer family charging people to see Diana's grave at the Althorp estate. The home itself is being turned into a Diana memorabilia museum. At an adult admission of $16.00, Althorp is now one of Britain's most expensive tourist attractions. Her island grave can be viewed only from a twenty-yard distance across the water. According to the *Mirror,* Burrell told friends: "The Princess would have hated people having to pay to come close to her."

Diana had always been a tourist attraction. She remains one in death.

Diana's personal tragedy soon became encompassed by the story of her mourners. An estimated billion people worldwide watched on television, making the funeral the most widely witnessed event in history, surpassing the previous record-holder—Diana's wedding. In Britain alone, 31.5 million tuned in, or fifty-nine percent of the population. Some fifty million Americans got up early or stayed up through the night to watch the live telecast, while another twenty million were estimated to have watched the rebroadcasts.

"We have never seen anything quite like it," said NBC network news anchor Tom Brokaw upon the conclusion of Diana's funeral.

"And that includes the media coverage," commented Pulitzer Prize-winning television critic Howard Rosenberg, in the *Los Angeles Times,* about the passing and mourning of the Princess. "The funeral and the Brits' response to it were quite a spectacle. But even more awesome was the crush of TV treating Diana's life and death as if they were biblical in size and she had parted the Red Sea."

According to the *Tyndall Weekly,* a newsletter that monitors broadcast network news, American network news organizations devoted more time in one week to her fatal accident and worldwide mourning than to any news event since the 1991 coup attempt against Soviet leader Mikhail Gorbachev.

The rest of the global media—newspapers, magazines, radio, the Internet—followed suit in its extravagant coverage and praise for a woman who, granted, did good works, but was hardly saintly or powerful in any conventional sense of the words.

In Britain, thirty-five percent of the total news coverage for the entire month of September was devoted to Diana, radio-television commentator Paul Harvey said on C-SPAN. "Not even the end of World War II got that much ink."

The funeral highlighted something that I'll come back to later: The media has only a few models for covering large, outdoor, public events—the JFK funeral, presidential inaugurations, the Macy's parade. There is very little hope of finding the right note for an extraordinary event like this one.

Who were these mourners? Did the public want more Diana or did it want more news? That is, did the media oversupply coverage or were they, as they claimed, merely responding to public demand?

Howard Rosenberg says he received death threats after he was slightly critical of Diana in the *Los Angeles Times*. Given that reaction, it seems the carnival celebrating Diana's death was just what the people ordered.

Norman Pearlstine, editor-in-chief for Time Inc., said in our interview that the Diana story was a difficult one to categorize. The traditional news sensibility defines news stories as politics, economics, diplomacy, and war. These are the lenses through which Bill Clinton, Iraq, and Newt Gingrich are viewed. "By that definition, a divorced princess got far too much attention and was taken to sainthood when objectively, if you believe the royals about Diana, she was a much more complicated woman," Pearlstine explains.

"But there is a different definition that says news is something that affects emotion, affects life, how you feel about yourself and the world around you," he continues. "[In that context], I don't think she was either sainted or over-covered. I don't think her death was something where the media created this monster story. When the bulletin [about her death] broke in on *Saturday Night Live* at 11:37 P.M. or whatever, East Coast time, on August 30—before *Time* closed its cover story the next morning at 9:00 A.M., before *People* did nineteen pages, before all of that—there was a popular reaction to this event that was unprecedented, a response that would make any editor have to say, 'This is news,' and go with the story. The sainting of her grew from a genuine heartfelt and global emotional response to her . . . but, particularly in the U.K. and U.S., I think the public appetite for the news of her death preceded the appearance of news or content about her, be it on television or in print. I absolutely believe that one-hundred percent."

Clemm Lane, bureau chief for the Western bureau of ABC News, agrees. "In terms of her historical importance, Diana was over-covered. But I don't think it was over-covered in terms of the public's appetite for it. Are we feeding the appetite? Well, maybe. But are they clamoring for it? Yes."

But some thought the media excesses and the public demonstrations could not be explained away by the laws of supply and demand. After a decade and a half of voyeurism, many people wanted absolution. The media, according to this theory, canonizes the dead to redeem itself for the negatives exposed about those people during life. "We demonize the well-known when alive, and tend to sanctify them when they are dead, almost out of guilt," nationally syndicated columnist Arianna Huffington pointed out in our interview. "And when someone dies suddenly and tragically, there will always be hyperbole."

Whether out of guilt or admiration, the descriptions of Diana that week sounded like exaggerations to Dan Okrent, former managing editor of *Life* and current editor of new media for Time Inc. "The coverage was audience-determined, but there was a discrepancy between my own perception of who she was and what the media said about her. To describe her as one of the great humanitarians of the century was weird."

New York Times television critic Walter Goodman wrote: "The worldwide slobbering over celebrities, often by celebrities, who became celebrities by slobbering over celebrities, is a felony only against journalism."

If the journalistic response was inappropriate, then the many who have called for curbs on the media should be taken seriously. But if the media simply responded to an unexpected demand for news about the Princess, then it is worth looking at the way we perceive our public figures. Why are so many of us as attracted to them as we are? What do they represent? And we should consider, finally, whether public figures manipulate our feelings. Did Diana not only understand how to control the media, but also how to appeal to the hearts of the millions who publicly demonstrated their sense of loss when she died?

Why was Diana mourned so passionately? There are two schools of thought. Around the world, people's emotional reaction to her death was immediately intense, making their grief justification for blanket coverage. Indeed, the mourning became the main story after the death itself. "No, the coverage wasn't overblown, because Diana was the most popular person in the world," Mitchell Fink, a contributing editor and regular on CNN's *Showbiz Today,* told me. Carla Hall, who covered the mourning and funeral in London for the *Los*

Angeles Times, agrees: "On a raw gut level, Diana was one of the most fascinating women."

A more cynical explanation of the copious media coverage is the intense competition amongst the media outlets. To fill the time and space that is growing steadily and rapidly with each introduction of another subsidiary, broadcasters have blurred the line between news and entertainment.

The Internet became a venue for global grief. Official condolence Web-site hits numbered 1.8 million by Labor Day, less than two days after Diana's death. MSNBC, CNN, and ABC each reported significant spikes in the number of "page views" of their news organizations' Web sites that week.

Buckingham Palace's Web site for the Princess received 13.8 million hits the week of September 1. A total of 352,157 messages of condolence were written on the site from Sunday through Friday. Yahoo, the on-line directory service, reported by week's end that more than a hundred Web sites were created to celebrate Diana's life.

There is plenty of evidence that the public had difficulty processing the fact of Diana's death. In chat rooms, the discussions began immediately with the news, but quickly jumped into reaction and response, from grief to speculation about a possible murder conspiracy and the paparazzi's role (the photographers were often called "scum" and "parasites"), according to Dom's Domain on the Internet.

The expressions were maudlin, the poetry often banal, Steven Levy wrote in *Newsweek,* but the "rawly sincere messages" were a breath of fresh air compared to the television commentators, long since out of new material, "whose sentiments were just as trite but couched in slicker prose." It connected people to other people in their sharing of emotion in a way that television, radio, or print could not, as illustrated by one Internet user's message: "It is with great sadness I sit here in front of my computer. I cannot be at the embassy to sign the condolence book. . . . I cannot be at the service to say goodbye to a wonderful human being. . . ."

Certainly, the grief of the British could be understood, as could the prominence of the story in the British media. Diana was their Princess. She promoted their causes and fashions and products and national pride. She updated the role of the monarchy, and she gave birth to an heir to the throne.

Tuesday's stories captured the high esteem in which citizens of all classes held the Princess, and their sadness at her death. *The Times* ran seven stories on grieving alone. The headlines: "Thousands Testify to their Sorrow"; "Silent Saturday for Mourning"; "Police Ready for Million Mourners"; "Extra Trains for Travelers to Funeral"; "Mourning Will Shut Harrods, the Store a Bomb Could Not Close"; "Grief for Diana is Without Borders"; "New Yorkers Mourn Queen of the World." There were five in *The Scotsman:* "Dawn of a Day of Mourning"; "Ordinary People Take Time to Pay Last Respects"; "Grieving for a Fairy Tale Princess We All Created"; "Country Faces Standstill for Farewell"; "Kings and Commoners Share Grief Worldwide." In the *Irish Times:* "A Divided Community Unites in Grief for Princess"; "Diana's Appeal Transcended Barriers in Northern Ireland."

Sales of flowers, records, and books were up. Everything else was down. These trends were attributed to the death of the Princess. The masses of flowers and condolence books that appeared outside British embassies—the impromptu creation of shrines to the Princess—seemed to belong to a very different, more religious or superstitious age. In the same way that pilgrims leave special offerings at holy places, crowds brought flowers and teddy bears and penned personal notes and left them at designated public places.

Outside Belfast's city hall, Debbie Wilson wrote, "We have lost the jewel in our crown and that's what she was. It is all so sad." In

Glasgow: "A piece of you is still with me and always will be," wrote an eleven-year-old girl who met the Princess during a skiing holiday." Said one man: "It's strange, I feel upset, as though she was someone I really knew, almost like a member of the family."

In London, outside St. James's Palace—where Diana's body lay in a private chapel for visits by family and friends and where crowds queued to sign books of condolence—one woman who had traveled overnight from a distant village with her daughter said: "We were at a concert, but as soon as we heard we just wanted to come and lay flowers."

British-born writer-broadcaster Martin Lewis theorizes that the ocean of flowers was a sort of political statement. For a decade, even blue-collar England backed Margaret Thatcher, who brought about fundamental economic changes at a devastating social cost. Diana's causes reminded the common people that those less fortunate than themselves paid the price. "The flowers were an atonement for their own cynicism, which Diana adamantly opposed," Lewis says.

Warren Hoge, writing for the *New York Times,* thinks the opposite. "The grief of the British people was utterly spontaneous," he says.

But why all the fuss in the United States and elsewhere, by media and public? The sheer numbers of people around the world who mourned publicly surprised even the most devoted Diana followers and friends, not to mention her detractors.

Was the media reporting on Diana? Or was it engaged in the cyclical process of covering the mourners for the gratification of other mourners and for the merely curious? It might be suggested that what we witnessed was yet another example of the existence of the global village. An unimaginable number of people needed a worldwide wake, an opportunity to grieve as a global community through the media.

Los Angeles KABC Radio talk show host and author Dennis Prager contended that Diana was the chosen one because she was young, beautiful, and a mother.

But the stories of ordinary people who suffer such tragedies rarely have much affect on us. In fact, it is often argued that television news, by making us accustomed to a steady diet of misfortune, has made us callous to suffering. The grieving for Diana seems to have been a much more complicated matter.

Fairy tales should not have unhappy endings, and Diana's life in the public eye began as the quintessential fairy tale. Did we mourn the loss of innocence? It seems unlikely. Diana's story had looked like material for melodrama, if not tragedy, for years. The Princess suffered with bulimia and had a loveless marriage. She clearly had personal demons she fought valiantly to overcome. To an outsider, any new romance might seem to offer a window of promise, a happy ending. One might hope that, after so many years of sadness, the fairy tale would resume. To have that dim, romantic possibility snatched away so soon was sobering. But a tragic end to a life of controversy and risk-taking was hardly paradoxical.

Author Nancy Friday strongly believes, however, that people grieved for their own lost promise as relived through Diana's untimely death. "Part of our misery was that she was beginning her life [again]. We saw her relax, have fun, become herself. We have all been there. Usually in our twenties, we say, 'Now I can become who I am.' We felt that with her because she was so public. We returned to that point in our own life, when we were ready to become what we wanted to be, we believed in ourselves, our tension was gone, we were happy . . . and then something happened, and we couldn't reach our full potential. Few of us do," Friday says.

"That hope was dashed again for everybody when Diana died. It seemed so f***ing cruel, so wrong. 'No, no, no, not her, not when she was on the brink . . .' we cried. I was never besotted with Diana, yet I wept like I lost a child. I think I lost myself, but myself of long ago."

Dr. Joyce Brothers, who discussed the nature of grieving on an early morning ABC newscast that week, expands the range of our vulnerability to "our own unresolved losses of any kind—job, friends, pet. This was an opportunity for us to deal with unfinished business in our lives."

That was precisely the experience for Margaret Trudeau Kemper. The ex-wife of the former prime minister of Canada had recently lost a friend to cancer in the spring of 1997. "She was an absolutely wonderful person. I was still mourning for her when Princess Diana died. Even though I did not know Diana, I found that throughout the coverage of her death—the comforts, the Queen's speech, the funeral—I missed my friend."

Even those who never gave Diana or most other celebrities two thoughts in their lives were swept away, much to their surprise. In *The New Yorker*, Francine du Plessix Gray wrote an incisive piece as to why she and her over-fifty cronies "who use ice tongs to carry copies of *People* to the trash can" were burning up the phone lines for two days after her death to talk about the Princess. These "progressive feminists" from the '60s and '70s had scorned Diana for years because of a perception of self-absorption with glamour, clothes, and self-improvement therapies, "and yet we were bawling."

The common denominator of their sadness: "Diana expressed . . . the melancholy solitude to many women's experience of marriage," Gray said. "The disappointments, humiliations of her experiences with men reflected the rage my friends and I still felt, decades later, toward all those fellows in our own pasts who had jilted or deceived us, the cads who had moved on to exploit others, deaf to our anxieties and quests."

Dr. Stuart Fischoff, professor of media psychology at Cal State University, believes the sentimentality of the coverage—its bathos, as he calls it—was key to puncturing the armor of most people's boredom. "Most of our lives are dull and a lot are miserable. We can't get a job or get in school. These things aren't pleasant but we numb ourselves. Diana's death exploded that shell and we feel the exquisite pain of our lives."

The mourning also was evidence of the celebrity cult that emerged after society lost faith in its establishments, from church to government to corporation. Diana was raised "to sainthood in the electronic church," wrote Richard Reeves in the *Los Angeles Times.* "She was necessary in this era of mobility, of aloneness and of declining institutions, one of them the British Crown."

And it was the electronic church—television and the Internet—that brought people together as a community to pay homage to Diana. Syndicated entertainment columnist Liz Smith calls it "a secular excuse to have the emotional feelings associated with having religious faith."

There was a paradox in the uniting of so many mourners through television. Generally, contemporary media fragments the audience. According to Joe Turow, professor of communications at the University of Pennsylvania's Annenberg School for Communications (cited in Larry King's 1998 book *Future Talk*), consumers will continue to a greater degree to isolate themselves because people will choose to gather their own information from media that reinforces their own preconceptions. Turow believes that continued "fractionalization" of the audience will lead to a lack of concern for others outside your own circle, bred by the demise of community. The funeral, however, seemed to bring together people widely separated from one another.

When Diana died, the grieving crossed all races and cultures, as motivation guru Tony Robbins was to find out firsthand. On Saturday, August 30, Robbins was getting ready to give a lecture to a cosmopolitan crowd in Hawaii. Two minutes before going on stage, he was informed of Diana's death. Having known and worked with the Princess since 1993, he was understandably shaken. The news was broken to his audience shortly thereafter.

"There were moans, cries, screams. People couldn't believe it. This was a crowd of two thousand from sixty-five countries and who spoke six languages. There was a universal feeling of shock and anguish. We sang 'Amazing Grace' and then said some prayers."

Does this anecdotal evidence demonstrate the genuine feelings of millions? Whether those in the audience were sincere mourners or innocent onlookers can't be determined. But most surveys support the idea that a huge portion of the public was obsessed with news of the death, the funeral, and the post-mortem analysis of Diana. Magazine publishers were stunned by the public interest, according to an *American Journalism Review* summary by Jacqueline Sharkey. *Time*'s first issue about Diana's death had newsstand sales of about 850,000— 650,000 more than normal. The commemorative issue one week later sold about 1.2 million copies. They are the two largest sellers in the magazine's history. After putting out two cover stories on Diana, *Newsweek* also published an ad-free, stand-alone, commemorative issue on September 11, and within one week, wholesalers were running out of the 1.5 million newsstand copies. *People* upped its newsstand run from 2.4 million to 3.3 million for its first Diana cover, which was selling out in spots around the country. The magazine kept the run for the second Diana cover at 3.3 million.

Newspapers caught the windfall too, Sharkey reported. *USA Today*'s total circulation the week after Diana's death was several hundred thousand above normal. The *Washington Post* sold more than twenty thousand additional copies of its Sunday edition the day Diana died and the day after her funeral.

Broadcast and cable networks saw huge ratings increases, as documented by trade publication *Electronic Media*. In the middle of the Labor Day weekend (and more than likely because of it) Diana news drew 7.2 million more people to their sets than had watched the week before, with 41 million viewers tuned in to watch four prime-time network specials that appeared simultaneously on Sunday night.

Network news-show ratings gained twenty to sixty percent. CNN's Saturday night coverage was the highest-rated cable show (6.5 Nielsen rating), drawing 4.6 million households from midnight to 12:30 A.M. Several CNN programs had their highest ratings ever during that weekend. MSNBC drew 223,000 households for its Saturday night coverage, with viewership peaking at 975,000 on Sunday morning. Sunday daytime was its strongest day ever (419,000 homes). On Monday, it averaged 1.1 (361,000 homes). In August, MSNBC's average daily viewing had only been 31,000 households. The Fox news channel drew a 1 rating (213,000 households) Saturday night, and throughout Sunday averaged a record 185,000 households, up from its August Sunday average of 12,000.

The Pew Research Center for the People and the Press reports that nearly nine out of ten Americans paid attention to the tragedy, with fifty-four percent following the tragedy very closely. No other story in 1997 came close.

A head count of viewers may not necessarily define their sentiments. How do we know that the viewer is actually *watching* what is on the screen? Jerry Seinfeld, talking about television, remarked to *Time:* "It's a habitual medium. Most people aren't really entertained. What they need is they need to watch TV. Entertainment is almost a luxury item. . . . Television is like a flier somebody sticks on your windshield. Who gives a damn what's on it?

It's iridescent wallpaper. Sometimes I think people just like the light on their faces."

The media stories published and broadcast after Diana's death, many based on slender evidence, could be compared with gossip. But gossip, which seems to saturate the media these days, has a useful purpose. In addition to unveiling hidden truths, gossip unifies social groups. There's no reason to believe its effect will be any different today even if the delivery system—electronic media—has changed.

"Humans have always liked gossip. We have known that since the Bible," says *People* creator/founding editor and current Time Inc. senior editorial adviser Richard Stolley. "Human beings are inquisitive. When we lived in small towns, you could see what was going on in front of your eyes. When we moved to industrialized urban areas, connections unraveled, so we turned to intimate news of friends—and strangers—to cement society. The way it was spoken, written about, and distributed became more formalized. The media democratized gossip in an industrialized society."

As mentioned earlier, Gail Collins, a member of the *New York Times* editorial board, also believes in the social usefulness of gossip. "People express their hidden fears through gossip," she says, "imposing on others the anxieties that they haven't resolved in their own lives."

Gossip has always been integral to media history. But because of technology, it moves faster and harder and therefore makes it seem more pervasive today. Says Time Inc.'s Norman Pearlstine: "Go back and read the Penny Press. Go back and read the coverage of Grover Cleveland's presidential campaign. The basic ingredients were always there. It's just that technology wasn't such that you had to do instant analysis eight minutes later and you didn't have an audience of sixteen million people. But the human instincts have been there."

Cultural historian Leo Braudy agrees. "People in the seventeenth, eighteenth, and nineteenth centuries were just as sleazy. It's just coming out in different ways and is more widespread because of technology—as people go on talk shows and tell their stories to large national audiences."

Media psychologist Dr. Stuart Fischoff adds that gossip is a social monitoring method based on our animal instinct to survive. In any social group—be it wolves or humans—the lower animals in the pecking order depend on the upper levels for their lives. The power elite of every social group needs to be tracked. "If the leader fails, an upstart will be quick to jump in and take over," Fischoff says. "On a gut level, we are genetically predisposed to be interested in celebrities because they are today's royalty." The members of Diana's audience of mourners, in other words, found comfort in the company of others.

We don't fully understand the dimension of celebrity relationships felt by many people—a sense of intimate knowledge and empathic connection. Some people imagine a direct, personal friendship with a celebrity whom they've never met. They feel a bond comparable, or perhaps even stronger, than they might have with an actual friend. (That there is a potential danger in this sort of relationship is obvious. The assassin of John Lennon and the would-be assassin of President Reagan both thought they had personal ties with celebrities.) Yet many ordinary, sane people imagine themselves close to famous people. They refer to them by their first names.

Apparently, millions of people unhappy or wearied by life found in Diana the antidote they needed. "People live vicariously through what they think is a perfect life. If it turns out not to be perfect, they can identify more," says Marilyn Beck, a syndicated gossip columnist for forty years.

Washington Post media reporter Howard Kurtz, who reported on the Donald Trump/Marla Maples ordeals in New York, agrees: "Probably only a psychologist could fully understand why millions are absorbed with the trials of families they never met. But there is something about watching the rich and famous go through divorce, affairs, and other trauma that makes them seem all too human. Perhaps it distracts them from their own petty problems. Celebrity *Sturm und Drang* serves as mass entertainment for those stuck in the house or getting on the subway every day."

In the following chapters we will look more closely at Diana's public and at the media which acted as intermediary between the Princess and those who were fascinated by her. We will also see how Diana's way of presenting herself to the world led to this extraordinary expression of public mourning. And we will explore the need the public feels for drama, story line, and closure, and consider the rules and limitations on the media as it feeds those needs in the packaging of celebrities.

The Coverage

> "... [T]he public is increas-
> ingly addicted to gossip and
> voyeurism and the media feed
> these addictions."
>
> —Dennis Prager
> *The Prager Perspective*

If you knew the world only through television and the newspapers, you might have thought that time was standing still. For days, BBC television covered virtually nothing but Diana. Much of Europe did the same. Across the Atlantic, CNN and most of the rest of North American television also focused on the death of the Princess, to the exclusion of almost everything else. American news anchors jetted to London. The networks devoted approximately ninety-five percent of Monday night's newscast to Diana, according to the *Tyndall Weekly* newsletter. On Monday, September 1, *The Times* of London, the venerable publication of British rulers, gave twenty-six of twenty-eight news pages to Diana's death. The *Daily Mail,* a paper with a more middle-class audience, gave the subject eighty pages. The *New York Times* devoted forty percent of its general news space to the tragedy.

The coverage of the accident and death dominated news coverage from the night of Saturday, August 30, through Monday, September 1. But then something unprecedented happened. Instead of subsiding after respectful obituaries, the story continued to run through the day of Diana's funeral, Saturday, September 6, and only slightly abated in the weeks following.

In the days leading up to the funeral, each day saw a new angle or spin on the story. On Tuesday, September 2, according to the *Tyndall Weekly*, the American television news networks focused on the criminal investigation of the paparazzi; on Wednesday, popular resentment of royals; on Thursday, the royals bowing to popular pressure; by Friday, Queen Elizabeth's TV address. All were legitimate stories resulting from the accident. But were they big enough to justify such extensive network coverage? There had been other news which, according to the *Tyndall Weekly,* received short shrift: Jerusalem suicide nailbombs killed seven (sixteen minutes), Mother Teresa died (sixteen minutes), and there was scrutiny of Vice President Al Gore's 1996 political fund-raising abuses (thirteen minutes).

Members of the public with longer memories certainly felt that there was overkill in the coverage. They remembered the reporting of World War II, the Kennedy assassination, Watergate, and Nixon's resignation. But part of their response was due to the increase in media outlets, each of which justifiably jumped on the story. All of us were bombarded from every side. "Diana died in her heyday at a time when there is more media in a world with an insatiable appetite for celebrities," explains Howard Kurtz, media reporter for the *Washington Post*. "Three decades ago, she would have been on the cover of *Life*. There was no *People* or *Entertainment Weekly* or five hundred cable shows to pant after her."

Vanity Fair contributing editor Cathy Horyn believes that these media realities "upped the ante and made it feel like Diana was sainted. But for this time and generation, her death was as memorable as the Kennedy assassination."

Part of the story of the death became the coverage itself. The charge that corrupt media pander to the baser instincts of an increasingly degenerate audience has been made for generations. Was it true now? Did the media exploit the tragedy?

"'This is what the public wants' is the very definition of prostitution," Dennis Prager wrote in *The Prager Perspective*, ". . . and also the motto of the drug dealer, and the parallel is meant literally. . . ."

Had Diana been hounded to her death by scoundrels and exploiters? But hadn't she also worked *with* these same tabloid journalists? The question no one wanted to address: Did Diana bear any responsibility for the crash in which she died?

Even before the statements of Rees-Jones, speech adviser Richard Greene told me: "I know a lot of people with limousines, and if you are driven, you control where you go and how fast to drive. . . . The speed of the car is not only the driver's decision." For all the desperate search to find new angles on the story, few in the media wanted to face the tough questions.

Sensible news judgment got burned up in the fever of the race, as aptly described by Richard Folkers in *U.S. News & World Report*. As the magazine's former photo editor, Folkers worked on many catastrophic stories, including Waco, the Atlanta Olympics bombing, Pan Am 103, Los Angeles earthquakes, and the Los Angeles riots. "When they happen, you move quickly—buying, dealing, assigning, trying to beat the agencies to the pictures. I rarely felt the impact of the story, at least until the coverage was over. When the race for images got heated, my biggest worry was that my competition would have something I didn't and that my editor would demand to know why."

Members of the media jump on the treadmill because without a scoop—whatever and wherever it can be found—you're obsolete. In the early contest to cover the car crash, CBS stumbled, launching network coverage more than an hour after its rivals and leaving its affiliates largely in the dark. While the other networks were reporting Diana's death, WCBS-TV in New York was showing professional wrestling.

Desperate for copy, the media covered every angle: the village where Diana was to be buried (*USA Today* cover story), Dodi's gift to her of a $200,000 diamond ring, the New Jersey couple for whom Diana had worked as a babysitter who were invited to the funeral, the French legal system, the funeral route, the royal strategy for the funeral, the fate of Princes William and Harry, the fate of Charles's mistress, the monarchy's future, Di's last words to Cindy Crawford, Hillary Rodham Clinton's funeral trip, Di books, and actresses who might play Di in the docudramas.

Syndicated tabloid television shows dug up even more sensational material. *Extra* gave us Di's nanny, Di's trainer, Di's hairdresser, Di's health club, even the dead driver's maid (who revealed the contents of his garbage on the air). Running out of fresh faces and angles, *Entertainment Tonight* interviewed Cathy Lee Crosby (who once flew in Dodi's jet) and Lucy Lawless (the television actress who plays Xena, the warrior princess).

Again and again we saw the mainstream media competing with the tabloids. Renowned journalists went toe-to-toe with supermarket rags, trying to outdo them in sentimentality. Senior editor Mark Harris noted in *Entertainment Weekly* that Barbara Walters announced that she could barely bring herself to reveal her friendship with Diana. Larry King also reflected on his encounters with the Princess. Geraldo Rivera told his viewers, "I believe that this woman was one of the most significant women of our time." Diane Sawyer beamed as she described Diana's last appearance on ABC's *Prime Time Live.*

Howard Rosenberg says, "There was a time when an anchor would have been chastised for breaking up on television over anything, [although] it was okay when Walter Cronkite lost composure as he announced the assassination of President Kennedy and Dan Rather teared up when Challenger exploded."

Now the messenger is celebrated over the message. The anchors are the stars of a new kind of play: the showbusiness of news. All of these news-coverage approaches—entertainment, tabloidization, hyperbole, dramatic performance—are used to attract an audience that is bombarded from every side by information.

Over and over again, television bioclips throughout the week flashed images of Diana the Fairy Tale Bride, Diana the Mother, Diana the Humanitarian, Diana the Betrayed Wife/Turned Divorced Wife/Turned Single Mother.

Different headings for the same story abounded, recycled with slight changes and updates: "The Death of Diana"; "Goodbye to the People's Princess"; "The Final Farewell." Dramatic license was often employed: "Diana dies just as she found true love" or "Diana dies just as she and Charles become friends again" or "Diana is reclaimed in death by the family that shunned her in life"—all contrived to make the Diana saga that much sadder, heightening the tension of the climactic funeral.

Freelance writer Christopher Hitchens experienced recycled mob reporting as an on-air commentator for scores of television and radio shows that week. As he detailed in *Vanity Fair*, he was called upon because of his anti-monarchist sentiments and because he criticized television for creating an artificial consensus.

Through most of the week, his was a voice opposed to the sentimental treatment of Diana's life. His clearly defined, contrary position made him highly sought-after by programmers who were seeking an appearance of balanced reporting. The first rule of "media rush," Hitchens wrote, is that "if you say something on one network, all the others want to book you at once so you can come on and say precisely the same thing. . . . I am offered slivers of 'equal time' to be disobliging about the idea of someone who has just died. . . ."

While round-the-clock coverage of one subject is an opportunity to delve deeply into various branches of the story, bringing in a range of viewpoints, Hitchens continued, the media instead were creating "an echo-chamber atmosphere, based on complete uniformity and regular repetition." By Friday, NBC asked Hitchens to appear on a *Nightly News* segment to argue that the coverage had gotten out of hand.

Bob Woodward, assistant managing editor of the *Washington Post* who won a Pulitzer Prize with Carl Bernstein for his Watergate coverage, says that the demand to fill broadcasts, hour after hour, day after day after day, "creates a hydraulic pressure within all news organizations to jump on something and then everything gets reported."

Even the most reputable print news organizations get sucked into the vortex. *Time*'s assistant managing editor and former science and technology senior editor, Philip Elmer-DeWitt, says: "Because competition has gotten worse, everyone pushes harder for fear of being left behind. . . . Media outlets used to be considered reliable because their information was true. Fact-checked news underscored value. It's not working that way now because everyone is racing to keep up with the Net."

But new electronic technologies have transformed journalism in positive ways as well. Technology has allowed newsgathering to be faster and more accurate, especially through the Internet network systems like Lexus Nexus.

Time's senior editor Bruce Handy says news organizations must buy into new technologies to stay competitive. "It makes us work harder. It pushes us to tell stories better, make them more colorful, more coherent, put new things to the forefront. I suspect fifty years ago people read *Time* because it was *Time*. Now there is more competition. You can't presume the reader's attention." This same line of thinking, however, leads Establishment media outlets to compete with tabloids.

I asked Carla Hall of the *Los Angeles Times*, "Is technology the enemy of reverence?" She was more optimistic: "I am not sure that you're wrong, and I am not sure that that's a bad thing. Technology has taken the color off of people who would have hid behind their mystery. I don't know that technology makes us better people, but it makes us more informed people. And information is not the enemy of the people. Information is the helpmate of the people."

But a story that gets to us quickly is not necessarily a better story. It is a story that, in practice, has not been carefully enough researched, thought out, or crafted. The real change in newsgathering and news reporting is that the historian's virtues—objectivity, substance, accuracy—have been replaced by the virtues of the marketplace: speed, polish, availability. In short, clever packaging.

Because instant history can be done by every major news source, there is no way for any one outlet to establish its superiority except through rhetorical one-upmanship. Journalists hype because they know big stories make careers. "We also build things up so we can justify our future coverage," admits Howard Rosenberg, television critic for the *Los Angeles Times*.

Television, in particular, lavishes coverage on public events—large and small—because advances in technology have made live reports easier and less expensive then ever before. "Satellite communications allow local newscasters to cover a far-flung disaster in the same way as a neighborhood kidnapping," G. Pascal Zachary wrote in the *Wall Street Journal.*

Technology often creates the story and gives it value it would not have otherwise. "Having a helicopter in the air allows you to follow a car chase. Couple that with satellite transmission, and you have the story in the moment," says Dr. Stuart Fischoff, professor of media psychology at Cal State University in Los Angeles. It's the chase, the visual story that's important; it doesn't matter what crime has been committed or who is being pursued.

"Why is a street crime a more important story than a major bank fraud and stock fraud? Because it's visual, although [the fraud] costs people far more in terms of money and lives than a guy who is shot on the street or in gang wars."

Virtually everyone agrees that television sound bites have corroded the quality of the news coverage. "What causes me the most concern," said Diane Sawyer on C-SPAN in December 1997, "is what I call 'bumper sticker' journalism and what that does to American politics. . . . In 1968, the average length of a sound bite on television was 42.3 seconds. By 1988, it was nine seconds—nine seconds to say things that will determine the future of the country."

Author and essayist Norman Mailer sees real danger in the innovations. Mass media deceives. "Each day a few more lies eat into the seed with which we are born, little institutional lies from the print of newspapers, the shock waves of television, and the sentimental cheats of the movie screen."

In his book *Suddenly,* essayist George Will describes how watching television deadens the senses simply from the firestorm of advertising. In the early 1990s, American viewers could be bombarded with as many as fifty messages in one prime-time hour, between thirty-second commercials, fifteen-second commercials, and five-second network promos.

In his book *The Medium is the Massage,* Marshall McLuhan theorized how this happens: The delivery of all media alters how we think and act by changing the "ratio of the senses," biological alterations that control behavior, even leading to fixation and semi-hypnosis.

Through repetition—either of news, entertainment programs, commercials, or all of these—television becomes like a drug. People get hooked without even knowing why. Two decades ago, journalist and critic Marie Winn aptly named television "the plug-in drug."

Entertainment Weekly's Richard Sanders admits to being a news junkie, a direct result of the nonstop coverage. When at home, he leaves the television on constantly. "My ear is cocked to catch that little new tidbit. I know when it's coming. There's a change of voice . . . and when I get it, an adrenaline rush happens again. I like to be in the know. It's kind of an addiction."

Matt Drudge has become the symbol for the best and worst of the media frontier opened by new technologies. Based in Hollywood, Drudge puts together *The Drudge Report,* an individually created Web site of gossip that is visited more than a million times a month. Sitting in his one-bedroom apartment, he scans wires, works phones, and checks out the tabloids daily for spicy tidbits about Hollywood and the Washington, D.C., Beltway.

What's positive about Drudge's approach is that it democratizes news. Anyone with a computer and a modem can become a maverick reporter and publish for their own audience. The downside of Drudge and his operating methods is that there are no gatekeepers or experienced editors to check for accuracy. It's the Wild West on the Internet; reputations can be damaged, lives ruined, perhaps, and not much can be done to safeguard the innocent.

In the midst of all this competition and information overload, each outlet tries to stand out from the clutter not just by being first, but also by becoming more sensational. "Noise makes news," said radio-television commentator Paul Harvey on C-SPAN. "One gunshot makes more noise than a thousand prayers. That does not mean it is more important. It just means that it sells more newspapers. Bad news pays."

After the death of Diana, many both inside and outside the media called for higher journalistic standards. In an ideal world, the people would stop watching sleaze and trivia. One way to resist temptation is simply by creating a purposeful life and adhering to better character standards, as Leo Braudy concluded in his 1997 afterword to *The Frenzy of Renown*: "We wouldn't be so obsessed with celebrities, or tear them down so quickly, if we had a higher opinion of ourselves. It's about time for a rebirth of personal honor and responsibility in which people no longer need to substitute their heroes for themselves."

ABC's Diane Sawyer believes individual reporters have the power to change the tone of reporting from shallow to substantive, simply through their interview techniques. "Watching politicians try to compress a discussion of balanced budgets into a seven-second sound bite is like watching a gymnastic contortion that can't be achieved," she said on C-SPAN. "If during campaigns we set aside a topic, a time, a forum in which [the candidate must] complete a thought to a sharpened question, that seems to me at least a beginning." But we can't forget that the media are working in a highly competitive market.

As Hitchens and others suggest, modern media, as it is increasingly changed by technological advances, has only a few ways of telling a story. There are only a few ways of packaging celebrities. We have to ask ourselves: How does packaging keep us from the truth?

Diana, the Investigation

> *"Meanwhile, the CIA has issued a statement saying "any assertion that the CIA played any role" in the death of Princess Diana is absurd."*
>
> —*People Daily*

The pageantry of the funeral over, the flowers at the embassies faded, swept up, thrown away, the newscasters and journalists turning at last to other subjects, the Diana story would have seemed to be over. But there was enough appetite, real or imagined, in the audience to elicit more coverage. The press, particularly periodical editors, stayed with the story. They did so in what has proven to be a successful journalistic strategy to perpetuate a story—they conducted investigations. There are excellent models for doing this: the first-rate investigative journalism of I. F. Stone, the myriad inquiries into the Kennedy assassination, the work of Woodward and Bernstein and others into the Watergate conspiracy. That there was little to be learned by taking this approach to Diana's death was immaterial. The hard-boiled style of investigative journalism could make articles and reports stand or fail on their own aesthetic merits.

Because they had been saturated with early coverage, the public knew the basic facts of the story. After the funeral, questions about Diana's death were again in the forefront: What was her relationship with Dodi al Fayed? What really happened the night of the crash? Who was responsible?

At first, the paparazzi looked like arch fiends. In Paris, the Sunday of the crash, pilgrims to the Pont de l'Alma underpass were bitter in speaking with reporters who elicited reactions to the Princess's death. "Right now I'd have to say I feel pretty angry with you," said Simon Neaverson, a thirty-two-year-old Australian tourist. "You guys push pretty hard, don't you? I think right now if you had one of those cameras with a long lens, I'd probably bop you one in the face." Thirty-three-year-old British tourist Jacqueline Sencier cried: "Everyone knows how much she hated the press—and now they've killed her. I hope because of this they will make some laws restricting the media."

Network television commentators seemed to agree that the paparazzi were responsible, as did Sunday morning callers to Phoenix talk radio station KTAR-AM. Host Charles Goyette summed up the majority opinion: "The media are clearly to blame. The consumers of this trash don't have the culpability the media do."

In the public eye, freelance photographers had been seen as outlaws for a long time. More than fifteen years earlier, *Time* predicted a disaster born from a royal chase. In a February 28, 1983, cover story entitled "Royalty vs. the Press," it captured the scene thus: "When game is afoot, royal watchers routinely engage in round-the-clock stakeouts, read lips with binoculars, suborn servants, chase their prey at crazy speeds in high-powered cars. There has been so much of this mad motoring that the wonder is that no member of the royal family or the public has been killed."

On BBC Radio 4, al Fayed spokesman Michael Cole described the paparazzi as predators. "The photographers were flashing off blitz lights into the eyes of the people inside the car. It was like a stage-coach surrounded by Indians, but instead of firing arrows, they were firing these lights into the eyes of the people. One of the motorbikes, a very powerful machine, was overtaking the car and pulling right-wards in front of the car to try to slow it down so that the other photographers could keep up."

At his home just outside Cape Town, South Africa, Earl Spencer—expressing a thought he would elaborate on in his eulogy—said: "I would say that I always believed the press would kill her in the end. But not even I could imagine that they would take such a direct hand in her death as seems to be the case. It would appear that every publication that has paid for intrusive and exploitive photographs of her, encouraging greedy and ruthless individuals to risk everything in pursuit of Diana's image, has blood on his hands today."

Warren Hoge, London bureau chief of the *New York Times,* recalls that the British media swiftly distanced themselves from the French media. "The photographers at the accident very quickly became their paparazzi, not ours."

At the outset, moreover, the reports on conspiracy allowed the mainstream media to disavow the vulgar paparazzi who usually sold their work to tabloids. The indictments reinforced antipathy toward the paparazzi, among the public and the mainstream media. In the opinion of *Vanity Fair* and *Time* contributing editor Kim Masters, the press was "focused totally on the paparazzi and not on the guy who was smashed. . . . During my appearance on MSNBC, I stated, 'What we only know at this time is that the driver was drunk.' I was greeted with some antagonism. The media did not want to let go of Diana's martyrdom."

Or, she adds, they were milking the opportunity to divorce themselves from tabloid tactics, which often beat them on legitimate stories, much to their chagrin. "It wasn't us, it was the bad people" is her summary of their attitude and spin, even though "when it came out, a lot [of the photographers] were legitimate. One in particular, Jacques Langevin, was a highly respected war photographer.

The paparazzi are not evil. They are simply responding to the free-market demand for photos. They were trying to make money. Tom Haley, an American freelancer with Sipa agency in Paris, explained the reasoning to the Associated Press later on the day Diana died: "For most of us, news is a profession. We might spend a month in Bosnia and barely cover expenses, but we could make a fortune by hanging around and spying on people like Lady Di."

The tabloids can and do pay higher prices for photos. "Pocketbook journalism also hurts mainstream media," Masters says. "Sources [for intimate stories] are expecting to be paid, but [mainstream media] doesn't do business this way, and yet they could get actual news [if they did]. So they have a certain amount of anger toward the tabloids."

"There is an antagonism between mainstream and tabloid media," adds Masters, also a former feature writer for the *Washington Post*. "One reason is because the tabloids have been forcing issues like Gennifer Flowers [and her alleged affair with then-presidential candidate Bill Clinton] into mainstream media. The *Washington Post* often had to decide if it should cover or ignore a story because the tabloids pushed it."

The line between the tabloids and the mainstream is not sharply drawn. Established sources can be salacious without appearing to pander to the lowest common denominator through "tabloid laundering." Wrote Margaret Carlson in *Time*: "There's an audience for celebrity pap, and when the mainstream press doesn't pander to it directly, it does so indirectly . . . writing about how crazy it is that the tabloids spend so much time covering a royal romance, and then running pictures of the tabs' pictures to say how invasive they are." The end result is that the mainstream press gets the gossip that they wouldn't originally write onto their screens or printed pages anyway.

As an example, *Newsweek* ran two stories during the Diana tragedy—one about the media's celebrity obsession, the other about the paparazzi phenomenon—illustrated with photos published by *The Sun* of Dodi and Diana. In one, her swimsuit straps had slipped down her arm; another showed the Princess walking down the street, hiding her face from a camera lens. *Newsweek*'s writer Jonathan Alter was unapologetic. He claimed that the use of these tabloid-style photos was necessary to illustrate serious pieces of writing.

Sensing that public opinion was against them, tabloid media around the globe promptly proceeded to separate themselves from the very paparazzi from whom they buy pictures. On Sunday, many announced they would not buy photos of the crash. The image of the Mercedes smashed into an accordion had already been flashed around the world on television, including CNN, CBS, NBC, and ABC; the announcement was referring to photographs allegedly snapped by photographers who had furiously descended upon the crash scene. Although the police had already confiscated some twenty roles of film from the seven detained freelance photographers, some shots from other photographers who had fled the scene were already in circulation.

Dick Belsky, editor of *The Star* based in Tarrytown, New York, declared in an Associated Press report that the paparazzi chasing Diana had "nothing to do with us. We're appalled and upset as anybody. We absolutely condemn that kind of journalism. [*The Star*] would never run these pictures [of the fatal accident]."

The BBC reported that *News of the World* said it passed on the offer of a picture of Diana dying in the car. Price: $300,000. On NBC's *Meet the Press* that Sunday, Steve Coz, editor of the *National Enquirer*, said crash photographs were being sold for $250,000. He turned them down and urged the world press to do so as well. Pete Hamill, editor-in-chief of New York's *Daily News*, stated his belief that printing such images would sensationalize Diana's accident and make members of the media "collaborators in a process that's sleazy and, to some extent, evil."

In Germany, media regulatory agencies like the Press Council and the Association of German Journalists called for "a spirit of responsibility," both in the gathering of news and pictures and in the use of crash photos, so as to respect the "editorial principles which govern investigation and publication of accidents." Despite these urgings, Germany's largest-selling tabloid, *Bild Zeitung*, on Monday, September 1, published a controversial photograph of emergency workers trying to free Diana from the Mercedes just after the crash.

In a Reuters report, Laurent Sola, director of the French picture agency LS Diffusion, said most tabloid outlets lied about never wanting to publish the accident photographs. The agency's paparazzi who shot photos and ran, escaping detention by the police, sold pictures by phone to scores of media outlets in dozens of countries for hundreds of thousands of dollars during the first five hours following the crash. "They were hungry for them," he told France 2 television. "Word spread like wildfire. I had calls from dozens and dozens of media who are now denying it and saying 'We never wanted to publish them.'" Sola withdrew the photographs early Sunday with the news of Diana's death.

In its finger-pointing and search for scapegoats, the media were doing more than deflecting attention from themselves. They were fueling their need for a story by covering the flurry of charges and countercharges. This was excellent material because it played to a general public cynicism about public officials.

The investigation—and the media's coverage of it—became a sequel to Diana's dramatic life as developments unfolded, bit by bit, over the months, like new episodes of a continuing serial.

Except in a debate about placing legal restrictions on the press (discussed in chapter 16), the attacks on paparazzi and tabloids burned out.

In France, however, the government had placed restrictions on several of the photographers found at the scene of the crash. Fearing overregulation of their activities, in Paris in October 1997 dozens of French photojournalists demonstrated to protest the charges of manslaughter still levied against their colleagues. At a weekly meeting of the French cabinet at President Jacques Chirac's Palais de l'Elysée, they laid down their cameras on the palace steps, forcing cabinet members to step over them. According to a Reuters report, the photographers asserted that they were being made "scapegoats for Diana's death."

The press coverage of the investigations had an odd twist. It's an old rule of investigative journalism that the writer stay out of the story. He or she assumes the role of an impartial, faceless bystander. Many of us were taught in school never to use "I" in a research paper. It was a way to maintain the fiction that we were unbiased. The growth of personal journalism changed the rules decades ago, but most good journalists today would probably still insist that the observer should not be part of the story.

In the story of Diana's death, from the beginning, the media were at the very center. Members of the media could now star in their own show.

Not wanting to shoulder the blame for the tragedy, the media in general turned from accused to accuser. Within a few days of the death, the headlines focused on the driver as a guilty party. From the Associated Press the afternoon of September 1: "Report: Diana's driver was drunk." From Agence France Presse on that same afternoon: "Blame for Diana's death shifts to drunken driver, and ultimately al Fayed."

The lead story headlines in British newspapers on September 2 looked like this: From *The Independent*: "Killed by Drunken Driving, Not Fame"; from *The Times*: Princess's Driver Was Drunk"; from the *Express*: "Driven to Her Death: Diana's Driver Had Drunk the Equivalent of Two Bottles of Wine"; from *The Scotsman*: "The Lethal Cocktail: A drunk driver three times over the limit at the wheel of car doing 132 kilometers . . . on a darkened city road . . . and the paparazzi in hot pursuit." *The Guardian* talked of the "disastrous decision of the Ritz, owned by Mohammed al Fayed, to allow Henri Paul to drive the Princess and her companion home." *The Times,* reporting that Paul had taunted the photographers to catch him, noted: "It would be hard to concoct a plot for more certain disaster than the fusion of alcohol, adrenaline and machismo that seems to have led to the deaths." The *Express* mused: "How quickly our certainties can crumble."

Upon first hearing of Paul's alcohol level, Paris lawyer Bernard Dartevelle, representing the al Fayed family, asserted that the photographers remained guilty. If they had not started the chase, "it is highly probable that the driver would not have driven at an excessive speed."

Al Fayed aggressively worked to deflect blame from driver Henri Paul. First, an al Fayed spokesman introduced a professor of forensic medicine from the University of Glasgow ". . . to introduce the O. J. question," wrote Richard Lacayo in *Time*. The professor asked, "Could the blood samples used by police have been contaminated?" No evidence of contamination was offered, however.

There were other angles the press could pursue: More answers raised more questions. Why did Diana and Dodi feel compelled to avoid photographers that night? Who authorized Paul to speed? When would the memory return to the sole survivor, bodyguard Trevor Rees-Jones, who suffered memory loss and a severely injured jaw? Did the Mercedes lose control when sideswiping another car, possibly the white Fiat Uno, as suggested by road debris and paint marks on the Mercedes?

Finally, there were also conspiracy theories to investigate. These cropped up especially on the Internet. In the Arab world, where the Dodi-Diana relationship was proudly welcomed, there was speculation that the British plotted to stop the Princess from marrying an Egyptian by killing her. *Time*'s Richard Lacayo dismissed that theory, writing that "the Windsors may have been thinking that marriage to Dodi, a man routinely described as a foreign playboy, would have been a public relations blunder for Diana and a badly needed plus for them. For once it would make their tweedy rectitude seem appealing to the British public."

But the conspiracy stories surely had an audience. In America, at least since the assassination of President Kennedy, conspiracy theories have been alive and well. It has been proven in the marketplace time and again that conspiracy sells.

Despite the unofficial conclusions about the accident's cause, Mohammed al Fayed continued to express his belief that his son and the Princess were victims of a conspiracy plot. He also kept insisting that the paparazzi were in part culpable.

Al Fayed's spin on matters was interpreted in part as a way to deflect responsibility from the Ritz. But the royal family and Diana's survivors did not buy into it. On December 21, advisers to Diana's estate were preparing to sue Mohammed al Fayed for the Princess's premature death. The minimum claim under consideration was eight million pounds, the amount of the inheritance-tax bill incurred because of Diana's death. There could also be a claim of another twenty-five million pounds, the interest that would have accrued on the money had she lived. It was expected that any claim would be contested.

Al Fayed began to play to the galleries. He claimed he was troubled by the conspiracy theories, including the rumors that the British intelligence service, M16, brought about the accident. And he could not erase from his mind "the horrible thought that his bitter battle with Britain's Establishment somehow played a part in the tragedy," wrote authors Thomas Sancton and Scott MacLeod in their book *Death of a Princess: The Investigation.* The book quotes al Fayed explaining that British racism would have been motive enough to break up the romance between Diana and Dodi: "It was a very serious matter. Maybe the future king is going to have a half brother who is a 'nigger,' and Mohammed al Fayed is going to be the step-grandfather of the future king. This is how they think, this establishment. They are a completely different type of human being."

The allegations captured the media's attention and stirred debate for about two weeks. But, by now, few serious readers could have regarded the controversies as news. Al Fayed, the photographers, the journalists, the broadcasters, and the editors themselves were trying to play exactly the game Diana had succeeded in. They were using the press to advance their personal agendas. None of them did it with half Diana's flair.

Mainstream media could cover the official inquiries. In its October 13, 1997, domestic and international issues, *Time* published a five-page story entitled "The Dossier on Diana's Crash." It divulged the most comprehensive, up-to-date details:

On September 29, at 9:20 A.M., Judge Hervé Stephan and a dozen police investigators had conducted an on-site investigation. Though nine photographers and one photo-agency motorcycle driver had been placed under investigation on charges of manslaughter and violation of the Good Samaritan law, police had yet to ascertain how close the paparazzi were to the Mercedes. It was reported that they now doubted that any of them actually made contact with the car.

The *Time* article concluded that drunk driving seemed to be the main cause of the accident.

A week later, in its October 20, 1997, issue, *Newsweek* reported that paparazzi appeared on the scene two minutes after the collision. The cause of the crash turned away from the paparazzi and onto the white Fiat.

Hypothetical answers to why the Fiat didn't crash were surfacing. This theory, however, posed new questions: Why haven't the passengers of the Fiat come forward? Might they be additional paparazzi?

By the end of October, the investigation began to zero in almost exclusively on the white Fiat Uno.

In its November 3 issue, *Newsweek* reported that the investigating judge had informed the lawyer for two of the photographers that charges were anticipated to be dropped at the inquiry's completion. The investigators had discovered that one photographer did call for help and then informed the others so they wouldn't tie up the phone lines. This would mean that the Good Samaritan law was not violated. In addition, none of the witnesses could vouch that any of the photographers pursuing the Mercedes made direct contact with the car, making the manslaughter charges groundless. "Now it appears that they may be guilty of nothing more than being obnoxious," wrote Rod Nordland.

In early November, reports came out about a controversy over the extent and cost of the investigation. At that time, forty thousand Fiats were being examined. Still working the case were two investigating magistrates and two dozen detectives from the criminal brigade of the Paris police—a quarter of the unit's staff. In addition, officers from across the country were asked to assist. Examination of the Mercedes alone had cost about $338,000. But at the end of the year, France's elite detectives were still searching for the white Fiat, while a suspected serial killer was terrorizing Parisian streets.

In a November 21 episode of *20/20*, photographers suggested that a flashbulb at the entrance to the tunnel might explain why the Mercedes picked up speed.

By the end of November, the U.S.-based tabloid *The Star* built up the angle of murder conspiracy with a compilation of details that supported the theory—a feeble attempt at life support for a story that seemed to be running out of steam. According to *The Star,* Diana was killed either because she was about to wed a Moslem, she was pregnant with Dodi's child, or powerful arms dealers were upset about her efforts to ban landmines. Unconfirmed assertions on how the accident happened ranged from the car's tires being shot out before the Mercedes entered the tunnel to the Fiat's occupants throwing a small explosive device that distracted Henri Paul.

By the end of December, the case seemed almost wrapped up. According to a six-hundred-page police report given to the investigating judge, investigators believed that the fatal crash was due to speed, liquor, and possibly a second car. An assassination plot was eliminated. Given that the police discovered no evidence that a camera flash had contributed to the cause of the accident, the paparazzi were considered to have played a secondary role in the tragedy. None were next to or in front of the car.

The judge refused to make the conclusions public because the search for the mysterious Fiat Uno was ongoing. But it seemed that there was little more to be said. According to *Newsweek,* though the victims were not ordinary, "investigators now believe that the accident . . . was just that, ordinary. . . . Diana and her boyfriend were killed in a routine drunken-driving accident."

And yet, in its media scrutiny, the crash and subsequent inquiry have been compared to the investigation of President John F. Kennedy's assassination. The rationale had less to do with the story than with the audience: the media could say they were reporting what the audience wants to know. And they were telling the story in a recognizable form—the exposé.

By mid-January of 1998, *Time* reported that after an exhaustive search the police were focusing on twelve Fiat cars. Still, nothing was conclusive. The investigation seemed nearly as dead as the story itself.

In early February, the release of the book *Death of a Princess: The Investigation* breathed new life into the story—or, more accurately, applied an oxygen mask. Serialized in *The Times* and excerpted in *Time,* for which authors Sancton and MacLeod had originally covered the story, it brought forward a few new and interesting details, some of which provoked dissension. Particularly controversial was their charge that the SAMU team could have saved Diana's life had they gotten her to a hospital sooner—and the fact that the book gave space to Mohammed al Fayed's conspiracy theories.

Diana's family and friends dismissed the book's assertions, believing the authors' agenda was profit rather than altruism. In the *Evening Standard,* a source close to the family remarked, "These suggestions are hurtful and unhelpful. It's rather a coincidence that the authors are trying to publicize a book." The Princess's mother, Frances Shand Kydd, who has a copy of the medical report, told the *Daily Express* that Diana's injuries were "unsurvivable" and that "the medical staff in Paris did everything they could."

Reactions also criticized Mohammed al Fayed for his stubborn adherence to the theory of a plot by the British Establishment, and the authors for printing it without much question. "How credulous are these claims?" asked Warren Hoge, London bureau chief for the *New York Times.* "Many took [the authors] to task. The book was cloaked under the notion that it was serious investigative journalism by *Time* reporters. How could they have fallen for these claims?"

One reason was that the book was written with the full cooperation—and approval—of Mohammed al Fayed. In the *Daily Mail,* Michael Cole, al Fayed's spokesman, explained that authors Sancton and MacLeod were granted access because, "They are not royal-watchers, they are just honest and well-respected American reporters. We thought it worthwhile to try to get one definitive book, one objective account."

Louder cries were levied, not surprisingly, against al Fayed himself, who resurrected the murder conspiracy theory in an interview with the *Mirror* around the same time as the release of *Death of a Princess.* He was awaiting a decision on his latest application for British citizenship at the time. Prime Minister Tony Blair was the most outspoken. Through official spokesman Alastair Campbell, he warned al Fayed to stop talking about conspiracy theories that fuel stories about Diana's death for commercial ends and hurt Princes William and Harry. "The prime minister regards this as tacky and inappropriate," Campbell said. The Queen was said to have shared his concerns.

The dust that *Death of a Princess* had stirred up settled by the end of February and the story lost steam again—until March 2.

After sessions with a psychiatrist, twenty-nine-year-old bodyguard Trevor Rees-Jones was recalling, in bits and pieces, events minutes before the crash. He revealed them in an interview published March 2 in the *Mirror.*

Except for the account in the *Mirror,* the Rees-Jones story was buried deep in the inside pages of British and French newspapers. On March 6, 1998, Rees-Jones recounted his flashbacks to a French magistrate.

Meanwhile, the search for the missing Fiat Uno continued.

Before many weeks had passed, a number of the reports and opinion pieces were, literally, non-news—proof that yet another previous possibility or rumor concerning the accident had turned out not to be so. The media were filling minutes and column inches telling a story that was not happening.

Cause Célèbre

> *"Anyone who has ever been*
> *chased like that, and who has*
> *had to live that sort of life, hit*
> *the wall with her."*
>
> —Madonna

Elisabeth Kübler-Ross, M.D., in her book *Death and Dying,* said that when confronting death we all first feel shock and disbelief, then anger, then a desire to bargain. Among the mourners of Diana Spencer, a similar pattern could be seen. As the first weeks in September passed, one saw first disbelief, then anger (directed mostly against the tabloid media), and then, from various quarters, a desire to do something positive, to put Diana's tragedy to some good purpose. In what may even have been an attempt to rewrite history, many channeled their energy into searching for ways to prevent other such ghastly misfortunes.

The outcry against the paparazzi spun off or gave force to a debate on both sides of the Atlantic about journalistic ethics. There was enough to sustain this controversy, independent of the crash, that it took on a life of its own apart from the various investigations. It contributed, however, to the false idea that Diana was merely a victim of rapacious paparazzi. The picture of Diana dying in a high-speed flight from "mercenaries of sensation," as *Newsday* described the paparazzi, may have enhanced the public's grief. Subsequent reactions from media and celebrities fanned the flames.

The debates on press restraint were conducted independently in England, the U.S., Canada, and France. As Geoffrey Robertson wrote in *The New Yorker*: ". . . in every country press freedom boils down to a bargain, a three-way deal between state power and popular instinct and the media's muscle." The covenant made with a country's press customarily expresses its national preferences and values.

In the U.K., discussion of the press law had been heated from the very beginning of Diana's marriage to Charles. As we saw earlier, often these debates centered on the representation of the Princess in the tabloids and they took on a new urgency after her death. In Britain, Lord Wakeman, chairman of the Press Complaints Commission, immediately began meeting with newspaper editors to talk about the insatiable demand for photographs of public figures. Foreign Secretary Robin Cook reportedly suggested the government should reconsider a privacy law, though *The Times* revealed that Cook subsequently recanted. A spokesman for the newly-elected prime minister, Tony Blair, confirmed that Labour was for self-regulation.

A privacy law—the one that Diana had spoken up for despite her collusion with the media—is problematic in an open society; while it could rein in excesses of the tabloids, it could also prevent the media from seeking out truths vital to the public interest, such as corruption, money laundering, conflict of interest, or obstruction of justice. But self-regulation is not a perfect method either. British newspapers informally monitor their activities through the PCC, set up by newspaper proprietors and described by a Parliament member as a "toothless watchdog" because it can scold for unfair actions but not levy fines.

Britain has no First Amendment protecting free press against government regulation and interference. It has no Freedom of Information Act like the one that allows reporters in the United States access to official documents filed on individuals for investigative purposes. Britain also is renowned for some of the world's most oppressive libel laws that routinely shield important facts about crime and malpractice. And yet there are no laws that protect personal privacy. Moreover, the country is home to one of the world's most reckless yellow press that joyously prints kiss-and-tell tales.

Writes Robertson: "This, after all, is a society that's known for its prurience and prudishness. The newspapers that are the most despised for invading private lives are also the most popular: they reflect rather than create the nation's character. This is a society in which tens of thousands of people report their neighbors for not paying their annual television license fee . . . in which telephone tapping and other forms of covert surveillance are permitted by the police without their first having to apply to a court. . . ."

According to Reuters, Britain's senior newspaper editors backed a call for "wide-ranging and rigorous reforms" to cover privacy, harassment, and the use of paparazzi photographs. The support of the editors followed a meeting of the code committee of the Press Complaints Commission which had been considering legal changes to the newspaper industry's Code of Practice.

As for a broad-brush privacy law intended to reign in the tabloids' excesses, the main question, *The Times* explained, was "where to draw the boundary between free speech and privacy. How far is personal privacy a human right in an open society? Should public figures [or their children] be endowed with special rights over and above the rest of us?"

The challenge was to find a distinction between the reporting of details essential to real investigative journalism and factoids that aroused prurient interest but in no way advanced the public welfare. Instead of passing one sweeping law, Britain's Chief Justice Lord Bingham of Cornhill suggested that a privacy law could be developed through individual cases coming before the courts.

(In a slightly surreal statement, Rupert Murdoch, at an annual meeting of his News Corp. in October 1997, argued that a paparazzi ban would save money for his papers because he would no longer have to pay exorbitant fees to "this crew." Regarding privacy laws, he urged resistance from journalists and others in publishing and television: "Privacy laws are for the protection of people who are already privileged.")

In late November, the Broadcasting Standards Commission (BSC) published a new code of practice effective January 1, 1998. It stated that violating privacy is justified if the program is detecting crime or disreputable behavior, protecting public health or safety, exposing misleading claims, or disclosing significant incompetence in public office. People caught up in the news should not be abused. Individuals in the public eye do not forfeit this right to privacy, the code said, and this protection of personal privacy extends to their friends and family, especially children under sixteen.

In late December, the PCC announced stricter codes, also effective January 1, 1998, for British newspapers and magazines. Sixteen points defined privacy, harassment, intrusion into grief, the rights of children, and the nature of public interest. This document included a ban on persistent pursuit and the use of telephoto lenses to take pictures of people in private places without their consent. It also contained rules against publishing telephone calls or other private conversations that have been intercepted.

However thorough or nicely crafted, there was serious doubt that either the PCC code or the BSC code could be enforced. With tabloid exploitation of celebrities already firmly established in practice, could sets of guidelines have any teeth? The sharpest penalty the PCC is able to inflict is a public apology from the errant news organization.

But the members of the press had gone as far as they wanted to go. PCC chairman Lord Wakeman argued against putting these codes into law because cost of enforcement would be prohibitive for most. He also favored self-regulation

In early 1998, a bill was introduced in Parliament which would have required "prior restraint"—the requirement that publishers seek consent before publishing photos. Tony Blair quickly quashed the idea, condemning it as a threat to press freedom.

As of March 1998, the new codes were being obeyed. "So far, there are no major violations," said Warren Hoge of the *New York Times* London bureau when we spoke. "But I think there will be. I can't imagine that the tabloids would obey them assiduously."

They seem, however, to have carefully respected the privacy of William and Harry. During a skiing holiday, the media shot pictures of the boys at a staged photo opportunity, but then left them alone. "I think they will continue to honor their privacy," Hoge adds. The public, he feels, demands that the boys be left alone.

The debate in the U.S. had a different character. Hollywood celebrities added their voices, describing their own problems with aggressive photographers. They pushed for legal restrictions. Only three hours after hearing of the paparazzi pursuit, Tom Cruise called CNN himself to recount how he and his wife, Nicole Kidman, had been chased by photographers through the same tunnel: "They run lights and they chase you and harass you the whole time. You don't know what it's like being chased by them." On *60 Minutes* the evening of August 31, Elizabeth Taylor dramatically told of her own frightening experiences of being dogged, then labeled the paparazzi that trailed Diana and Dodi as murderers.

There followed a deluge of complaints by celebrities about overly aggressive photographers, the invasion of privacy, and the sacrifices required of those in the public eye. "The paparazzi are like a hydra," said David Duchovny. "Last weekend this twice-convicted sex offender got my address from a tabloid. . . . They're drawing a map for every maniac in America!" Fran Drescher said, "They should stop buying from freelancers, because they're putting a bounty on your head." Referred to by *People* years earlier as a "slugaholic" after he punched a photographer who was trailing him and his then-wife, Madonna, Sean Penn piped up: "I've been in traffic accidents myself. I've been baited and lured. I've ended up in jail and called a bully for defending myself against stalkers." Madonna, hardly a reclusive or retiring public personality, also complained that an intrusive press made her daily life difficult.

Responding to the argument that the media only gives the public what they want, Paul Reiser called for the public to boycott certain media. Tom Selleck told the media to stay out of his life, saying he would pursue his career without publicity. ABC reported that a group of celebrities was organizing to give tabloid media a taste of their own medicine; they were putting together a multi-million-dollar fund to probe the private lives of, and stalk, the heads of the *National Enquirer*, *The Star*, and *The Globe*.

At a media conference held at the Screen Actors Guild in L.A., actor George Clooney vowed to take on the First Amendment by trying to eliminate the requirement that a plaintiff prove "malicious intent" in a lawsuit. (The previous year, Clooney had boycotted Paramount Television's *Entertainment Tonight* because of paparazzi footage of him used in a sister tabloid program, *Hard Copy:*

"[Malicious intent] are the two words that every ethical journalist says is the loophole tabloids hide behind. Change these two words and all journalists are held accountable in a civil trial.") At about the same time, the Screen Actors Guild released a statement that indicated it had been meeting for two years with elected officials—including California's two U.S. Senators, Diane Feinstein and Barbara Boxer, and Los Angeles Mayor Richard Riordan—on drafting legislation that would affect libel and privacy issues as they relate to the lives of performers.

SAG raised several important issues. For example, should the laws of libel be reconsidered "to allow for protection of persons who are the object of libelous statements"? SAG also urged a serious dialogue about appropriate standards of newsgathering. It urged a prohibition on ambush methods in public places by "stalkerazzi" and stakeouts by photographers. Finally, it opened for debate the expansion of the statutory right of privacy: Should a private person be able to bring a case against not only those whose conduct was considered unacceptable by law, but also against those news organizations "who know or have reason to know" that the photograph or information was gathered illegally?

At the same time, California state legislators Tom Hayden, Charles M. Calderon, and Diane Watson vowed to introduce legislation in the next session to curb paparazzi behavior with an enforceable code of conduct.

Specific rules governing the American press are usually brokered in the courts. A classic case was the 1973 scuffle between Jacqueline Kennedy Onassis and photographer Ronald Galella. He had gone beyond the reasonable limits of newsgathering by intentionally assaulting Onassis and intruding into her son's school, imperiling their safety in car chases, and interrupting her children's riding lessons. Result: Galella was forbidden to come closer than twenty-five feet from Onassis and thirty feet from her children. Otherwise, picture-taking and selling was unrestricted.

As in the U.S., Canada's privacy laws are a matter of provincial or local jurisdiction. In April 1998, Quebec photographer Gilbert Duclos lost a suit brought by a private citizen who, when still a teenager, had been photographed by him as she sat on the steps of a library building in Montreal. A magazine had printed the photo without her permission. Duclos claimed that the ruling, which might establish precedent in four other provinces, would make it very difficult for him to do his work.

In the United States, as in the U.K., there seemed little likelihood that a federal privacy law would be passed. In February 1998, Senator Diane Feinstein of California announced her sponsorship of the Personal Privacy Protection Act, a federal law that would crack down on actions by photographers who jeopardize public safety. The announcement came on the heels of guilty verdicts against two paparazzi who had pursued actor Arnold Schwarzenegger and his wife, NBC News correspondent Maria Shriver, as they drove their three-year-old son to preschool in Santa Monica. The bill would also expand the definition of trespassing to include telephoto lenses and other enhancement devices.

The American Civil Liberties Union questioned the bill's constitutionality and did not believe it could back it. "It burdens the First Amendment," the executive director of the ACLU of Southern California told the *Los Angeles Times*. She added that the crimes mentioned are already forbidden by state laws. "We don't need more national crimes regulating the press."

In our conversation, Norman Pearlstine, editor-in-chief at Time Inc., agreed with the ACLU, though he conceded that the Feinstein bill seems "precisely drawn, carefully considered, and should be taken seriously and evaluated carefully. It's clearly an effort to address First Amendment issues."

Nevertheless, he believes that state and local laws adequately address the actions as crimes without having to make them federal crimes. In addition, legislating technology is new and "potentially troublesome," on a par with legislating editorial judgment.

The *Los Angeles Times* blasted the bill in an editorial, particularly attacking the redefinition of trespassing to include the use of zoom lenses and other enhancement devices. ". . . this provision blatantly limits information-gathering by the legitimate press as well as the celebrity stalkers. As such, it is an unacceptable curb on the First Amendment. As the Schwarzenegger case shows, existing law protects against clearly dangerous behavior."

Preeminent First Amendment lawyer Floyd Abrams told me that the proposed law would be held unconstitutional. "The broad protection against photographers following people is unlikely to hold up."

Abrams clearly thought the issue of privacy for celebrities was contrived. He concluded, "Princess Diana died because of reckless driving, and it is singularly unattractive for the Hollywood set in the name of Princess Diana's memory to endeavor to avoid the public scrutiny that many seek on their own terms and that most profit from."

There are others who doubt that the outrage in Hollywood is genuine, since so many of the outspoken celebrities continue to court the attention of the press as Diana did. Indeed, many celebrities were making themselves visible, getting their faces in magazines and on television, by speaking out for privacy.

Stuart Fischoff of Cal State was as skeptical as Abrams: "The 'iron curtain' people let it be known they are not interested in being public. The Pecks and Redfords have absolute control. The 'peek-a-boo' people occasionally get out of control. . . . The 'glass house' people are savvy about where and when to expose themselves. . . . Diana promoted herself. She gave the media information on herself. Once you do that, you have already crossed the Rubicon." If a celebrity seeks attention, what is the point of laws that restrict activities of the press?

Celebrities who genuinely value privacy must go to extraordinary lengths to protect themselves. Paul McCartney, who took up residence in the country after the breakup of the Beatles, was reported to have been unnerved by the assassination of his former partner John Lennon. He has guarded his privacy carefully for decades. In the spring of 1998, Paul's wife, Linda Eastman McCartney (who began her career as a photographer), died of breast cancer. The death occurred, apparently, at the McCartney ranch in Tucson, Arizona. The family representatives, however, reported that Linda died in Santa Barbara, California. The time bought by the lie gave McCartney and his children privacy to grieve and to return to England. It also made it possible to have the body cremated in Arizona where, by state law, death certificates are kept confidential.

Various scholars and public relations experts criticized McCartney for lying. And a television reporter was quoted as having said, "There was a deliberate attempt by the McCartney family to mislead the media and, in doing so, to mislead millions of loyal and faithful fans." The reporter, describing a candlelight memorial service organized in Santa Barbara, referred again to "the slap on the face of those fans who'd learned that they'd been misled." Clearly many, such as this reporter, hold the belief that celebrities belong to the general public as if they were features of the landscape. The argument they make is that, if one seeks fame, one must be willing to deal with the consequences. It is not clear by any means, however, that spouses and children of famous persons are seeking fame.

If one becomes famous by accident, so to speak, what is the appropriate response? Leo Braudy describes Diana's own ambivalence toward her fame with a perfectly contradictory term: willful victim. Her mismanagement of the conflict finally did her in.

It would seem that the relationships between the public, the media, and the celebrity are too complex to be settled by legislation. But we can hope that they do not continue to ruin lives. *Time* senior writer Richard Zoglin, who examined press ethics for the magazine's commemorative Diana issue, told me he believed that the death of Diana in itself would change the way the press operates.

"There will still be cameras when stars come out of courtrooms, but with an accident site, people will remember Diana's case in the back of their minds," he said. "We won't be able to restrict paparazzi, so it's up to the buyers to hold the line. They in the back rooms can make cooler judgments. Even the tabloids. Diana's death was a milestone for them. They tried to position themselves like the mainstream media. That moved them a little closer to the mainstream and they will become a little less unscrupulous."

Landon Jones, vice president of strategic planning for Time Inc., had a similar opinion: "I think those [subjects] who are most victimized will take legal action more often. And I think the media will be more restrained about using stalkerazzi film footage or paparazzi photos taken in bushes or with telephoto lenses."

Right after Diana's death, James Fallows in *U.S. News & World Report* called for journalists to rise to a higher ethical level: "The constraints and incentives come from within. An inner awareness of the struggle to remain human is what has made police, soldiers, and doctors respectable. It can make the public respect the value of our work again."

But *Washington Post* media reporter Howard Kurtz is less hopeful that Diana's death will teach the media to clean up their act. "If we've learned anything from this tragedy, it's clear that the media will stoop to any level, use any aggressive tactics in chasing after celebrities. All this hand-wringing about the press exercising self-restraint will be a short phenomenon. There is so much press it will be difficult to get them all to play by the same rules."

Amidst the indictments against the media, a few maintained clear heads about the proven strength of existing press laws.

William F. Buckley Jr. insisted that privacy laws have already gone too far in the United States. In his syndicated column, he maintained that photos from innumerable instances could shed important light on the circumstances of crimes and accidents. Case in point: Paparazzi photos taken of Diana with her hand raised to shield the left side of her face might be critical evidence in the investigation.

In an Internet article entitled "The Paparazzi Excuse," lawyer Alan Dershowitz brought the discussion back to the circumstances of that tragic night with a simple question: Who broke the law? "The right to photograph a celebrity is protected by freedom of expression. The 'right' to drive at more than double the speed limit with a blood alcohol level three times the legal limit is not protected. That is why the fault for these deaths should be placed squarely at the feet of those responsible for driving, rather than those trying to take their pictures."

I would argue that no law, no set of standards would have been sufficient to guarantee Diana privacy. She was no ordinary celebrity; she had learned how to work with the media, how to keep them interested, and she used her genius to hold the attention of millions. Laws that give lesser lights something comparable to the freedom of ordinary people could never have kept the paparazzi from Diana.

Queen of the Media Age

> *"Warm and fuzzy sells, but*
> *warm and fuzzy plus a*
> *tragedy equals*
> *stratospheric sales."*
> —*Entertainment Weekly*

We've seen how Diana used the media for her own purposes. The other half of the equation is what did the media see in her that made her so irresistible to them? To be sure, they had packaged her. But why was Diana so perfect for packaging?

Princess Bride, number-one cover girl, most photographed woman in the world—these were the accolades showered on Diana in the early 1980s. What did she do to deserve the distinctions? She married a prince. She was made to look beautiful by stylists and given an enormous budget for designer clothes. She pressed the flesh at routine royal occasions. She bore two sons—a feat accomplished by millions of women around the world. Why was she so adored?

"What many will typically say," responds Landon Jones, former managing editor of *People* and current vice president of strategic planning at Time Inc., "is that she was beautiful, she led a fantasy life, women in particular were fascinated with her, she had a sense of style. This is the wooden answer. Diana is a media-age phenomenon. She lived during the rise of a celebrity culture in which fame and accomplishment are delinked. Because of her extraordinary beauty, she was also the right person for the technological methods of media distribution. One color photo can be instantly transmitted to every newspaper, magazine, television show, and the Internet."

It was of critical importance that she was beautiful. Many of the people interviewed for this book were asked, "If Diana had been fifty pounds heavier, would she have captured the attention of the media and the public? Would there have been this outpouring of love, even adulation?" Many thought not. Beauty captivates and holds people. Without good looks, Diana would not have captured so many imaginations. (The same need to be beautiful obviously does not apply to men. Hitler, Churchill, Gandhi, were immensely powerful and physically unattractive men.) But Diana was exceptionally photogenic in a media age. Would so many people have been so enthralled with her, overlooking Charles and making Diana feel more important than she was, if she had been homely, even average-looking? Essayist William F. Buckley Jr. thinks not. "How different it would have been if she had been ugly. The marriage, contracted under such circumstances, would probably have lasted, and the grief over a mortal accident would have been formalistic," he wrote in the *National Review.*

Because of television there has been a shift in our culture, adopted by journalists, from résumé criteria to dating criteria. We would not choose a lover or a friend based on writing samples. And it was never the case until recently that we would consider someone a viable presidential candidate because of the twinkle in his eye.

Some disagree. They believe that the allure imbued by her association with the most visible royal family in the world would have been enough to make Diana the center of global media attention. Heather Vincent, senior coordinating producer of *Dateline NBC,* said to me, "I think that a charismatic person is a charismatic person is a charismatic person. Fifty pounds heavier, Diana would not have been a fashion maven, but she would have still been married to Prince Charles and, frankly, a woman with those connections and those means would still catch the eye in places that lead to car chases in Paris in the middle of the night." Diana's beauty was enhanced by her context. Her appearance easily outshone anyone else's in the royal family. The *New York Post*'s Cindy Adams described their appearance to me as "a family who looks like you threw oatmeal up against a ceiling and it dried. Even if she weren't beautiful, she would have been a knockout because they all look like Dodge hatchbacks."

To take the argument to the other extreme, would Diana have been universally embraced by media and viewers if she had been truly extraordinary to look at? Nancy Friday says absolutely not because she would have evoked jealousy, especially from women. "Beauty is a double-edged sword. Beautiful women are envied. Diana's appeal at the beginning was that she didn't have a sexual element. Her beauty lacked that movie-star sexuality like [a young] Elizabeth Taylor."

Both men and women agree that Diana could be attractive but was not always stunning. But through the camera's eyes, according to Myrna Blyth, editor-in-chief and publishing director of *Ladies' Home Journal,* Diana was unsurpassed. She had a love affair with the lens. "She was extremely photogenic. She had wonderful hair. And she had a kind of faith that managed to convey great personality through her wonderful smile and wonderful eyes. You could tell what she was feeling. That made for extremely interesting photographs." Blyth's own experience in preparing a special issue on Diana for *Ladies' Home Journal,* two weeks after the Princess died, drove home to her the laws of supply and demand for Diana's image. "We were putting together a very personal photo album, but I thought, 'I can't get pictures. Everybody else had them because everyone was doing their specials too.' Within a day, I had five thousand pictures in my office. Diana was the most photographed person the world had ever known."

She was wholesome, like the homecoming queen. And who won the most votes for homecoming queen? Not the great beauty, because she provoked jealousy. Not the brain, because she made people feel inadequate. But the girl who was pleasant enough to look at, cute, maybe even pretty, with "a great personality."

Once established and recognizable from the photos of her wedding, Diana had what American politicians call momentum. The more times her image—which by satellite or through wires could be acquired at a cheaper cost than through a one-on-one interview or photo shoot—was splashed on pages or screens, "the more famous she got, and then people could not get enough of her," says Richard Stolley, *People* creator/founding editor and current Time Inc. senior editorial adviser.

She had star quality. The public saw in her what they themselves held in high regard—youth, beauty, then introspection, a desire for self-improvement, and a need to be loved—values that the modern media has itself molded for society. The media became infatuated. A *Sunday Observer* editorial said that Diana ". . . was the first popular icon to be manufactured by the media. . . . Diana, too, became steadily infatuated by her own image." Like all lovers, she fell in love with being loved. She returned the adoration of the media by falling in love with what the media loved in her.

But certainly the same kind of symbiosis can be seen between the media and other public figures. How was she able, more than people with more analytical intelligence, to make the media do what she wanted? The answers can be found in history, economics, and communications technology.

To begin with, Diana didn't have to *do* anything to attract media attention. Experts from a variety of fields have said for years that image and appearance are touted more than substance in our society. It isn't just the rockstars and social elite who have become performance artists, wrote Meg Greenfield in *Newsweek,* but so have a lot of other people—in politics and government, of course, but also in substantially less visible professions. "People who are rarely under the gaze of a television or other camera are hiring public relations consultants to guide them in what to say and how to try to look and be perceived. . . . People . . . are willing to self-censor their conversations with professional colleagues and friends on the theory that protection of their image comes first. I don't think this is all the doing of TV. . . ."

Eminent historian Daniel J. Boorstin explained why and how our society planted the seeds for living under perceptions rather than realities in his 1961 seminal book *The Image—or What Happened to the American Dream.*

We want and believe "illusions because we suffer from extravagant expectations," Boorstin said, especially "of what the world holds" and of our "power to shape the world." This leads to the creation of events and heroes when there are none. We need illusions to be happy and so we reward people who deceive us—professionals in advertising, public relations, politics, entertainment, manufacturing, merchandising, even journalism and publishing. "The making of illusions which flood our experience has become the business of America. . . ." Europeans, who have grown up with movies and the Wild West and Disney, know we are a nation that manufactures dreams.

We have disassociated accomplishment and fame and think of celebrities as heroes, Boorstin explained.

Of the subjects of biographical profiles appearing in the *Saturday Evening Post* and *Collier's* between 1901 and 1917, seventy-four percent came from politics, business, and the professions, Boorstin noted. After 1922, more than half were from the world of entertainment. Among those, a decreasing proportion hailed from the serious arts—literature, fine arts, music, dance, and theater—and an increasing proportion came from fields of popular entertainment, sports, and the nightclubs.

"The machinery of information brought into being a new substitute for the hero, who is the celebrity, and whose main characteristic is his well-knownness," Boorstin wrote. "In the democracy of pseudo-events, anyone can become a celebrity, if only he can get into the news and stay there."

Charles Lindbergh, who made the first nonstop solo flight over the Atlantic Ocean in 1927, is the first example of a true hero transfigured into celebrity through mass-media coverage. Yet, despite little hard news, the *New York Times* gave Lindbergh's feat the entire first five pages. Other papers devoted as much if not more, and radio commentators discussed him by the hour.

When Lindbergh returned to New York three weeks later, the *New York Times* continued through sixteen pages. A deluge of "non-stories" continued in subsequent editions. At this point, Boorstin wrote, "The biggest news about Lindbergh was that he was such big news." This kind of news manufacture went on for five years, interrupted by two legitimate stories—his marriage in 1929 to Anne Morrow and, of course, the kidnapping of his infant son in 1932.

Lindbergh was the prototype of Diana.

The advent of television, followed by the early 1960s launch of the geostationary satellites that could bounce broadcast signals around the planet, allowed events to be watched live around the world. When videotape replaced film in newsgathering, broadcasters could package a story in words and pictures which can be transmitted worldwide, twenty-four hours a day. This allows people in the news to be seen faster, more frequently, and by more people, making them instantly famous. Or infamous.

It took several years of technological advances and major changes in social structure before a global icon could be sold easily. The events of the 1970s laid the groundwork for Diana. Extensive coverage of such things as Vietnam, Watergate, and consumer advocacy, combined to diminish the respect the press showed toward public figures. And economic good times made it possible for almost every family in America, and high percentages in the rest of the industrial world, to buy television sets.

From this spiritual desert and "waning sense of historical time" arose the "me generation," explained social critic Christopher Lasch in his 1979 book *The Culture of Narcissism, American Life in an Age of Diminishing Expectations*. Lasch identifies an increasing focus on personal interests, a loss of communal sentiment, that he says evolves naturally out of the technological and social changes of the post-war period. He sees "new consciousness and therapeutic cultures, pseudo-confessional autobiography and fiction" as symptoms of a culture-wide narcissism. Diana's personal struggles, lived out on a very public stage, may have been more appealing to the 1980s and 1990s audience than they would have been a generation earlier.

The merger of these technological and historical forces created a celebrity culture defined and kept alive by the media.

"People become famous in a variety of ways other than by actual achievement," Braudy wrote.

Interestingly, he continued, the word "superstar" has been replaced of late with the word "icon." The word was once used to describe religious figures, from pagan gods to saints. Celebrities have replaced saints as idols and the term pays homage to the technology that has created them.

There were also smaller, less tangible, less visible qualities about Diana Spencer that made her perfect for the role. Some great performers never let us forget that they are performing. Olivier was that kind of actor. Marlon Brando, Meryl Streep, Robert DiNero never let us think that they are lost in a role. Diana in her own way seemed also always to be playing. She never became the queen, but she could *play* at being queen and she was better than the real thing.

"[Queen Elizabeth] had a brilliant sense of pageantry and when to lay it on the public," says Barbara Hower, who produced a two-hour syndicated television special on the royal family in the late 1980s. "She knew when to orchestrate a wedding, when to throw a pole dance. She understood the pomp and circumstance, the golden coach coming around the corner heading towards St. Paul's Cathedral."

But she was unaware of how to be appealing and sympathetic during a time when audiences demand personal connection with their celebrities through the camera's eyes. Hower continues: "[The Queen] didn't understand how every time she lifted an eyebrow, every little housewife in Des Moines was apprised of it seconds after it happened. She didn't get the fact that the world was watching. She didn't understand the technology. Not until she made that speech [during the week of mourning for Diana] that said, 'We will all miss [Diana]."

In an era of image, Diana knew that the media determines how one gets noticed, how one loses or keeps attention. Understanding how the media operates is part of the game. Part of what captivated the media must have been that she knew how to wrap them around her finger.

As an icon of the times, Diana could have come from Central Casting. She married a prince and projected the self-image and values that mirrored the self-absorbed society created by history and technology. The advances and economics of modern media technology made her a universally recognizable face, catapulting her to worldwide celebrity.

According to *The Economist,* Diana made good business sense for the global media shortly after she appeared on the scene. When Diana married Charles in 1981, 750 million people watched the event, making her instantly known by almost twenty percent of humanity at the time. Because she was royalty in a democratic age, she was almost unique.

Being a woman helped because both men and women admire female beauty. Being English and English-speaking was critical, however, because the global news and entertainment industries are dominated by people who speak English.

Even her weaknesses made her attractive. She was very human, even vulnerable. *People* creator Richard Stolley rattles off the "fame" checklist for most of the twentieth century: "She was beautiful, young, married a prince, was accessible, had two beautiful children, had money, took care of herself, and suffered ailments that many could sympathize with or suffered themselves. She had all the qualities that make for celebrity and some in far greater measure."

The evidence that Diana had acquired a superhuman status could be seen reflected in the memorabilia sold around the globe. The number and variety of these mementos increased after her death. They reveal not only the innate qualities that made us pay attention to her, but also the human need to have charismatic figures and relics of them in our lives. As of mid-February 1998, the Diana souvenir industry was estimated to be worth $165 million a year worldwide. Some 25,000 products bear her image or name, only a handful of which have been produced with the consent of her estate. The Internet reveals 36,000 sites linked to Diana memorabilia, including Diana sex lines (voiced by coarse Diana sound-alikes) and a tasteless computer game involving a high-speed chase in a Mercedes. Among the other products are dolls, ashtrays, rose bushes, photos, stamps, books, crockery, lottery cards, CD and video tributes, margarine, and pizza.

Three months after Diana's death, items already manufactured skyrocketed in value. The black velvet gown that Diana wore to the 1985 *Les Miserables* opening was resold by philanthropist Barbara Jordan at a benefit auction for $200,000—almost six times what she had paid in June of 1997 at the Christie's auction. Diana birthday mugs more than tripled in price to $120. In Hong Kong, collectors spent up to $950 on commemorative postage stamps. In the *San Diego Union-Tribune,* classified ads were run by collectors wanting to cash in on memorabilia, including a sterling silver Diana-and-Charles wedding coin for $450 and a Princess Diana bride doll for $3,500. The Franklin Mint issued plates, jewelry, and sixteen-inch fine porcelain dolls, including one wearing a hand-beaded gown.

On December 1, Columbia Records released an all-star charity CD entitled "Diana, Princess of Wales—Tribute," with exclusive tracks by Annie Lennox, Sinead O'Connor, Peter Gabriel, Aretha Franklin, and Mariah Carey, plus previously released tracks by Paul McCartney, Barbra Streisand, Michael Jackson, Luciano Pavarotti, and Bruce Springsteen. As this book goes to press, there is a Diana Barbie on the drawing boards.

The market for information continued as well. *The Independent* reported in early October 1997 that the late Princess's estate stopped publication of seventeen new unauthorized books, but could do nothing about eight more that were already published and distributed or about to be released in the following two weeks. In February 1998,

St. Martin's Press brought out *Death of a Princess: An Investigation* by *Time*'s Thomas Sancton and Scott MacLeod. St. Martin's has also committed to a full-fledged biography to be written by Anne Edwards and published in 1999. Times Books plans an August 1998 publication of a book by Sally Bedell Smith focusing on the last year of Diana's life.

Videos and audios kept pace with publishing. In October 1997, Simon & Schuster Audio released taped versions of the Morton and Kelley books. Working in cooperation with the Palace and Charles Spencer, the BBC is producing *Diana: A Tribute,* a two-cassette, two-hour audio with material from BBC documentaries, interviews, and news broadcasts during the last seventeen years, from the wedding to the births of William and Harry, to the divorce, to Diana's life after, and then her death. It includes Diana's first interview after she became engaged, her first public speech as Princess of Wales, excerpts from the *Panorama* interview, the Queen's address to the nation before the funeral, and Spencer's eulogy.

By early 1998, the television movie *The People's Princess: A Tribute* was being filmed at various European hot spots. Starring top English stars Amy Clare Seccombe and George Jackos, the story focused on the last year of Diana's life, in particular on the Diana-Dodi love affair.

Althorp is being turned into England's Graceland, to be open every July and August, beginning in 1998. Visitors will be able to dine at a restaurant, buy a select range of goods, view Diana's island grave from across the lake, and tour a stable hall converted into a museum. It will exhibit glamorous dresses as well as everyday wear, mementos like Diana's wedding tiara, and home movies shot by Diana's late father. The museum's content will change constantly, in keeping with the modern woman who kept up with the times.

In January 1998, the Spencer family began selling tickets. Two-thirds of the 152,000 available tickets sold out in a week. Profits, of course, will go to the memorial fund.

At the same time, battles began to be waged by lawyers for Diana's estate and memorial fund against companies that used Diana's name, voice, or image without authorization, whose products were inconsistent with her image, and whose profits didn't go to charity. Official souvenirs approved by the family and fund then began to be identified by a logo—Diana's looping signature in purple, over the words "Princess of Wales Memorial Fund."

An editorial in *The Guardian* called the strategy faulty, conceptually and legally. ". . . it fails to see that humanity's most cherished icons have all been transformed into trinkets and junk. . . ." The editorial noted that Diana's image might not be protected because the memory of the face of the most famous woman in the world is shared by everyone. "It could no more be copyrighted than Einstein's haircut or Chaplin's walk: it is part of the visual landscape of our century." We can assume that the Diana industry will continue to thrive indefinitely.

Without any further real news about Diana, the tabloids started to exploit the paranormal stories by January 1998. "Psychic Predicted Di's Death," said *The Globe*. "Di & Dodi Pledge Their Love From Beyond The Grave," cried the *National Enquirer*. And, of course, there were the typical sex stories, with a slightly different spin. "Royal Family Searching For Dodi & Di Sex Tapes," revealed the *National Enquirer*. For all her other qualities, in the end, as Diana herself knew, she was a commodity, a prototype for tchotchkes.

CHAPTER 18

Diana, the Movie

"She was the star of the Lady Di Show."

—Peter Weir
Director of *Truman*
NPR *Morning Edition*

We saw Diana Spencer, in life, packaged as if she were a commodity—a fairy-tale princess, a model, a victim, a saintly figure. In death, the media treated her as if she were a fallen head of state, then used her as the center of a sequence of mostly dead-end pieces of investigative journalism. In retrospect, it is clear that the events of her life were always handled as if they were entertainment rather than news.

Entertainment Weekly senior editor Mark Harris seized on this point in his scathing analysis of the Diana coverage. "As the first tragedy to test the maturity of the 100-channel, 24-hour-coverage, satellite-dish media era, Diana's death made an unreasonably steep demand of the medium—it was supposed to offer us solace while defining our age and serving as a counselor, an investigator, a leader, and a conscience. What tens of millions of Americans may have discovered instead was TV's oldest and most familiar essence.

289

Television—all television, even television news—is show business, and so the bulletins that first arrived from Paris as a cold, hard shock were quickly repackaged as overproduced spectacle and pageantry."

Harris is right. But it seems to me that news has been show business for a long time. Don Hewitt claims that the success of *60 Minutes* had a huge effect on television programming. The pioneering news magazine show proved that viewers will routinely absorb tougher, more complicated issues if told like a story with an interesting cast of characters. The show was in the top ten for twenty years. It made more than a billion dollars for CBS, Hewitt says. Not surprisingly, the show has been frequently imitated.

The new television magazine shows are slotted as if they were entertainment. Appearing years after *60 Minutes* began, for example, *20/20*, scheduled at 10:00 P.M. Fridays, was "the first time a news show was competing with regularly scheduled prime time [programming]," says Heather Vincent, senior coordinating producer for *Dateline NBC*. Other magazine shows are in a similar situation. *Dateline*'s competition, Vincent says, is not *60 Minutes, Prime Time Live, 20/20,* or other news magazines. On Mondays it's *The Practice.* On Tuesdays it's *NYPD Blue.* And that competition determines the content and presentation of the news. "We have to tell stories with no fiction in them that are interesting enough and produced quickly enough to hold the attention of the people who might want to change the channel for a full-fiction story," Vincent explains.

There is something chilling in her use of the term "full-fiction." Are there shows on the air that are one-quarter fiction? One-half?

At *People Magazine Television,* says producer Karen Jackovich, "We look for stories that are driven by likable characters and have resolutions." That is to say, they look for stories that have the same construction as "full-fiction" movie and television dramas.

The demand for stories that deliver ratings and sales has intensified as the number of media outlets has multiplied and the competition for viewership and readership has heated up. This was described by *Los Angeles Times* media critic David Shaw in the *Columbia Journalism Review*: "All those 24-hour TV news channels. All those TV tabloid and magazine shows. All those supermarket tabloids. All those Web sites. It's a vast maw, craving information—infotainment—around the clock."

Sensational stories don't need to be degenerate or corrupting. These types of stories have touched a primal chord for centuries, said *Entertainment Weekly*'s Richard Sanders. "Sensationalism goes back to the Greek tragedies, which were about murder, crime, lust, fate— basic emotional stories—not about policy or taxes. People are fascinated by stories that touch on life-and-death issues. Reflections on their own mortality arouses interest and holds them." Problems arise, however, when news-gatherers only seek out stories that contain these elements or, even worse, distort stories to make them sensational.

Top-level members of the media say news coverage has devolved into entertainment because we live in calmer times than we have in decades. With less hard news to report, the fervor to beat out rival outlets, whose numbers are expanding daily, has spurred media to focus on celebrities rather than heroes, on secular saint Diana rather than the more conventionally saintly Mother Teresa.

Thirty years earlier, Diana's death would not have received the blanket mainstream media coverage it did in 1997. That is partly because there weren't as many media outlets, and also because celebrities at that time were not considered valid news. They were constant fodder for the tabloids, fan magazines, and monthly feature magazines, but hadn't penetrated the front covers of mainstream print news media or become lead items on the national television news.

The differences between news and entertainment have blurred progressively over the past decades. "In the absence of events and heroes, celebrity and entertainment does fill the gap," says Norman Pearlstine, editor-in-chief at Time Inc.

"There has been a bit of a news void. We don't have international tensions that either Vietnam or World War II created. Except for the Gulf War in 1990, the Bush and Clinton years have been good times but relatively static times. There has not been a huge international story. The economic policies have been relatively consistent and successful."

No crises, no heroes either, at least not in the traditional sense. And even if there was an occasion to rise to, would the public believe in those who were in charge? Possibly not, Pearlstine continues. "I think Lyndon Johnson and Richard Nixon did a lot to undermine our belief in the presidency and in government and government institutions for different reasons. Our belief in the military has come back a bit with Generals Colin Powell and Norman Schwarzkopf."

But not enough to deflect our attention from entertainment figures, who are today's heroes. Between 1946 and 1950, the Gallup Organization polled Americans on who they admired most in the world; singer Kate Smith was the only person in the top ten who was not a political, religious, or military leader. Between 1989 and 1994, Gallup's most-admired lists have included Magic Johnson, Cher, Bill Cosby, Rush Limbaugh, Donald Trump, Michael Jordan, Elizabeth Taylor, Oprah Winfrey, and Diana.

Because of the void in major news and major heroes, those in the news business have filled the time and space with entertainment figures, Pearlstine says, "and I do include the royals as entertainment, just like Michael Jordan and O. J. Simpson."

Essayist Lance Morrow, in the *Columbia Journalism Review,* contends that the standards enforced by the older journalistic fraternity are now considered stuffy, if not outright elitist. Media managers cater to the least common denominator because of the difficulty, if not impossibility, of "pinpointing uniform standards of propriety and ethics" in a multicultural society.

Mounting bottom-line pressures from media conglomerates also have accelerated the emphasis on entertainment-oriented news, summarized Jacqueline Sharkey in the *American Journalism Review.* Stockholders expect high profits in the short term, and entertainment products deliver.

Moreover, print advertisers are cautious in the placement of their materials. Many which used to be interested in mass-market appeal now want to attract wealthy, well-educated readers. So they place ads in sections that aren't controversial and have strong human-interest components.

Howard Dickman, assistant managing editor at *Reader's Digest,* thinks that many editors are guilty of serious cynicism in their buying and selling of materials. "I think the media held Princess Diana in . . . contempt, but they are sophisticated and cynical and knew they could glom onto her, ride the wave, make a lot of money, without any political or cultural downside."

Since tragic and dramatic stories will continue to interest every media outlet, news that looks like entertainment will continue to be successful.

And whether or not we believe that our times are more stressful than those of our grandparents, most of us at the end of the day are looking for some sort of escape. Sensationalism, when available, will continue to permeate the media and the situation can only worsen.

That is a matter of concern for us as individuals and for society as a whole. Attention to nonsense hurts us deeply, for without devotion to what is important our lives lose meaning. Without meaning we lose purpose. Without purpose we lose ourselves.

Sheer sensationalism of the tabloid variety is easy enough to spot. But there are other types of distortion and misrepresentation that may arise when news is treated as entertainment. Don Hewitt of *60 Minutes* suggests networks produce better entertainment shows so that they do not feel compelled to fill prime-time schedules with entertaining nonfiction disguised as news. "News is news. Entertainment is entertainment. When entertainment is replaced with news, you ruin both."

If ever there was an institution which lent itself to infotainment, it is the British monarchy. As a nonpolitical, completely symbolic head of state, do the royals make news? Or do they entertain and instruct the public?

The hybridization of entertainment and news tells us a great deal about the way Diana was packaged and the way she used the package.

In Hollywood, the writing of most feature films is based on one of a small number of formulas or else a combination of formulas from films or characters that have worked well in the past. At first, Diana was a fairy-tale figure, but one that reflected the realities rather than the fantasies of modern women. In Hollywood the first years of the Diana story might be called *Cinderella* meets *Sleepless in Seattle*. As it went along, her story tracked the enormous changes that many women have undergone in the last fifteen years, "from the Prince Charming generation to the post-Prince Charming generation," says Ellen Goodman of the *Boston Globe,* who writes frequently about women's issues. Hollywood might call that Sleeping Beauty meets Tina Turner.

"A lot of women believed that if you put the slipper on, you'll live happily ever after," says Goodman. "But you might not live happily ever after. The prince might turn into a frog. How you survive and make a life of your own—that was Diana's story. She went in one direction, walked into a propeller, struggled to create a new life, with the same weaknesses and strengths of others—all an indication of [the change] in women's roles too."

There are other ways to pitch the Diana story. *Rumpelstiltskin* accurately represents the experience of Diana and many other women, believes Leopold Katz, an affiliate of the William Alanson White Institute of Psychoanalysis in New York and expert in the psychoanalytic significance of fairy tales.

Cinderella is about marrying well and living happily ever after. *Rumpelstiltskin* is about betrayal, loss of innocence, coming of age, and personal empowerment; a young lass frees herself from an exploitive man with her innate resourcefulness and creativity.

There is surely some truth in these comparisons. All of them, however, prevent us from seeing what really went on in Diana's life. On a deeper level, Diana's life story follows the pattern of other beautiful and tragic figures of our times. Diana is part of that elite club whose members include James Dean, Elvis Presley, Marilyn Monroe, Jimi Hendrix, Jim Morrison, John F. Kennedy, Dylan Thomas, and John Lennon. All were beautiful, lived hard, and died tragically young. Many seem to have been self-destructive and their deaths often related to their vices.

People's Mitchell Fink believes that women are particularly attracted to such tormented figures: "I remember watching the coverage of [Diana's] funeral and listening to people on television, like Tom Brokaw, Peter Jennings, to name a few, who generally seemed surprised by the overwhelming turnout and emotion. They were surprised because they hadn't been watching her story unfold over the years. It had everything—divorce, awful in-laws, eating disorders, adultery. It was a perfect soap opera, and I knew women all over the world would react to her death the way they did."

Essayist Lewis H. Lapham elaborated in *Harper's Magazine*: "Her fans cherished her for her neediness, which was as desperate and as formless as their own. . . . We live in an age that casts the victim as the hero of the play. Who listens to the stories of the people who don't make of their lives a chronicle of endless woe?"

It is tempting to dismiss such stories as melodramatic and shabby or to say that they demonstrate a culture-wide despair or boredom. But confessional literature is as old as civilization. The *Odyssey* wouldn't have been written if there hadn't been an audience for a man who had had many misfortunes and loved to talk about them.

All members of the media—even those disenchanted with the inordinate media coverage that they believe unduly glorified her—were moved by the funeral itself. Vice president and editor-in-chief of *Variety*, Peter Bart, describing the funeral, says, "In movie terms, it was the third act of her story, brilliantly devised, with great music." It is a profound insight. Almost all contemporary films are written in three acts: In the first act, a character faces a problem. (Diana was courted by a prince, engaged, married, had beautiful children, but was never really accepted by her husband or his family.) In the second act, the character takes steps to overcome the problem. (Diana became a fashion symbol, did good works to prove her worthiness, challenged her husband, went public, had affairs, divorced.) In the third act, the central character either overcomes or is destroyed. Diana's story is a drama perfect for the films.

In its themes, as well, Diana's story has universal appeal. It is a tale of love gone wrong, surely the most common theme of dramatic literature since Shakespeare and Molière. It has the poignancy of *Casablanca* and the inevitability of *Titanic*.

Diana was also the perfect heroine. She met the standards of a variety of archetypes. She was a shy, ordinary girl without direction metamorphosed into a sleek, sophisticated beauty. She was warm and emotional and, therefore, out of place in a cold, grim family. She was a scorned woman, a jilted wife who got revenge. She learned compassion from her own suffering. She was an underdog who won. "In human journalistic terms, Diana was a very good story," says Richard Stolley at Time Inc. "Her problems could have doomed a more fragile person." It is material for more than one drama.

But when we start speaking of real-life events as though they were fiction, we open the door to distortion. We can see, for example, that sort of myth-making going on in the way the press treated the royal family in the days following Diana's death.

The tabloids are the masters of emotional manipulation in the pursuit of news. The prime example, wrote Charles Krauthammer in *Time,* was turning the public wrath against the paparazzi at the beginning of the week into anger toward the unexpressive Windsors for not sufficiently mourning Diana, ". . . one of the greatest acts of misdirection since Houdini—pulled off, amazingly enough, by the very tabloids that were originally so under siege."

Other media also reformatted the truth to suit their own ends. To sustain viewer interest there had to be not only pageantry, tragedy, and familiar faces, but also dramatic tension. Reporters had no choice but to move in on the royal family. Indeed, the only tension in the week's events was in trying to understand what the royals felt, trying to anticipate what they would do.

The mainstream media scrutinized the royal family's every gesture or failed gesture. They were relentless in demanding that the Commonwealth's symbolic family mirror the emotions of the people in the street. The brief statement of sorrow that the royal family issued shortly after it heard of Diana's death was insufficient: Grieve with us and comfort us in our grief. "SHOW US YOU CARE," demanded the *Daily Express*. "What is the nation to make of silence and absence at a time of vocal and visible lamentation?" asked *The Times*.

For most of that week, eyes were focused on Charles. Could he pick up the torch that Diana passed to him in her death to make the monarchy relevant for the twenty-first century? At every turn, his decisions were an opportunity to resolve the country's doubts that he was the right man for the job.

Was he grief-stricken? He received bad reviews for taking his sons to church the Sunday morning of Diana's death, but later that day, escorting Diana's body home to England, he appeared distraught and red-eyed.

Complaints arose that the funeral procession was too short for all the mourners. At Prime Minister Tony Blair's urging, Charles convinced the Palace to triple the length of the route. Charles and his sons influenced the Queen to return to London from Scotland earlier and face her subjects. On Friday, the three led the way in a royal walkabout outside Kensington Palace, shaking hands and accepting flowers; the Queen and Prince Philip joined them a little later. The crowd applauded.

The Queen then addressed the nation and the world live on television, finally putting the royal seal on the anguish that her subjects had already expressed so poignantly: "No one who knew Diana will ever forget her. Millions of others who never met her, but felt they knew her, will remember her." Speaking live was unprecedented; her annual Christmas address is always taped. And then an act that was not only unprecedented, but the most telling of all: When Diana's cortege drove away from Westminster Abbey, the Queen bowed her head.

By week's end, reports surfaced that Charles was the one arguing for these changes. The monarchy indeed seemed to be transforming right in front of the cameras.

This desire to see the Prince and the royal family as redeemed by Diana's death is natural. But did it really happen? Wrote Morton in *Diana, Her True Story—In Her Own Words*: "Those few days after her death captured forever the contrast between the Princess and the House of Windsor: her openness, their distance; her affection, their frigidity; her spontaneity, their inflexibility; her glamour, their dullness; her modernity, their stale ritual; her emotional generosity, their aloofness; her rainbow coalition, their court of aristocrats."

One might ask, too, whether the royal family had done anything so terrible that they needed to be redeemed.

Correctly analyzing the mood of the people, and perhaps even reading their own press, the royals played the roles called for by the story.

After the funeral, the Palace immediately offered to restore Diana's royal title. This was an undoubted acknowledgment of the masses' sentiment for a modern monarchy that represents and embraces them, not lords over or ignores them. It also was an antidote to Charles Spencer's eulogy that slammed a monarchy that rejected Diana and her warm, inclusive, nonpredjudicial ways. The Spencer family declined the offer.

Prince Charles must have felt himself under tremendous pressure to live up to his new role. During a royal trip to Africa in November 1997, Charles, dressed in shirt sleeves, roamed back from first class on the plane to chat and clown with reporters, impersonating a Swazi king choosing a bride from a pack of bare-breasted dancers. He was trying to lighten up. "Re-born to Rule," exclaimed *The Sun*, a previous relentless critic of Charles. The normally anti-royalist *Guardian* wondered, "Could the death of Diana have had a liberating influence on our future King?" By February 1998, A. N. Wilson told in the *Evening Standard* of a love affair going on between the "royal hacks" and the new "Prince of Hearts."

Whether Diana's passing has mellowed Charles or, sadly, removed a shadow that allows people to see the Prince more clearly than before, is not quite apparent. Charles is said to be spending more time with his sons than ever before.

The rewriting of the story to suit dramatic formulas was even clearer in the case of Dodi al Fayed. There was not much known to say about him. My impression was that he was an introverted man who enjoyed his life but wanted very much to impress his father. Given the short deadlines, shallow reporting was bound to occur. Early broadcast profiles on him noted that he financed the Oscar-winning feature *Chariots of Fire*, and so he was portrayed in television reports as a big-time producer in Hollywood. The portrait "was absurd," laughs *Variety*'s editor-in-chief, Peter Bart. "He was the ultimate fringe player, yet the networks talked like he was Irving Thalberg." In reality, Dodi was known for talking the talk in Hollywood, partying with beautiful women, and investing his father's money in movies, among them *F/X*, *Hook*, and *The Scarlet Letter*. He was rarely, if ever, seen on the set doing any real work as a producer.

Bart believes Dodi was overplayed, in part, to live up to Diana's illustrious aura. The world's darling Diana couldn't die with a boy-man who lived on an allowance from his father and only dabbled in projects through investments backed by his father. That would tarnish her image when she was being portrayed as equivalent to the angels. Without the perception that the Diana as people imagined her had finally found true love with her match, the drama of the tragedy would dissipate into tragicomedy. And that kind of story won't earn ratings.

The build-up of Dodi began the first day. "Reporters or producers saw Dodi's [credit on] *Chariots of Fire*, and then rushed to put something on the air." Hearing the report by legitimate media, another outlet on deadline used it without checking it out. "There's a lot of scalping. It's the easy way out," Bart says.

The second day, stories were about the romance, which was blown up into something more serious than a summer fling by al Fayed's press agents. That day, the tape of the couple together at the Hotel Ritz was released. This, too, was swallowed because video-feeds are quick, easy ways to fill time and space.

By the end of the week, the print media could spin the more complete profile that they'd by then had time to research.

One wants to like Dodi, to believe that he was a better man than he seemed, to believe his love for Diana was real and that she had taken him seriously. If none of that was true, Diana must seem to have died stupidly and pointlessly. None of us wants to believe that such random disaster, such chaos, is possible.

We make the truth fit the plots we already know. We need only to take a few steps further to see that we may have been fascinated by Diana's death because it touched us at some almost instinctual level. It had a mythic quality. In an article entitled "Fatted Calf" for *Harper's Magazine,* Lewis H. Lapham compared the slashing of a heifer's throat, the removal of limbs, and the burning on skewers—as described in the *Odyssey* for the dedication to the Greek goddess Pallas Athena—to the fate of Diana: "The wonders of modern technology make it possible to render the burning of every bone and the tasting of every organ as a sequence of pleasant images. . . ."

On that particular night in Paris, the price of fame as defined by the media age literally resulted in ripping out the heart of its anointed queen.

"In a twisted way, she died in the line of duty, not to country but to the age she came to represent," summarized Jonathan Alter in *Newsweek.*

"Princess Diana was killed not just by a speeding car but by a speeding culture—by what the author Leo Braudy calls 'the frenzy of renown'. . . . Only the most determined literalist could fail to see a connection between her death and her epoch, a time—our time—when celebrity obsession seems as out of control as a hurtling Mercedes on a late summer night in Paris. . . . Ultimately, nothing much can change because media coverage is the oxygen of modern public life . . . for it is the mighty communications culture that made Diana and shapes the world she left. The Princess will never be queen. . . . The England in which she lived will never be remembered as Elizabethan. It will be The Di Era. So sad she had to die for it."

But it makes a great story.

CHAPTER 19

The Princess Was the Package

> "... She was once asked what
> she would want as an epigraph
> on her grave. 'A great hope
> crushed in infancy' was
> her reply."
>
> —Andrew Morton
> *Diana, Her True Story*
> *—In Her Own Words*

I could not have written this book without the observations, ideas, and support of the more than fifty people who contributed their comments and opinions in interviews. Through the diversity of beliefs and talents they represent, they have given me a wealth of insights. I went to them for feedback on my theory that Diana must have been an extremely skillful manipulator of the media, that she had used the media to make a powerful contact with millions of people around the world.

I came to this conclusion while watching the extraordinary outpouring of grief from around the world at the news of her death. My image of Diana was a long way from the one most commonly described. I thought she had not been victimized by the media, I thought she had handled them well. I thought she was not always the one pursued, I thought she had been a hunter herself; she'd pursued

Prince Charles, then the press and television, and ultimately an adoring public. It was unclear to me whether she had strategized intellectually or whether she had remarkable instincts, but the latter possibility seemed the most likely.

In my work as a publicist I have worked with film stars who had an innate gift for knowing how to position themselves with their public (Demi Moore comes to mind). Diana's EQ, as described by Daniel Goleman in his book *Emotional Intelligence,* placed her in the genius category.

My image of the late Princess put me at odds with the major books and articles about her. Most do describe Diana as an innocent victim. A few go too far the other way, calling her stupid, a twit, a pathetic sentimentalist. I thought my version of Diana was at times critical, but more appreciative of her as well. I expected she could be a formidable adversary and I admired her for her toughness, for her record of achievement, for guessing right so much of the time what packaging she needed in order to achieve her goals. I couldn't think of another celebrity who has been so skillful.

To my surprise, my unconventional, even iconoclastic picture of the Princess was endorsed by almost everyone I spoke to. Some journalists continued to feel that Diana was misused by the royal family and by the press in the early days. Some felt that she was reckless, even suggesting that she might not have died as she did if she had learned to moderate her attitudes toward tabloid photographers. Many believe that the media need a higher set of standards for themselves, and I agree. But no one I spoke to could envision laws strong enough to safeguard a megastar like Diana that didn't also put unacceptable restraints on press freedom.

In the community of editors, journalists, executives, and scholars, there is a surprising consensus about Diana's gift. These people recognize a master craftsman in their own field.

To one question, however, I received no clear answer: Who might be Diana's heir apparent? Who might be the media age's next icon that delivers golden rewards for the media? It's an obvious question. It could be treated as a sort of parlor game. I asked it because it was a way to find out what the people felt was the quintessential quality Diana possessed. In *Mirabella* earlier this year, Ruth La Ferla had suggested a few names: Carolyn Bessette Kennedy, wife of John F. Kennedy Jr., the star of America's de facto royal family; music-world superstars Jewel or Alanis Morissette; megamodel Kate Moss; screen sirens Uma Thurman, Claire Danes, or Gwyneth Paltrow.

None of these resonated with me. It seemed to me, as is the case with other big stars, that Diana was the right person in the right place at the right time with the right message. In general, top-level media figures agreed. The reason, they say, is that such an icon would suddenly emerge when there was the right combination of social, historical, and personal forces. "Part of what gives them visibility is the surprise," notes David Shaw, media critic for the *Los Angeles Times*. "They just come on the scene."

Adds Peter Bart, editor-in-chief of *Variety*: "The next one will arrive at a fortuitous moment in history. Even five years later, that person would not be right for the time." There's no way to research this, Bart continues, but there is a way to earmark the media's next queen or king: sales and ratings. "*People* puts someone on the cover as a gamble. The magazine might sell out. Then everyone else looks out for that person. *People* tends to be the harbinger."

Cultural historian and author on the subject of fame, Leo Braudy, feels that any Joe or Josephine, average or otherwise, with a penchant for self-publicity can aspire to fame through the Internet because there are no gatekeepers. "Anyone can have their own Web site that tells who they are, what they do, who their friends are, what they think," he says.

Vanity Fair's Cathy Horyn imagines that the Diana of the next millennium—and it may take a few years before the blessed one arrives on stage—might actually communicate with people on-line. "What if this person had a chat room? What would that do? He or she could be huge. The reach would be tremendous if millions felt they could talk personally and have any kind of direct access."

But it takes more than technology to make a star. Daniel Okrent, editor of new media for Time Inc., says, "A media celebrity can't be created simply by publicity." Okrent thinks that personal qualities are the ones that count. "Someone with imputed dignity," he says, will be the next big celebrity. "Not a Hollywood star. We never care about showbusiness people as much."

Martha Smilgis, *Time* correspondent and former supervising producer for *Extra,* agrees: "Someone in an exalted position due to fate. We relish looking at someone regal because wearing sweats and sitting by the computer we all have dull lives." Valerie Steele, chief curator of the museum at New York's Fashion Institute of Technology, told *Mirabella* that the coming star must have "radiant vulnerability."

But we will fail to learn what Diana taught us if we think that natural gifts or qualities alone can keep a celebrity in the spotlight. The megastar has to maintain position. They must have an air of mystery, many think. Stature can evaporate through overexposure of intimate details, real personality, even voice. Staying power is achieved through "opacity," said La Ferla in *Mirabella.*

"A mega-celebrity has to have a certain inaccessibility," concurs Richard Sanders of *Entertainment Weekly.* "It's better for people to talk about you than for you to talk. A chat room would devalue the mystery element. Diana's great advantage was that she did not have to do press. She had no reason to speak so she could be very selective about who she saw, what she promoted."

Movie stars don't have this luxury because if they want their films to do well, they do interviews with the media not just once, but many times. "If they accomplish something, they do have to promote it," says Sanders. And then—if not sooner, certainly later—showbusiness reporters must see clearly that these "stars" are just people, and write profiles that reveal their worst sides, including bland, real-life personalities.

The "next Diana" will reflect our progress or deterioration as a society. The challenge to the media is to take a stand: give the people what they need, not necessarily what they want. Exalt a person who has truly done something of importance first. Set an example with a true role model rather than a fantasy figure.

There are signs that media news outlets are seriously reconsidering their public role. CNN, a company which depends on exciting, late-breaking news, might have been likely to move toward entertaiment in its reporting and programming in order to hold on to ratings. But instead, they have just hired Jeff Greenfield, a news analyst of impeccable credentials and integrity. They are taking the high road.

A half-century before the beginning of the media age, Karl Marx wrote that great events and characters in history always occur twice, first as high tragedy and later as low farce. Had he lived into our times he might have considered how major historical events evolve beyond tragedy and farce to soap opera to sound bite to commercial endorsement, and so on. It is difficult to separate Diana from the network of people and circumstances through which we see her. It is impossible for journalists to avoid comparing her with other glittering, promising, tragic figures. In the *Spin Cycle* audiotape, Howard Kurtz makes the same point regarding journalists who cover the White House. Kurtz says of Rahm Emanuel, a special consultant to President Clinton: "He was convinced that the press operated within paradigms—neat little belief systems that fit the contours of elite opinion. The notion of objective reporting [is] hogwash." Enough time has passed, however, that we can begin to make guesses about Diana's legacy.

For many women, Diana may occupy a unique role, one that is more difficult to fill. Many believe that she may symbolize the feminine figure of our age. By the time of her death, after many struggles, she had integrated all the roles that women have been exploring since the women's liberation movement began—femininity, career, motherhood, individuality, dependence, independence. In *The Guardian*, feminist Camille Paglia admired Diana as "a woman who came along at a time when feminism seemed to have sexually redefined woman as simply the white upper-middle-class professional with an attaché case. It was her freshness, her femininity, her desire for marriage and children, her glamour."

But Diana was more than the pretty, soft thing that her admirers sometimes believed her to be. Broadcaster Martin Lewis says she ennobled British women living in a misogynist British society. "The women in Britain were behind the women's movement in the United States. Margaret Thatcher was the toughest man in her party. She did not embrace women's rights. The British media is an old boys' club. . . . Women's roles in charity were to make tea and sandwiches, and judge dresses, not to take a leadership role. Diana is an excellent role model as to how women can empower themselves and not be browbeaten."

Diana got even—a very specific reason for her enormous appeal to women worldwide. Like so many average women, she was a woman spurned, but unlike so many typical women, she fulfilled her fantasy of retribution. Author and journalist Richard Reeves admits he was clueless about Diana's appeal until he was enlightened by a smart CBS News reporter, Martha Teichner: ". . . it had to do with how badly ordinary women are so often treated by husbands, parents, and in-laws. They suffer, mostly in silence, and were moved by the public pain and revenge of this young woman so different from them."

Newsweek's Barbara Kantrowitz was more brutally honest: "... by the time of her death, she was an object of intense fascination because of the woman she had become on her own. At every step of her journey, women could say: 'Been there, done that ... wish I'd done that.' Diana was a woman scorned who developed a masterful fury. She got mad and then got even in world-class style."

In so doing, Diana symbolizes today's feminists. She was not a '70s feminist who might have learned lessons from the behavior of men. Nor was she an '80s superwoman feminist who thinks she can juggle career and family. Diana was a '90s feminine feminist, who accepts her human frailties and lauds her womanly gifts, unapologetically expecting respect for their value. And like many modern women, she was willing to go outside Establishment concepts and values to get what she wanted. The Princess, with her astrologers, her diets, her interest in Oriental philosophy, tapped into a spiritual undercurrent in society and appealed to emotional rather than intellectual intelligence.

Diana's fame does not have long legs, author Leo Braudy believes, not even as a symbol of women's modern-day identity conflicts, because she was privileged. "Over time, it will be hard for most to sympathize with a single mother with millions, who lived in a palace and went on a Mediterranean vacation for weeks, as one who was struggling to maintain her integrity and self."

But for the moment, Diana is a symbol for single women in their thirties who have emerged as a constituency to be heard and taken seriously, further dissolving the stereotypical image of Britain as a white, male-dominated society. "That group responded in a way no one would have ever guessed," said Warren Hoge from the London bureau of the *New York Times*. "Through Diana, they saw their own troubled selves on a quest for self-improvement and never quite getting there."

As a historical figure Diana may become more important than anyone could have imagined. Many believe that she, combined with the forces that brought a new Labour government to power, may have a lasting effect on the monarchy.

It will be Charles's responsibility, then will continue under William's reign, to make the monarchy adjust to the times. One small lesson is a practical one: Let the monarch marry whomever he or she likes. The royal rule that the king-to-be must wed a virgin is foolish by late-twentieth-century standards. "Had Charles married the non-virgin he loved," says Dennis Prager, "the royal family might have had to endure some men speaking to tabloids about their experience with Britain's princess. But that would have been nothing compared to the problems the royal family had to face when the Prince and Princess divorced."

The stiff-upper-lip approach—the importance placed on self-restraint so long associated with the British ruling class—is discredited after the tremendous outpouring of grief, heartfelt love, and remembrance during the week following Diana's death, which, speech adviser Richard Greene believes, "changed the emotional landscape of Britain." Consequently, the royal family and others in positions of authority acknowledge their humanness if they are to hold the people's loyalty and guide them.

But Diana's longest-lasting contribution to British institutions may be through her children. That was what Ellen Goodman of the *Boston Globe* said when interviewed for this book. "She tried to keep her kids on track in real life in the face of centuries of tradition." Richard Stolley agrees: "It will be interesting to see how the boys, especially William, try to invoke her name. That would continue to keep her impact alive longer than would be expected."

She may have some impact on other institutions as well. Diana as a humanitarian will be long remembered, but her lasting impact is dubious. There is some evidence already that the Princess of Wales Trust, set up in her name, is unclear about its direction. (The trust takes a royalty from every company that uses Diana's name. In a celebrated example, Diana's signature appeared on tubs of margarine sold in the U.K. A friend's opinion was that she would be amused to find herself in so many refrigerators.)

Her friends hope she will be remembered for the example she set and that she will be imitated. Tina Brown, in her eulogy in *The New Yorker,* describes her as a model: "Now she is frozen in bas-relief, forever kneeling to comfort some hurt." Says Martin Lewis: "Her biggest legacy, I hope, will be her spirit behind the charity. She supported those causes that were not fashionable. Yes, she enjoyed the spotlight, but she had a calling."

Extending herself to the less fortunate is exactly what redeemed her in the eyes of many who hardly, if ever, gave Diana a second thought. "Diana made herself appealing with her good works. Without that, she was a ten-minute story," believes Kim Masters, contributing editor for *Vanity Fair* and *Time.* "It gave her a depth and dimension that someone as cynical as myself respected. It separated her from Madonna. She used her fame to do something that mattered."

So powerful was Diana's example that the charities she supported have continued to draw substantial increases in donations after her death, defying the usual experience of fund-raisers. Her association with the British Red Cross on an anti-landmine campaign, for example, boosted its intake $1.6 million in 1997. "Usually when a celebrity dies, within six months you hear very little of them," Edward Matthews told *People* in February 1998. He is executive director of United Cerebral Palsy, for which Diana doubled the 1994 intake to $2 million in 1995 by attending an annual banquet. "We're just about at that point now, and you see no diminishing." The Princess of Wales Memorial Fund is anticipated to increase by $60

million from sales of the CD produced in her memory. A charity concert at Althorp on June 27 will also bring in revenues.

Inevitably, her strength as a fund-raiser will weaken, some
believe. Richard Stolley questions whether invoking her name to collect money will last more than three years. "It's hard to believe she will
have a lasting impact," he says. "She did semi-good works, but she
didn't conquer cancer. The work she did, her contributions to research
and landmines, that will go on, with others emerging as leaders. She
will be remembered ultimately as one who illuminated our lives."

"Diana fought in her life our era's central battle between service
and self-absorption, between the impulse to give and the craving for
pleasure," explains nationally syndicated columnist Arianna
Huffington. "Most people play out that conflict in life and rarely win.
Our culture says if you are troubled, take a pill or go shopping. Diana
did all that too, but she also didn't lock herself up and give in entirely
to narcissism. She was willing to be vulnerable in public and then go
beyond that to reach out and comfort others, and in the process find
solace. She realized there was not much healing in self-absorption."

In *Newsweek,* Jonathan Alter expressed his hope that Diana
inspired us to act face-to-face, not just to talk or write checks. "How
many of Diana's devotees have taken their children to visit the homeless? How many actually talk to the poor and disenfranchised? That
impulse—in fact, a social conscience in general—has been out of
fashion for at least a quarter century. We give to the poor, but we
don't engage them and love them as these two women [Diana and
Mother Teresa] did. By burying a secular saint and a real one in the
same week, maybe we will plant some seeds of commitment."

Through her visits to the critically ill and dying, Diana showed
us that each person's contribution, no matter how small, is significant. Dennis Prager believes that those who found Diana wanting
when comparing her to Mother Teresa, for example, missed the

point of Diana's contribution. "The question all of us must ask ourselves is not whether we did as much good as Mother Teresa, but whether we did as much good as we could do. Each one of us has a different role to play in making the world better."

The deeper lesson of Diana's life may be that if you are sick, you can heal yourself—and others—by coming out of yourself. ". . . far from being obsessed with her own injuries, she would forget herself in the injury of others. It was the secret of her appeal to the sick and the wounded," wrote ITV talk show host Clive James, one of Diana's longstanding media advisers, in *The New Yorker*. As Dennis Prager said in his newsletter, *The Prager Perspective*, "Many people do good works precisely because they feel unworthy and want to raise their self-esteem. This is the opposite of the contemporary foolish belief that high self-esteem fosters good works."

At least this is the spin that some members of the media would like to put on things. In December, the *Mail on Sunday* profiled twenty-two women who have followed in Diana's path, including a model working for an orphanage, a filmmaker helping disadvantaged teenagers, and a former merchant banker teaching at a school for underprivileged children in Pakistan. "It's starting to become clear now: Princess Diana has irrevocably changed our attitude to charity," the *Mail* wrote.

It is difficult to predict the qualities of the next media superstar because one appears on the scene, as I said earlier, when a combination of circumstances is so right that the appearance seems almost inevitable. Diana was a figure who bridged distinctions of age, class, and gender not only in Britain but in North America and the rest of the world as well. She represented the power of a new generation and the attitudes of those poorer and less fortunate than she. Diana found a way to enfranchise herself and other women too. Her image was, in fact, distorted by the people who needed her most. She was not a commoner, nor did she share all the values and problems of ordinary people. But ordinary Britons thought she was like them and counted her as one of them. Increasingly, she did reach out to them because she was genuinely charitable and because her own neediness made her want to reach out. But on the other side many hands were stretched towards her as well.

Richard C. Robertiello, M.D., a psychiatrist and psychoanalyist interviewed for this book, says that gays are powerfully attracted to Diana, as they have been to Judy Garland, Elizabeth Taylor, Shirley Bassey, and Jackie Onassis, because all of them "are people who can be exhibitionist about femininity, which gay men can't do without censure. Gay men envy them for flouting their emotionality." Gay men made up only one of a number of groups who found solace in the fact that Diana's struggle with her demons was so highly visible.

Historical figures who bridge major social differences or who try to unite antagonistic groups always attract or create tremendous energy, positive and negative, around themselves. True or not, John and Robert Kennedy seemed to be breaking down distinctions in the U.S. between Protestant and Catholic, rich and poor, old and young. They had passionate admirers and detractors. The same was true of Martin Luther King. Even figures in entertainment who take strong political and social positions may arouse strong passions, both positive and negative.

Diana's image—or, more appropriately, each of her multiple images—reflected the self-images of so many around the world. "Diana had that ability to straddle the whole, from Gucci to the ground floor," says *Dateline NBC*'s Heather Vincent. She had something for everyone, author Leo Braudy elaborates, saying that those who top the fame totem pole in modern society pull together contradictory images. Diana was the premier example of someone who did that "double thing." She was an aristocrat by birth, but also Cinderella—the assistant kindergarten teacher whose foot fit the slipper. And, of course, she maintained the popular appeal. "Even though she came from a family with longer lineage in England than the Windsors, she was ill at ease playing an empty ceremonial role," Braudy explains.

She had wealth and power, but also little children. "She was more at home with them," he adds, "than with soldiers wearing tall fur hats, making her one of everyone." She was noted for being a fashion connoisseur, which is perceived as vacuous and elitist, but also for her charity work, which gave her emotional dimension.

Diana's *coups de theatre* were her confessions of suffering. Here, she stretched the greatest distance. She had always treated everyone with equal respect on her official visits, but through the newspaper reports, the Morton book, and especially the *Panorama* interview, ordinary people felt that, despite her title and money, she was one of them. They loved her for being normal, a mirror of their narcissistic, troubled, introspective selves, rather than an example of achievement and higher purpose, which she was attempting through her charity work. The public affection for her ordinariness turned her into an icon.

"The rewards of fame accrue differently to celebrities," according to *The Economist*. "One sort of reward is public approbation. That is something that a society can produce inexpensively; and the approbation that ordinary citizens can produce costs no more than it costs the rich. So fame is essentially an egalitarian commodity and society's approval is most readily earned by those celebrities who are seen to have the common touch—or, in Diana's case, to be 'the People's Princess.'"

Mediating between social groups and forces can place a famous person in a dangerous position. Nancy Friday suggests that by acting upon the many desires she felt or the demands placed on her, Diana may have taught us to be more careful, not to try for so much, whether it's love, fun, privacy, notoriety. Friday adds, "I hate that message. Diana would have hated it too. But it seems as if her destiny was a punishment." Conversely, Friday muses, Diana's early death could give an opposite message: "Gather ye rosebuds while ye may," as poet Robert Herrick wrote.

But I would agree with Arianna Huffington that the next Diana will be someone who can "bridge the gap" between the haves and have-nots. "Glamour and beauty will be essential to draw attention to him or her, but once noticed, this person must be willing to be wounded in public and transcend barriers. By example, this person will remind the public of the less fortunate, even if the pundits aren't paying attention to them."

Dick Morris, former political consultant to President Clinton, says, "Diana forged a new genre of leadership and communication based on vulnerability. As Kierkegaard said, 'The wound is the hole through which God enters.' Her vulnerability permitted us to enter her. Whether she understood it or it just happened, she got the concept that vulnerability is more important than strength, like Gandhi. People identified with and embraced Diana because she was normal. They don't trust anyone who is trying to sell them something, but they look to someone who lives a normal life as a role model."

Of course, as I have said in this book, Diana's life was anything but normal. It was as far from normal as a modern life can be. Was our image of Diana unreal? I'd argue that it was surreal, that it was hyperreal, that it had a reality that transcended ordinary experience. It was a life lived with more colors in the spectrum than most of us have ever seen.

Diana's story is the Tiffany package that makes the gift seem even more valuable than it actually is.

Source Notes

I have wanted, in this book, to reinterpret the life of the Princess of Wales focusing on the ways she and the media interacted. My intention was not to present new information about Diana. I wanted to avoid sensationalism. In fact, I hoped to stay close to the events of her life as they are commonly known to the general public, to tell Diana's personal story in a way that would not be open to dispute. Therefore, for biographical details, I've drawn on a small number of respected books and documentaries on her life and have shied away from assertions that could not be substantiated by several sources.

Below, I've listed references for each chapter. A full bibliography and a separate list of interviewees can be found in the sections that follow.

Introduction

BOOKS
McLuhan, *The Medium is the Massage.*

BROADCASTS
Bashir, BBC *Panorama*, "The Interview: Princess Diana, Queen of Hearts."

Chapter 1

BOOKS
Campbell, *Diana in Private.* Kelley, *The Royals.* Morton, *Diana, Her True Story—In Her Own Words.*

BROADCASTS
Bashir, BBC *Panorama*, "The Interview: Princess Diana, Queen of Hearts."
PBS *Frontline*, "The Princess and the Press."

Chapter 2

BOOKS
Campbell, *Diana in Private.* Erikson, *Identity and the Life Cycle.* Kelley, *The Royals.* Morton, *Diana, Her True Story—In Her Own Words.* Peck, *The Road*

Less Traveled. Seward, *Diana: An Intimate Portrait.* Solomon, *Narcissism and Intimacy.*

BROADCASTS
Bashir, BBC *Panorama,* "The Interview: Princess Diana, Queen of Hearts."
PBS *Frontline,* "The Princess and the Press."

INTERVIEWS
Dr. Joyce Brothers. Alan Entin. Martin Lewis. Richard Stolley.

Chapter 3

ARTICLES
Walleye, *People.*

BOOKS
Campbell, *Diana in Private.* Kelley, *The Royals.* Morton, *Diana: Her True Story.* Peck, *The Road Less Traveled.*

BROADCASTS
A&E *Biography,* "Diana, the True Story." PBS *Frontline,* "The Princess and the Press."

INTERVIEWS
Martin Lewis. Carole Willcocks.

Chapter 4

BOOKS
Braudy, *The Frenzy of Renown: Fame and its History.* Gardiner, *A Student's History of England.* Kelley, *The Royals.*

BROADCASTS
PBS *Frontline,* "The Princess and the Press."

INTERVIEWS
Leo Braudy.

Chapter 5

ARTICLES
Appel, *The New York Times,* "Charles and Lady Diana Wed Today." Brook, *Mail on Sunday,* "I Lost My Husband, My Children . . ." Castro, *Time,* "The Vows Heard Around the World." Cocks, *Time,* "Magic in the Daylight." Downie, *Washington Post,* "Wedding to be Royal Revel for Harvard Britons." *The Economist,* "Prince's Peace." Fedcamp, *The Christian Science Monitor,* "London Fashion." Hallett, *Time* (Commemorative Issue) "To Our Readers." Hyde, *Washington Post,* "The Royal Wedding." Langway, *Newsweek,* "A Fairy Tale Come True." *U.S. News & World Report,* "Amid the Threat of Bloodshed." Shales, *Washington Post,* "The Royal Wedding." Willcocks,

National Catholic Register, "A Royal Reunification."

BOOKS
Braudy, *The Frenzy of Renown.* Campbell, *Diana in Private.* Friday, *The Power of Beauty.* Morton, *Royalty Watching.*

INTERVIEWS
Leo Braudy. Howard Dickman. Nancy Friday. Martin Lewis. Richard Stolley. Carole Willcocks.

Chapter 6

ARTICLES
Cocks, *Time,* "Magic in the Daylight." Collins, *Time,* "Talking Trash." Morrow, *Columbia Journalism Review,* "Journalism After Diana." Shaw, *Los Angeles Times,* "Simpson Legacy."

BROADCASTS
PBS *Frontline,* "The Princess and the Press."

INTERVIEWS
Cindy Adams. Mitchell Fink. Bruce Handy. Howard Kurtz. Martin Lewis. Daniel Okrent. Norman Pearlstine. Howard Rosenberg. Richard Sanders. Bernie Weinraub.

Chapter 7

ARTICLES
Castro, *Time,* "The Vows Heard Around the World."

BOOKS
Campbell, *Diana in Private.* Kelley, *The Royals.* Morton, *Diana: Her True Story.* Solomon, *Narcissism and Intimacy.*

BROADCASTS
A&E *Biography,* "Diana, the True Story." PBS *Frontline,* "The Princess and the Press."

INTERVIEWS
Leo Braudy. Jonathan Rader.

Chapter 8

ARTICLES
Anderson, *Chicago Tribune,* "High Fashion Drops in at Di's Place." Associated Press, "People in the News." Brown, *The New Yorker,* "A Woman in Earnest." *Charleston Daily Mail,* "Princess Di Put British Fashion on Map . . ." Fallon and Conte, *Women's Wear Daily,* "Diana, Fashion Star." Givhan, *Washington Post,* "A Beautiful Sight to Behold." Honigsbaum, *The Spectator,* "Diana and

the Tabloids." Jones and Gooding, *The Star,* "The Secret Di." Jones, *Mirror,* "She Changed Face of Fashion." Levine, *Los Angeles Times,* "Princess Diana Adds Glamour to London's Spring Fashion Shows." Mower, *Sunday Telegraph,* "Goodbye to All."

BOOKS
Braudy, *The Frenzy of Renown.* Campbell, *Diana in Private.* Kelley, *The Royals.* Morton, *Diana: Her True Story.*

BROADCASTS
A&E *Biography:* "Diana, the True Story." Bashir, BBC *Panorama,* "The Interview: Princess Diana, Queen of Hearts." PBS *Frontline,* "The Princess and the Press."

Chapter 9

In this chapter, unless otherwise noted, all quotes attributed to the following are from the PBS Frontline *"The Princess and the Press": Sir Peregrine Worsthorne, Ken Lennox, Richard Stott, James Whitaker, Simon Jenkins, Lord Deedes, Lloyd Turner, Max Hastings, Lord McGregor, Andrew Knight, Glenn Harvey.*

ARTICLES
Duffy, *Time,* "Separate Lives." Green, *People,* "Prince of Wiles"; "A Princess in Peril"; "Diana Under Fire"; "Prince of Pique"; "Diss and Tell." Jones, *Princeton Alumni Weekly,* "Tea with Diana." Lacey, *Life,* "Alone Together: Charles and Diana." Lague, Denworth, and Terry, *People,* "Foul Play." *People,* "Di Launches a (Decolleté) Counteroffensive."

BOOKS
Campbell, *Diana in Private.* Kelley, *The Royals.* Morton, *Diana, Her True Story—In Her Own Words.*

BROADCASTS
A&E *Biography,* "Diana, the True Story." Bashir, BBC *Panorama,* "The Interview: Princess Diana, Queen of Hearts." PBS *Frontline,* "The Princess and the Press."

INTERVIEWS
Alan Entin.

Chapter 10

ARTICLES
Brooks, *The Observer,* "Hurt Princess Seeks to Win Back Nation's Hearts." Brown, Cusick, MacDonald, *The Independent,* "Bitter Princess Seals Her Fate." Coles and Culf, *The Guardian,* "A Parting Shot?" Denworth, *People,* "Last Tango in Buenos Aires." Elliott and Pedersen, *Newsweek,* "'I Won't Go Quietly.'" Green, *People,* "Price-Less Diana." Hardman, *Daily Telegraph,*

"Princess to Give up HRH Style, £15M Settlement Means Divorce Next Month." Hellen and Rayment, *Sunday Times,* "Diana's Prime Time Revenge." Honigsbaum, *The Spectator,* "Diana and the Tabloids." Horyn, *Vanity Fair,* "Diana Reborn." Hubbard, *People,* "At Her Service." Luscombe, *Time,* "Now on TV: Diana, Goddess of the Haunt." *People,* "Princess Diana, With a Stunning Confession to the BBC, She Opens a Bid to Become 'Queen of People's Hearts.'" Peter and Brown, *The Independent,* "Diana Accepts Charles' Divorce Terms." Pilkington, *The Guardian* "Princess of Wales Agrees to Divorce . . ." Rayment, *The Times,* "Diana, The Princess Who Would Be Kingmaker." *The Times,* "Drama and Divorce." Wynn Davies, *The Independent,* "£17M Divorce for Charles and Diana."

BOOKS
Braudy, *The Frenzy of Renown.* Davies, *Diana, the People's Princess.* Kelley, *The Royals.* Morton, *Diana: Her True Story.* Pasternak, *The Princess in Love.*

BROADCASTS
A&E *Biography,* "Diana, the True Story." Bashir, BBC *Panorama,* "The Interview: Princess Diana, Queen of Hearts." PBS *Frontline,* "The Princess and the Press."

INTERVIEWS
Leo Braudy. Richard Greene. Cathy Horyn. Barbara Hower. Landon Jones. Steven Levy. Martin Lewis. Michael Medved. Dick Morris. Cable Neuhaus. Anthony Robbins. Liz Smith. Richard Stolley.

Chapter 11

It is sad to report that the institutionalization of Margaret Trudeau Kemper (p. 204), according to several Canadian and U.S. news accounts, was occasioned by her growing obsession with William and Harry, the sons of Diana. Though Kemper had never met the children, she became convinced that she had some important connection to them.

ARTICLES
Baldacci, *Chicago Sun-Times,* "Di Reaches Out to City and We Embrace Her." Barbash, *Washington Post,* "Royal Spin." Beck, *Chicago Tribune,* "A Royal Flush: Princess Di's Visit Gave Chicago the Vapors, But Why All the Fuss?" Bohlin, *Boston Globe,* "Bidding on Princess Diana's Gown to Begin at $36,000." Brown, *The New Yorker,* "A Woman in Earnest." Bumiller, *The New York Times,* "Diana Cleans out Her Closet." Carpenter, *Chicago Sun-Times,* "Princess Bids Fond Farewell." Deedes, *Daily Telegraph,* "The Private and Public Princess." Elgood, *Chicago Tribune* (Reuters), "Princess Diana Issues Heartfelt Plea for Ban on World's Land Mines." Gibbs, *Time,* "The EQ Factor." Groer and Gerhart, *Washington Post,* "The Reliable Source." Hitchens, *Vanity Fair,* "Tarnished Crown." Horyn, *Vanity Fair,* "Diana

Reborn." Hubbard, *People,* "Howdy, Dodi!" Kappstatter, *Daily News,* "2 Stars Glow in BX, but Saint Outshines Princess." Kay, *Daily Mail,* "The Diana I Knew." Lamb, *Sunday Times,* "Minefield." Miller and Osnos, *Chicago Tribune,* "City's Ethnic Neighborhoods . . ." Neal, *Sunday Telegraph,* "Princess Diana Joins Forces with Clare Short." *People,* "Di Wows Chicago." Royko, *Chicago Tribune,* "Media Have Made Diana What She Is: Princess of Hype." Smith, *Vanity Fair,* "Dodi's Life in the Fast Lane." Worthington, *The Independent,* "Going, Going, Gone."

BOOKS
Erikson, *Identity and the Life Cycle.* Goleman, *Emotional Intelligence: Why It Can Matter More than IQ.* Morton, *Diana: Her True Story.* Pasternak, *The Princess in Love.* Peck, *The Road Less Traveled.* Spoto, *The Decline and Fall of the House of Windsor.*

BROADCASTS
Vester, NBC News, "Princess Diana's Dress Sold for $36,000 at June Auction . . ."

INTERVIEWS
Nancy Friday. Richard Greene. Christopher Hitchens. Cathy Horyn. Martin Lewis.

Chapter 12

ARTICLES
Bellon, Agence France Presse, "'You Won't Catch Me' Said Driver of Diana's Doomed Car." Castelnau, Agence France Presse, "Row on Diana's Treatment is 'Medical Culture Clash.'" Coleman, *USA Today,* "French Conclusion: No Di Conspiracy." Judd and Wilkins, *The Times,* "Princess 'Told Crash Driver to Go Faster.'" Lacayo, *Time,* "Who Shares the Blame?" Marmis, Associated Press, "Photographer Took Diana's Pulse and Found She Was Alive." Rosser, *Evening Standard,* "I Heard Diana Calling Out His Name, Claims the Body Guard." Sancton, *Time,* "The Dossier on Diana's Crash." Sawer, *Evening Standard,* "Delay at Crash Scene 'May Have Killed Diana.'" Smith, *Vanity Fair,* "Dodi's Life in the Fast Lane." Swardson and Trueheart, *Washington Post,* "Headlong Flight from the Paparazzi Ends in Carnage."

BOOKS
Morton, *Diana, Her True Story—In Her Own Words.* Sancton and MacLeod, *Death of a Princess.*

BROADCASTS
Jarrel, Downs, Walters, ABC *20/20,* "Are They to Blame? Paparazzi's Story of Princess Diana's Fatal Crash."

INTERVIEWS
Don Hewitt.

Chapter 13

ARTICLES

Agence France Presse, "Australia Mourns Diana as Media Questions Its Own Role." AP Worldstream, "13 Million Hits on Diana Website." Arnaud, *The Scotsman,* "Kings and Commoners Share Grief Worldwide." Churchill and Leathley, *The Times,* "Extra Trains for Travellers to Funeral." *Daily Record,* "£50,000 For Butler." della Cava, *USA Today,* "Demand for Anything Di Unaffected by Time." Dodd, *Mirror,* "The Whole Country Will Remember Her with the Deepest Affection and Love . . . That Is Why Our Grief Is So Great Today." Gilbert, World Broadcast News, "Diana's Funeral: The BBC Coverage for the World." Gray, *The New Yorker,* "Dept. of Second Thoughts: What Women Talk About When They Talk About Princess Diana." Hamilton and Lee, *The Times,* "Thousands Testify to Their Sorrow." Hitchens, *Vanity Fair,* "Princess Di, Mother T., and Me." Horyn, *Vanity Fair,* "Diana Reborn." Huff, *Daily News,* "U.S. Paid Its Respects by Tuning In To Funeral." Hundley, *Chicago Tribune,* "Hundreds of Curious Go to Crash Site, Express Anger." *Irish Times,* "Divided Community Unites in Grief for Princess." Jones, *The Age Online,* "Without Diana, the Magazine Industry Wonders Which Way to Turn." Kennedy, *Entertainment Weekly,* "Diana, 1961–1997." Lafayette, *Crain Communications Electronic Media,* "Di Tragedy Spikes TV Viewership." Leeman, AP Online, "Britain Argues Over Diana-abilia." Levy, *Newsweek,* "World Wide Wake." *Los Angeles Times,* "Ads Focus on Grief Over Diana's Death." Markon, Slackman, and Nundy, *Newsday,* "The Death of Princess Diana / A Tragic Ending / Charles Escorts Body Back to London After Paris Crash." McVeigh, Rougvie, Smith, *The Scotsman,* "Ordinary People Take Time to Pay Last Respects." Mirsky and Owen, *The Times,* "Grief for Diana is Without Borders." Montalbano, *Los Angeles Times,* "Ticket Run for Opening of Diana's Family Estate." Morton, *Newsweek,* "Her True Face"; *The Scotsman,* "Grieving For a Fairy Tale Princess We All Created." O'Mara, *The Sun,* "After a Sea of Onlookers, a Final Island of Privacy." http:/www.sunspot.net/diana. O'Shea, Stewart, and McVeigh, *The Scotsman,* "Country Faces Standstill for Farewell." Pierce, *The Times,* "Mourning Will Shut Harrods, the Store a Bomb Could Not Close." Prager, *The Prager Perspective,* "Princess Diana: Why So Much Grief?" Rosenberg, *Los Angeles Times,* "1961–1997: A 'Masterpiece Theatre' of Pomp and Puff." Sorkin, *The New York Times,* "Diana's Death Expands Web's New Role." Tendler, *The Times,* "Police Ready for a Million Mourners." *Tyndall Weekly,* "Di's Death Breaks Records." Walker, *The Arizona Republic,* "Did Paparazzi Chase Princess to Her Death?" Whitaker, *Mirror,* "Diana Would Have Hated People Paying to Be Close to Her." Wilkins, *The Times,* "Two Most Trusted Servants Remain at Their Post." Wingett and Rice, *Sunday Mirror,* "I'll Cry on Your Shoulder, You Cry on Mine . . . Diana's Heartbroken Butler and the

Troubled TV Funnyman." Woods, Associated Press, "Press Role in Princess Diana's Death Angers British."

BROADCASTS

PBS *Frontline,* "The Princess and the Press."

INTERVIEWS

Peter Bart. Mitchell Fink. Stuart Fischoff. James Hewitt. Clemm Lane. Kim Masters. Dan Okrent. Norman Pearlstine. Dennis Prager. Anthony Robbins. Howard Rosenberg. Liz Smith. Richard Stolley. Bernie Weinraub. Richard Zoglin.

Chapter 14

ARTICLES

Braxton and Hall, *Los Angeles Times,* "Critics See Double Standard in Planned Funeral Coverage; Television: Mother Teresa's Rites Will Draw Fewer Crews and Less Live Air Time Than Princess Diana's." Brown, *The Guardian,* "BBC Reviews Royal Coverage." Bury and Koppel, ABC *Nightline,* "Battle Lines Hunt for Truth in New Media Jungle." Byrne, *Sunday Telegraph,* "Diana, Princess of Wales: BBC Muffles Audience Complaints Over Coverage." Colford, *Newsday,* "Ink / Elegies For a Princess / Scope of Public Interest in Diana Stuns Publishers." Deveney, *Wall Street Journal,* "U.K. Sales Hit by Death of Princess." Dobnik, Associated Press, "International Media Shying Away From Diana Accident Photo." Dodd, *Mirror,* "The Whole Country Will Remember Her with the Deepest Affection and Love . . . That Is Why Our Grief is So Great Today." Greenfield, *Newsweek,* "The News Business: Have the Media Abandoned Serious Journalism for the Trivial or are We Looking in the Wrong Places?" Harris, *Entertainment Weekly,* "A Critical Look at the Most Viewed Event in History and the Story Behind Elton John's Moving Tribute." Hosenball and Dickey, *Newsweek,* "Case Very Nearly Closed." Kroker, from *Technology and the Canadian Mind:* "Digital Humanism: The Processed World of Marshall McLuhan." Kurtz, *Washington Post,* "Extra! Read All about It! Over-coverage Shocks Press!"; *Spin Cycle.* New York: Simon & Schuster, 1998. Kurtz and Koppel, ABC *Nightline,* "Digital Dirt—Fact, Fiction and Cyberspace." McMasters, The Freedom Forum Online, "The Princess and the Press: How Good Was the Coverage?" Moore, *USA Today,* "Technology Alters Journalists' Job." Pfaff, *Los Angeles Times,* "Diana Was Killed by the Attention She Craved." The Pew Research Center For The People and The Press, "Diana's Death Interested Everyone—Rare News Event." Tuttle and Rauscher, U.S. Newswire, "70 Front Pages Show How Newspapers Report Death of Princess Diana." Will, *Suddenly: The American Idea Abroad and At Home, 1986–1990,* New York: The Free Press; *The Woven Figure,* New York: Scribner, 1997.

INTERVIEWS
Philip Elmer-DeWitt.

Chapter 15

ARTICLES
AFX News, "French Magistrate Charges Photographer With Manslaughter."
Agence France Presse, "German Media Calls For Press Restraint After Diana's
Death"; "Paparazzi Charged over Diana Death Crash"; "Paparazzi Hunted
Diana Like American Indians." Alderson, *Sunday Times*, "Fayed Faces £8M
Diana Lawsuit." Boffey and Wastell, *Sunday Telegraph*, "Blair Warns Fayed:
You're Hurting the Princes." Bremner and Pierce, *The Times*, "Princess's Driver
Was Drunk." Coleman, *USA Today*, "French Conclusion: No Di Conspiracy."
Dahlburg, *Los Angeles Times*, "Investigators of Diana's Death Begin Examining
Fiats." Dunn, *Mirror*, "Trevor Hits Back at Lies: Trevor Rees-Jones Hits Out at
The Sun for Making Up a Story About Him." Elliott, *Newsweek*, "Diana's
Britain." Evans, *Daily Mail*, "Could Diana Have Lived?" Foege, *People*,
"Searching His Memory." Ford, *Dateline NBC*, "Death of a Princess: Authors
Thomas Sancton and Scott MacLeod with Surprising New Information About
the Night Princess Diana and Dodi Al Fayed Were Killed." Gould, *The Star*,
"What Really Happened Night Di Died." Herbert, *Daily Telegraph*, "Diana
Bodyguard Confirms 'Flashbacks.'" Hosenball and Dickey, *Newsweek*, "Case
Very Nearly Closed." Lacayo, *Time*, "Images '97." Lichfield, *The Independent*,
"Killed By Drunken Driving, Not Fame." Midgley, *The Times*, "Editors in
Talks to Curb the Paparazzi." Nordland, *Newsweek*, "Focusing On The Fiat."
Noveck, Associated Press, "Report: Diana's Driver Was Drunk." Nundy and
Wilson, *The Scotsman*, "Pursuit by the Paparazzi That Led to Tragedy." Nundy,
Luckhurst, and Wilson, *The Scotsman*, "The Lethal Cocktail." Perry, Agence
France Presse, "Blame for Diana's Death Shifts to Drunken Driver and
Ultimately Al-Fayed." Reuters, "Press Photographers Back Colleagues in Diana
Probe." Sancton, *Time*, "Just Follow That Car"; *Time*, "The Dossier on
Diana's Crash." Sawer, *Evening Standard*, "Delay At Crash Scene 'May Have
Killed Diana.'" Shaw, *Los Angeles Times*, "The Simpson Legacy; Obsession:
Did the Media Overfeed a Starving Public?; Chapter Three: Tabloid Tornado,
Mainstream Mania: 'The Godzilla of Tabloid Stories.'" Swardson and
Trueheart, *Washington Post*, "Headlong Flight From Paparazzi Ends in
Carnage." Tye, *Boston Globe*, "Doctors Had Little Hope of Success."

BOOKS
Robertson, *The Diana I Knew*. Sancton and MacLeod, *Death of a Princess*.
INTERVIEWS
Jonathan Alter. Warren Hoge.

Chapter 16

ARTICLES

Alter, *Newsweek*, "Dying for the Age of Diana"; "Diana's Real Legacy."
Andrews, *The Hollywood Reporter*, "Brits Get Post-Diana Code." Arieff,
Agence France Presse, "Britain's Press Barons Promise Post-Diana Reform."
Boshoff, *Daily Telegraph*, "New Radio and TV Code Puts Accent on Privacy."
Burgess, *Washington Post*, "British Judge Says Press Can Publish Name of
Home Secretary's Accused Son; Ruling in Drug Case Overturns Tradition and
Codes on Privacy." Chang and Beals, *Newsweek*, "Too High a Price for
Fame." *The Detroit News*, "Media: Many Celebrities Eager to Give Paparazzi
Taste of Own Medicine." Eastham, *Daily Mail*, "Blair Says No to New
Privacy Law." Fennell, *The Times*, "The Great Media Debate." Fiore, *Los
Angeles Times*, "Senator, Actors Focus on Bill to Curb Paparazzi." Fisher,
Toronto Sun, "The Hunt for Royal Gossip: Will Media Respect Privacy Pact or
Serve Britain's Unquenchable Thirst?" Friedman, *U.S. News & World Report*,
"A Bull Market in Dianas"; *Time*, "From Squidgy to Saint." *The Independent*,
"Paparazzi Ban? That'll Save Us Money, Sneers Rupert Murdoch." Robb and
Chetwynd, *The Hollywood Reporter*, "Diana Death Brings Flash of Paparazzi
Legislation." Robertson, *The New Yorker*, "Privacy Matters." Robson, AAP
Newsfeed, "UK: Paparazzi Set for Court Appearance." Skelton, *Los Angeles
Times*, "Maybe 'Paparazzi Politicians' Have a Point." Welkos, *Los Angeles
Times*, "Paparazzi Guilty in Schwarzenegger Case."

INTERVIEWS
Floyd Abrams. Leo Braudy. Landon Jones.

Chapter 17

ARTICLES

Anderiesz, *The Scotsman*, "Little Hope of Stemming Tide of Ashtrays and
Dolls." Binswanger, *Newsweek*, "After the Tragedy, a Compelling Desire for
Anything Diana." Collins, *Los Angeles Times*, "Selling News Like Hotcakes
(Click Here)." della Cava, *USA Today*, "Demand for Anything Di Unaffected
by Time." *The Economist* (U.S. edition), "Faustian Bargain." *The Globe*,
"Psychic Predicted Di's Death." Greenfield, *Newsweek*, "The Last Word: Life
Under the Lens." Greenslade, *The Guardian*, "Diana and the Media: The
Making of an Icon." Kurtz, *Washington Post*, "Extra! Read All about It!
Overcoverage Shocks Press!"; "In the Storm Of the CBS Eye: After the Diana
Debacle, the News Hasn't Gotten Any Better for Andy Heyward." Leeman,
AP Online, "Britain Argues Over Diana-abilia." *Los Angeles Times*, "Ads Focus
on Grief Over Diana's Death." Madore, *Newsday*, "The Merchandising of the
Princess." Morrow, *Time*, "A Nasty Faustian Bargain." Montalbano, *Los
Angeles Times*, "Ticket Run for Opening of Diana's Family Estate." Prager,
The Prager Perspective, "Princess Diana: Why So Much Grief?" Quinn,

Publishers Weekly, "Still No Letup in Flow of Princess Diana Books."
Quintanilla, *Los Angeles Times*, "The Stuff: Move Over, Barbie." Rosenblum,
Publishers Weekly, "Following Princess's Death, Diana Audios Hit the Stores
This Month." Sauer, *San Diego Union-Tribune*, "Diana Artifacts Flood
Market: Collectibles Worth More Sentiment than Money."

BOOKS
Boorstin, *The Image—Or What Happened to the American Dream*. Kelley, *The
Royals*. Lasch, *The Culture of Narcissism: American Life in an Age of
Diminishing Expectations*. Morton, *Diana: Her True Story*. Sancton and
MacLeod, *Death of a Princess*. Wolf, *The Beauty Myth: How Images of Beauty
Are Used Against Women*.

INTERVIEWS
Myrna Blyth. Nancy Friday. Barbara Hower. Landon Jones. Clemm Lane.

Chapter 18

ARTICLES
Elliott and Pedersen with Underhill and Hall, *Newsweek*, "I Won't Go
Quietly." Harris, *Entertainment Weekly*, "A Critical Look at the Most Viewed
Event in History and the Story Behind Elton John's Moving Tribute."
Hubbard, *People*, "At Her Service"; "Missing Mummy"; "Touched By Diana."
Krauthammer, *Time*, "The Great Di Turnaround." Lapham, *Harper's*,
"Notebook: Fatted Calf." Mungo and Burrell, *The Independent*, "Estate
Struggles to Maintain Diana's Image." *National Enquirer*, "Di and Dodi
Pledge Their Love from Beyond the Grave." Paglia, *The Guardian*, "A Gift
Diana Squandered." Reeves, *Los Angeles Times*, "'Our Lady of Perpetual
Celebrity'; Opinion: Richard Reeves." Shaw, *Los Angeles Times*, "Hunger for
Heroes, Villains Rooted in American Psyche." *Sunday Observer*, "Diana, a
Modern Parable" (editorial). Zachary, *Wall Street Journal*, "Junk History: It's
Bigger than Big; It's More . . ."

BOOKS
Morton, *Diana, Her True Story—In Her Own Words*.

INTERVIEWS
Jonathan Alter. Peter Bart. Mitchell Fink. Stuart Fischoff. Ellen Goodman.
Karen Jackovich. Dick Morris. Richard Sanders. Bernie Weinraub.

Chapter 19

ARTICLES
Bart, *Daily Variety*, "Fayed's Odd Odyssey: Would-be Player Dabbled in
H'wood Waters." *Daily Record*, "Di's Butler Backs Free Grave Visits; Princess
Diana's Butler Paul Burrell Is Backing the Campaign for Free Admission to
See Her Grave." *The Globe*, "Di's Boys Face to Face with Charles' Mistress."

Hoffmann, *New York Post*, "Harry and Will to be Will-Off: Princes Get $22M from Di." Hoge, *The New York Times*, "Diana's Two Sons Share the Bulk of Her $21.45 Million Estate." Huffington, *Los Angeles Times*, "*Living* With Sinners, Burying Saints."

BROADCASTS
Bashir, BBC *Panorama*, "The Interview: Princess Diana, Queen of Hearts."

INTERVIEWS
Kim Masters. Arianna Huffington.

Bibliography

"Ads Focus on Grief Over Diana's Death." *Los Angeles Times*, February 28, 1998: B5.

Alderson, Andrew. "Fayed Faces £8M Diana Lawsuit." *Sunday Times*, December 21, 1997.

Alter, Jonathan. "Dying for the Age of Diana." *Newsweek*, September 8, 1997: 39.

_____. "Diana's Real Legacy." *Newsweek*, September 15, 1997: 59–62.

"Amid the Threat of Bloodshed, The Pomp of a Royal Wedding." *U.S. News & World Report*, July 27, 1981: 22.

Anderiesz, Mike. "Little Hope of Stemming Tide of Ashtrays and Dolls." *The Scotsman*, February 16, 1998: 4.

Anderson, Lisa. "High Fashion Drops in at Di's Place." *Chicago Tribune*, March 20, 1988: Tempo, 1.

Andrews, Sam. "Brits Get Post-Diana Code." *The Hollywood Reporter*, December 22, 1997: 6.

Apple Jr., R. W. "Charles and Lady Diana Wed Today; Beacons Burn Across a Joyful Britain." *The New York Times,* July 29, 1981: A8.

Arieff, Irwin. "Britain's Press Barons Promise Post-Diana Reform." Agence France Presse, September 17, 1997.

Arnaud, Stan. "Kings and Commoners Share Grief Worldwide." *The Scotsman*, September 2, 1997: 11.

"Australia Mourns Diana As Media Questions Its Own Role." Agence France Presse, August 31, 1997.

Baldacci, Leslie. "Di Reached Out to City, and We Embraced Her." *Chicago Sun-Times*, June 9, 1996: 4.

Barbash, Fred. "Royal Spin: Princess Diana, Since Leaving the British Royal Family, Has Won a Following as a Benevolent Alternative Monarch." *Washington Post*, February 14, 1997: A23.

Bart, Peter. "Fayed's Odd Odyssey: Would-be Player Dabbled in H'wood Waters." *Daily Variety*, September 2, 1997: 1.

Bashir, Martin. "The Interview: Princess Diana, Queen of Hearts," BBC *Panorama*. November 20, 1995.

Beck, Joan. "A Royal Flush: Princess Di's Visit Gave Chicago the Vapors, But Why All the Fuss?" *Chicago Tribune*, June 6, 1996: 29.

Bellon, Remy. "'You Won't Catch Me' Said Driver of Diana's Doomed Car." *Agence France Presse*, September 2, 1997.

Binswanger, C. K. "After the Tragedy, a Compelling Desire for Anything Diana." *Newsweek*, September 15, 1997: 8.

Blitz, James and Andrew Jack. "Demands for Curbs on Intrusion Grow." *Financial Times*, September 1, 1997: 6.

Boffey, Chris and David Wastell. "Blair Warns Fayed: You're Hurting the Princes." *Sunday Telegraph*, February 15, 1998: 1.

Bohlin, Virginia. "Bidding on Princess Diana's Gown to Begin at $36,000." *Boston Globe*, September 28, 1997: G29.

Boorstin, Daniel J. *The Image—Or What Happened to the American Dream.* Kingsport, TN: Kingsport Press, Inc., 1961.

Boshoff, Alison. "New Radio and TV Code Puts Accent on Privacy." *Daily Telegraph*, November 25, 1997: 9.

Braudy, Leo. *The Frenzy of Renown: Fame and Its History.* New York: Vintage Books, 1997.

Braxton, Greg and Jane Hall. "Critics See Double Standard in Planned Funeral Coverage; Television: Mother Teresa's Rites Will Draw Fewer Crews and Less Live Air Time Than Princess Diana's." *Los Angeles Times*, September 12, 1997: F2.

Bremner, Charles and Andrew Pierce. "Princess's Driver Was Drunk." *The Times,* September 2, 1997: 1.

"British Royals Expand Internet Site." AP Online, October 16, 1997.

Brook, Danae. "I Lost My Husband, My Children, My Home and My Business. . . . But Now I'm Back; I Won't Be Beaten Again; Royal Wedding Designer Elizabeth Emanuel's Defiant Return." *Mail on Sunday*, January 12, 1997: 52–53.

Brooks, Richard. "Hurt Princess Seeks to Win Back Nation's Hearts." *The Observer*, November 19, 1995: 1.

Brown, Colin, James Cusick and Marianne MacDonald. "Bitter Princess Seals Her Fate; MPs Rule out Chance of Diana Being Queen after Admitting Marriage Is Over." *The Independent*, November 21, 1995: 1.

Brown, Maggie. "BBC Reviews Royal Coverage." *The Guardian*, September 22, 1997: 10.

Brown, Tina. "A Woman in Earnest." *The New Yorker*, September 15, 1997: 58–61.

Buckley Jr., William F. "Enough Outrage to Strengthen Privacy Law?" *Houston Chronicle*, September 11, 1997: A32.

____. "On The Right: Princess Di, R.I.P." *National Review*, September 29, 1997: 66.

____. "Princess Di, R.I.P." *Opinion On The Right*, September 2, 1997.

Bumiller, Elisabeth. "Diana Cleans Out Her Closet, and Charities Just Clean Up." *The New York Times*, June 26, 1997: A1.

Burgess, John. "British Judge Says Press Can Publish Name of Home Secretary's Accused Son; Ruling in Drug Case Overturns Tradition and Codes on Privacy." *Washington Post*, January 5, 1998: A15.

"Burial, The." *The Austin-American Statesman*, http:/www.austin360.com.

Bury, Chris and Ted Koppel. "Battle Lines—Hunt for Truth in New Media Jungle." ABC *Nightline*, March 5, 1998.

Byrne, Ciaran. "Diana, Princess of Wales: BBC Muffles Audience Complaints Over Coverage." *Sunday Telegraph*, September 14, 1997: 9.

Campbell, Lady Colin. *Diana In Private: The Princess Nobody Knows.* New York: St. Martin's Press, 1992.

____. *The Royal Marriages,* New York: St. Martin's Press, 1993

Carlson, Margaret. "Blood on Their Hands?" *Time*, September 8, 1997: 46.

Carpenter, John. "Princess Bids Fond Farewell: Visit Raises $1.4 Million for Charity." *Chicago Sun-Times.* June 7, 1996: 8.

Castelnau, Brigitte. "Row on Diana's Treatment Is 'Medical Culture Clash'." Agence France Presse, February 12, 1998.

Castro, Janice. "The Vows Heard Round the World." *Time*, August 10, 1981: 66.

Chang, Suna. "The Royal Line." *Entertainment Weekly*, November 21, 1997: 37–38.

Chang, Suna, Anna Holmes, and Degen Pener. "Diana: Let Us Count the Ways." *Entertainment Weekly*, December 26, 1997: 100.

Chang, Yahlin and Gregory Beals. "Too High a Price for Fame." *Newsweek*, September 15, 1997: 16.

Churchill, David and Arthur Leathley. "Extra Trains for Travellers to Funeral." *The Times*, September 2, 1997: 2.

Cocks, Jay. "Magic in the Daylight; Prince Charles Weds His Lady Diana in The Century's Royal Match." *Time*, August 3, 1981: 20.

Coleman, Fred. "French Conclusion: No Di Conspiracy." *USA Today*, March 3, 1998: D2.

Coles, Joanna and Andrew Culf. "A Parting Shot?" *The Guardian*, November 15, 1995: T2.

Colford, Paul D. "Ink / Elegies For a Princess / Scope of Public Interest in Diana Stuns Publishers." *Newsday*, September 18, 1997: B2.

Collins, Gail. *Scorpion Tongues.* New York: William Morrow, 1988.

Collins, James. "Talking Trash." *Time*, March 30, 1998: 63–66.

Collins, Ronald K. L. "Selling News Like Hotcakes (Click Here)." *Los Angeles Times*, December 11, 1997: B9.

"Costner's Princess?" *Los Angeles Times*, November 19, 1997: F2.

"Crown to Diana's Staff: Out." *People*, November 9, 1997: http:/www.pathfinder.com/people/daily.

Dahlburg, John-Thor. "Investigators of Diana's Death Begin Examining Fiats." *Los Angeles Times*, November 8, 1997: A3.

Davies, Nicholas. *Diana: The People's Princess*. Secaucus, NJ: Carol Publishing Group, 1997.

Deedes, W. F. "The Private and Public Princess." *Daily Telegraph*, December 27, 1997: 22.

della Cava, Marco R. "Demand for Anything Di Unaffected by Time." *USA Today*, March 3, 1998: D1.

Denworth, Lydia, Laura Healy Sanderson, and Rachel Raney. "Last Tango in Buenos Aires? As Di Returns from Argentina, The Queen May Be Wishing She'd Stayed There." *People*, December 11, 1995: 153.

DeRosa, Robin. "Diana Dollars." *USA Today*, September 10, 1997: D1.

Deveney, Paul J. "U.K. Sales Hit by Death of Princess." *Wall Street Journal*, October 23, 1997: A13.

"Diana, a Modern Parable" (editorial). *Sunday Observer*, September 7, 1997.

"Diana and Divorce." *The Times*, February 29, 1996.

"Diana and Dodi: Decline and Fall of House of Windsor." *Dateline NBC*, November 17, 1997.

"Di and Dodi Pledge Their Love from Beyond the Grave." *National Enquirer*, January 6, 1998: 40.

"Di and Dodi's First Kiss as Created for TV Movie." *The Star*, March 17, 1998: 31.

"'Diana Effect' Hurts Spending in Britain." *USA Today*, October 23, 1997: 2D.

"Diana, The True Story." A&E *Biography*.

"Diana's Death Interested Everyone—Rare News Event." The Pew Research Center For The People and The Press, September 12, 1997.

"Diana's Family Said to Plan to Sue Fayed." *Los Angeles Times*, December 21, 1997: A18.

Dickinson, Emily. *The Complete Poems of Emily Dickinson*, edited by Thomas H. Johnson. Boston, MA: Back Bay Books, 1996.

"Di Launches a (Decolleté) Counter Offensive." *People*, July 18, 1984: 31.

"Di's Boys Face to Face with Charles' Mistress." *The Globe*, December 30, 1997: 9.

"Di's Butler Backs Free Grave Visits; Princess Diana's Butler Paul Burrell Is Backing the Campaign for Free Admission to See Her Grave." *Daily Record*, January 12, 1998: 7.

"Di's Death Breaks Records." *Tyndall Weekly*, September 1–5, 1997.

"Di's Secret Obsession With Kevin Costner." *The Star*, December 2, 1997.

"Divided Community Unites in Grief for Princess." *Irish Times*, September 2, 1997: 11.

"Di Wows Chicago." *People*, June 17, 1996.

Dobnik, Verena. "International Media Shying Away From Diana Accident Photo." Associated Press, August 31, 1997.

Dodd, Sheree. "The Whole Country Will Remember Her with the Deepest Affection and Love . . . That Is Why Our Grief Is So Great Today." *Mirror*, September 1, 1997: 8–9.

Dowdnay, Mark. "Di's Brother Loses Fight for Privacy Law." *Daily Record*, January 17, 1998: 4.

Downie Jr., Leonard. "Wedding to Be Royal Revel." *Washington Post*, July 26, 1981: A1.

Duffy, Martha. "Here Comes Wills." *Time*, July 22, 1996: 44–50.

____. "Separate Lives." *Time*, November 30, 1992: 52–58.

Dunn, Justin. "Trevor Hits Back at Lies: Trevor Rees-Jones Hits Out at *The Sun* for Making up a Story about Him." *Mirror*, March 3, 1998: 2.

Eastham, Paul. "Blair Says No to New Privacy Law." *Daily Mail*, February 6, 1998: 13.

Elgood, Giles. "Princess Diana Issues Heartfelt Plea for Ban on World's Land Mines." *Chicago Tribune*, February 10, 1997: 2.

Elliott, Michael. "Diana's Britain." *Newsweek*, September 15, 1997: 37.

Elliott, Michael and Daniel Pedersen with William Underhill and Carol Hall. "I Won't Go Quietly." *Newsweek*, December 4, 1995: 63.

Erikson, Erik H. *Identity and the Life Cycle*. New York: W. W. Norton & Company, 1980.

Evans, Christopher. "Could Diana Have Lived?" *Daily Mail*, February 9, 1998: 1–4.

Fallon, James and Samantha Conti, *Women's Wear Daily*. "Diana, Fashion Star." No. 44, Vol. 174: September 2, 1997: 1.

Fallows, James. "Are Journalists People?" *U.S. News & World Report*, September 15, 1997: 31–34.

"Faustian Bargain, The." *The Economist* (U.S. edition), September 6, 1997: 21.

Fedkamp, Phyllis. "London Fashion: A Season for Courtly Romance; Designing Lady Diana's Dress." *The Christian Science Monitor*, May 21, 1981: 17.

Fennell, Edward. "The Great Media Debate." *The Times*, October 14, 1997.

"£50,000 For Butler." *Daily Record*, December 22, 1997: 9.

Fiore, Faye. "Senator, Actors Focus on Bill to Curb Paparazzi." *Los Angeles Times*, February 16, 1998: A1–23.

Fisher, Matthew. "The Hunt for Royal Gossip: Will Media Respect Privacy Pact or Serve Britain's Unquenchable Thirst?" *Toronto Sun*, January 4, 1998: 7.

Foege, Alec. "Searching His Memory." *People*, November 3, 1997: 75–78.

Folkers, Richard. "When Our Worlds Collide." *U.S. News & World Report*, September 15, 1997: 40.

Ford, Jack. "Death of a Princess: Authors Tom Sancton and Scott MacLeod With Surprising New Information About the Night Princess Diana and Dodi Al Fayed Were Killed." *Dateline NBC*, February 9, 1998.

"French Magistrate Charges Photographer With Manslaughter." AFX News, September 2, 1997.

Friday, Nancy. *The Power of Beauty*. New York: HarperCollins Publishers, 1996.

Friedman, Dorian. "A Bull Market in Dianas." *U.S. News & World Report*, January 12, 1998: 8.

____. "From Squidgy to Saint." *Time*, March 23, 1998: 93.

Gaines, James R. "The Way She Was." *People*, September 22, 1997: 97–98.

Gardiner, Samuel. *A Student's History of England.* New York: Longmans Green & Co., 1891

"German Media Calls For Press Restraint After Diana Death." Agence France Presse, August 31, 1997.

Gibbs, Nancy. "The EQ Factor: New Brain Research Suggests That Emotions, Not IQ, May Be the True Measure of Human Intelligence." *Time*, October 2, 1995: 60.

Gilbert, Philip. "Diana's Funeral: The BBC Coverage for the World." *World Broadcast News*, November 1997.

Givhan, Robin. "A Beautiful Sight To Behold: Diana Loved Fashion, Promoted It and Understood Its Power." *Washington Post*, September 2, 1997: C1.

Glancey, Jonathan. "The Age of Diana: Three Steps to Immortality." *The Guardian*, September 2, 1997: 4–5.

Gleick, Elizabeth. "The Men Who Would Be King." *Time* (Commemorative Issue), September 15, 1997: 44–48.

Goleman, Daniel. *Emotional Intelligence.* New York: Bantam Books, 1995.

Gould, Martin. "What Really Happened Night Di Died." *The Star*, November 25, 1997: 24–25.

Gray, Francine du Plessix. "Dept. of Second Thoughts: What Women Talk About When They Talk About Princess Diana." *The New Yorker*, September 15, 1997: 30–31.

Gray, Paul. "Princess Diana, 1961–1997." *Time* (Commemorative Issue), September 15, 1997: 36–40.

Green, Michelle. "A Princess in Peril." *People*, September 5, 1994: 77–70.

____. "Diana Under Fire." *People*, September 14, 1992: 106–116.

____. "Diss and Tell." *People*, October 17, 1994: 38–45.

____. "Prince of Pique." *People*, October 31, 1994: 46–56.

____. "Prince of Wiles." *People*, July 18, 1994: 28–33.

____. "Prince-less Diana." *People*, March 11, 1996: 76–82.

____. "Separate Lives." *People*, December 21, 1992: 38–43.

____. "True Confessions." *People*, December 4, 1995: 92–98.

Greenfield, Meg. "The Last Word: Life Under the Lens." *Newsweek*, September 22, 1997: 94.

____. "The News Business: Have the Media Abandoned Serious Journalism for the Trivial, or Are We Looking in the Wrong Places for Stories?" *Newsweek*, November 3, 1997: 92.

Greenslade, Roy. "Diana and the Media: The Making of an Icon." *The Guardian*, September 8, 1997: 4.

Groer, Annie and Ann Gerhart. "The Reliable Source." *Washington Post*, June 26, 1997: 1.

Haley, Larry. "Royal Family Searching for Dodi and Di Sex Tapes." *National Enquirer*, January 27, 1998: 28.

Hall, Unity and Ingrid Seward. *Royalty Revealed*. New York: St. Martin's, 1989.

Hallett, E. Bruce. "To Our Readers." *Time* (Commemorative Issue), September 15, 1997: 4.

Hamilton, Alan and Adrian Lee. "Thousands Testify to Their Sorrow." *The Times*, September 2, 1997: 3.

Handy, Bruce. "It's All About Timing." *Time*, January 12, 1998: 77–83.

Hardman, Robert. "Princess to Give Up HRH Style; £15M Settlement Means Divorce Next Month; Couple Agrees to Confidentiality Clause; The Queen Will Regard Her as Member of the Royal Family." *Daily Telegraph*, July 14, 1996: 18.

Harris, Mark. "A Critical Look at the Most Viewed Event in History and the Story Behind Elton John's Moving Tribute." *Entertainment Weekly*, September 19, 1997: 24–28.

Hebert, Emily. "Technology, Consolidation Top Media Issues; Media Experts Discuss Trends." *Indianapolis Business Journal*, February 9, 1998: 35.

Hellen, Nicholas and Tim Rayment. "Diana's Prime Time Revenge." *Sunday Times*, November 19, 1995.

Henderson, Mark and John Goodbody. "Silent Saturday for Mourning." *The Times*, September 2, 1997: 1–2.

Herbert, Susannah. "Diana Bodyguard Confirms 'Flashbacks.'" *Daily Telegraph*, March 7, 1998: 2.

Hitchens, Christopher. "Princess Di, Mother T., and Me." *Vanity Fair*, December 1997: 114–123.

____. "Tarnished Crown." *Vanity Fair*, September 1997: 120–131.

Hoffmann, Bill. "Harry and Will to Be Will-Off: Princes Get $22M from Di." *New York Post*, March 3, 1998: 2.

Hoge, Warren. "Diana's Two Sons Share the Bulk of Her $21.45 Million Estate." *The New York Times*, March 3, 1998: A5.

Honigsbaum, Mark. "Diana and the Tabloids: The Real Story." *The Spectator*, September 27, 1997: 9–11.

Horyn, Cathy. "Diana Reborn." *Vanity Fair*, July 1997: 70–79, 137–138.

Hosenball, Mark and Christopher Dickey. "Case Very Nearly Closed." *Newsweek*, December 22, 1997: 65.

"How Not to Control Paparazzi." *Los Angeles Times,* February 19, 1998: B8.

Hubbard, Kim. "At Her Service." *People*, November 10, 1997: 71–72.

____. "Howdy, Dodi!" *People*, August 25, 1997: 48–55.

____. "Missing Mummy." *People*, December 1, 1997: 134–140.

____. "Touched By Diana." *People*, February 2, 1998: 82–91.

Huff, Richard. "U.S. Paid Its Respects By Tuning In To Funeral." *Daily News*, September 8, 1997: 23.

Huffington, Arianna. "Living With Sinners, Burying Saints." *Los Angeles Times*, April 10, 1996: B9.

Hundley, Tom. "Hundreds of Curious Go to Crash Site, Express Anger." *Chicago Tribune*, September 1, 1997: 14.

Hyde, Nina. "The Royal Wedding; The Glorious Garb: Tulle, Taffeta & Train." *Washington Post*, July 30, 1981: C1.

James, Clive. "Requiem." *The New Yorker*, September 15, 1997: 51–57.

Jarriel, Tom, Hugh Downs and Barbara Walters. "Are They to Blame? Paparazzi's Story of Princess Diana's Fatal Crash." ABC *20/20*, November 21, 1997.

Jewel, Dan and Simon Perry. "Designing Di's Memorial." *People*, January 26, 1998: 125.

Jewel, Dan, Simon Perry, and Nina Biddle. "Carrying On." *People*, January 12, 1998: 56–61.

Johnson, Marilyn. "Picture Perfect: Her Favorite Photographers, Her Favorite Photos" and "The Princess Bride." *Life*, November 1997: 42–64.

Jones, Barbara and Richard Gooding. "The Secret Di: Her Closest Friends Reveal the Real Woman Behind the Legend." *The Star*, November 4, 1997: 25.

Jones, Landon. "Tea With Diana." *Princeton Alumni Weekly*, October 8, 1997: 71–72.

Jones, Megan. "Without Diana, the Magazine Industry Wonders Which Way to Turn." *The Age Online*, September 20, 1997.

Judd, Terri and Emma Wilkins. "Princess 'Told Crash Driver To Go Faster.'" *The Times*, March 2, 1998.

Kantrowitz, Barbara. "Pictures of 1997: Princess of the World." *Newsweek*, December 22, 1997: 60–65.

Kappstatter, Bob with Jere Hester. "2 Stars Glow in BX, but Saint Outshines Princess." *Daily News*, June 19, 1997: 7.

Kay, Richard. "The Diana I Knew." *Daily Mail*, September 1, 1997: 4–5.

Kearney, Richard. "People's President." *Irish Times*, September 13, 1997: 60.

Kelley, Kitty. *The Royals*. New York: Warner Books, 1997.

Kennedy, Dana. "Diana, 1961–1997." *Entertainment Weekly*, September 12, 1997: 12–14.

Key, Wilson Bryan. *The Age of Manipulation: The Con in Confidence, The Sin in Sincere*, Lanham, MD: Madison Books, 1993.

King, Larry. *Future Talk*. New York: HarperCollins, 1988.

Kinsley, Michael. "In Defense of Matt Drudge." *Time*, February 2, 1998: 41.

Kneeland, Carole. "Model of Excellence." Edited by Valerie Hyman. *Poynter Report*, Winter 1998: 6–9.

Krauthammer, Charles. "The Great Di Turnaround." *Time*, September 22, 1997: 104.

Kroker, Arthur. "Digital Humanism: The Processed World of Marshall McLuhan," excerpted from *Technology and the Canadian Mind*.

Kurtz, Howard. "Extra! Read All about It! Overcoverage Shocks Press!" *Washington Post*, September 5, 1997: D1.

_____. "In the Storm Of the CBS Eye: After the Diana Debacle, the News Hasn't Gotten Any Better for Andy Heyward." *Washington Post*, October 15, 1997: D1.

_____. *Spin Cycle*, New York: The Free Press, 1998.

Kurtz, Howard and Ted Koppel. "Digital Dirt—Fact, Fiction and Cyberspace." ABC *Nightline*, January 8, 1998.

Lacayo, Richard. "Images '97." *Time*, December 22, 1997: 41–43.

_____. "Who Shares The Blame?" *Time* (Commemorative Issue), September 15, 1997: 52–55.

Lacey, Robert. "Alone Together: Charles and Diana." *Life*, August 1992: 26–32.

Lafayette, Jon. "Di Tragedy Spikes TV Viewership." *Crain Communications Electronic Media*, September 8, 1997: 1.

La Ferla, Ruth. "Looking for Diana: Who Will Be Our Next Fashion Icon?" *Mirabella*, March 4, 1998: 77.

Lague, Louise. "Foul Play; When Di Flirts with a Rugby Star, His Angry Wife Dresses Her Down." *People*, August 28, 1995: 55.

_____. "Going It Alone." *People*, November 30, 1992: 47–42.

_____. "If This Dress Could Talk; From Atelier to Auction Block, This Gown Has Led a Charmed Life." *In Style*, June 1997: 190.

Lamb, Christina. "Minefield." *Sunday Times*, January 19, 1997.

Landler, Mark. "From Gurus to Sitting Ducks." *The New York Times*, January 11, 1998: 1.

Langway, Lynn. "A Fairy Tale Come True." *Newsweek*, August 10, 1981: 40.

Lapham, Lewis H. "Notebook: Fatted Calf." *Harper's*, November 1997: 11.

Lasch, Christopher. *The Culture of Narcissism: American Life in An Age of Diminishing Expectations*. New York: W. W. Norton & Co., 1978.

Leapmam, Michael. "Private Passions and the Public Interest." *The Independent*, February 8, 1998: 19.

Lederer, Edith M. "British Ask: Has Diana's Death Softened Stiff Upper Lip?" *Sunday Gazette Mail*, January 4, 1998: P2A.

Leeman, Sue. "Britain Argues Over Diana-abilia." AP Online, February 19, 1998.

Levine, Bettijean, "Princess Diana Adds Glamour to London's Spring Fashion Shows." *Los Angeles Times*, October 13, 1986: Part 5, 1.

Levy, Steven. "World Wide Wake." *Newsweek*, September 15, 1997: 6.

Lichfield, John. "Killed By Drunken Driving, Not Fame." *The Independent*, September 2, 1997: 1.

Luscombe, Belinda. "Now on TV: Diana, Goddess of the Haunt." *Time*, December 4, 1995: 91.

Madore, James. "The Merchandising of the Princess." *Newsday*, September 10, 1997: A50.

Markon, Jerry, Michael Slackman, and Julian Nundy. "The Death of Princess Diana / A Tragic Ending / Charles Escorts Body Back to London After Paris Crash." *Newsday*, September 1, 1997: A3.

Marmie, Nicholas. "Photographer Took Diana's Pulse and Found She Was Alive." Associated Press, September 2, 1997.

McGrath, Peter. "Exposing the Magic." *Newsweek*, September 8, 1997: 50.

McLuhan, Marshall. *The Medium is the Massage.* San Francisco: HardWired, 1967.

McMasters, Paul. "The Princess and the Press: How Good Was the Coverage?" The Freedom Forum Online, December 15, 1997.

McVeigh, John Ross, James Rougvie, and John Smith. "Ordinary People Take Time to Pay Last Respects." *The Scotsman*, September 2, 1997: 4.

"Media: Many Celebrities Eager to Give Paparazzi Taste of Own Medicine." *The Detroit News*, September 5, 1997: A7.

Midgley, Carol. "Editors in Talks to Curb the Paparazzi." *The Times*, September 2, 1997: 13.

Miller, Sabrina L. and Evan Osnos. "City's Ethnic Neighborhoods Take the Princess' Visit in Stride." *Chicago Tribune*, June 6, 1996: 8.

Mirsky, Jonathan and Glen Owen. "Grief for Diana is Without Borders." *The Times*, September 2, 1997: 8.

Montalbano, William D. "Ticket Run for Opening of Diana's Family Estate." *Los Angeles Times*, January 6, 1998: A6.

Moore, Martha T. "Technology Alters Journalists' Job." *USA Today*, February 11, 1998: A1.

Morrow, Lance. "A Nasty Faustian Bargain." *Time*, September 15, 1997: 76–77.

_____. "Journalism After Diana." *Columbia Journalism Review*, November/December 1997: 38.

Morton, Andrew. *Diana, Her True Story—In Her Own Words.* New York: Simon & Schuster, 1997.

_____. "Her True Face." *Newsweek*, September 15, 1997: 64–65.

_____. *Royalty Watching: Where to Find Britain's Royal Family.* New York: Fodor's Travel Publications, 1987.

Morton, Tom. "Grieving For a Fairy Tale Princess We All Created." *The Scotsman*, September 2, 1997: 4.

Mower, Sarah. "Goodbye to All." *Sunday Telegraph*, May 18, 1997: 18.

Mungo, Paul and Ian Burrell. "Estate Struggles to Maintain Diana's Image." *The Independent*, October 5, 1997: 11.

Nachman, Jerry. "The Diana Effect: Will Anything Change?" *Columbia Journalism Review*, November/December 1997: 40.

Neale, Greg. "Princess Diana Joins Forces with Clare Short." *Sunday Telegraph*, May 18, 1997: 1.

Nordland, Rod. "Focusing On The Fiat." *Newsweek*, November 3, 1997: 6.

_____. "The Diana File." *Newsweek*, October 20, 1997: 34–38.

Noveck, Jocelyn. "Report: Diana's Driver Was Drunk." Associated Press, September 1, 1997.

Nundy, Julian and Sarah Wilson. "Pursuit by the Paparazzi That Led to Tragedy." *The Scotsman*, September 1, 1997: 3.

Nundy, Julian, Tim Luckhurst and Sarah Wilson. "The Lethal Cocktail." *The Scotsman*, September 2, 1997: 1.

O'Mara, Richard. "After a Sea of Onlookers, a Final Island of Privacy." *The Sun*, September 7, 1997: http:/www.sunspot.net/diana.

Orsatti, Ken. Untitled press release regarding Princess Diana's death. Screen Actors Guild, September 2, 1997.

O'Shea, Suzanne, Graeme Stewart, and Karen McVeigh. "Country Faces Standstill for Farewell." *The Scotsman*, September 2, 1997: 1.

Paglia, Camille. "A Gift Diana Squandered." *The Guardian*, September 4, 1997: 17.

"Paparazzi Ban? That'll Save Us Money, Sneers Rupert Murdoch." *The Independent*, October 8, 1997: 1.

"Paparazzi Charged over Diana Death Crash." Agence France Presse, September 2, 1997.

"Paparazzi Hunted Diana Like American Indians." Agence France Presse, September 1, 1997.

Pasternak, Anna. *Princess in Love*. New York: Dutton, 1994

Peck, M. Scott. *The Road Less Traveled: A New Psychology of Love, Traditional Values and Spiritual Growth*. New York: Simon & Schuster, 1978.

People, June 13, 1994: cover.

People, December 6, 1993: cover.

People, August 3, 1992: cover.

"People in the News." Associated Press, April 9, 1987.

Perry, Alex. "Blame for Diana's Death Shifts to Drunken Driver and Ultimately Al-Fayed." Agence France Presse, September 1, 1997.

Pfaff, William. "Diana Was Killed by the Attention She Craved." *Los Angeles Times*, September 3, 1997: B7.

Picton Jones, Ollie. "She Changed Face of Fashion." *Mirror*, September 2, 1997: 26–27.

Pierce, Andrew. "Mourning Will Shut Harrods, the Store a Bomb Could Not Close." *The Times*, September 2, 1997: 2.

Pimlott, Ben. *Elizabeth II, The Queen* (excerpt). New York: HarperCollins, 1996. http://www.pbs.org/wgbh/pages/frontline/shows/royals/readings/

Pilkington, Edward. "Princess of Wales Agrees to Divorce as Wrangles Run On." *The Guardian*, February 29, 1996: 1.

Prager, Dennis. "Princess Diana: Why So Much Grief?" *The Prager Perspective*, September 1, 1997: 1–4.

_____. *Think a Second Time*. New York: Regan Books, 1995.

"Presidential Adviser Sues America Online." *The New York Times*, August 28, 1997: D6.

"Press Photographers Back Colleagues in Diana Probe." Reuters, September 23, 1997.

"Prince's Peace." *The Economist*, August 1, 1981: 11.

"The Princess and the Press." PBS *Frontline* Documentary, November 16, 1997.

"Princess Diana Gown Installed at the Franklin Mint Museum on Valentine's Day." *Business Wire*, February 11, 1998.

"Princess Diana 101." *Newsweek*, November 10, 1997: 8.

"Princess Diana's Estate Worth $35M." AP Online, March 2, 1998.

"Princess Diana: With a Stunning Confession to the BBC, She Opens a Bid to Become 'Queen of People's Hearts.'" *People*, December 25, 1995: 50.

"Princess Di Put British Fashion on the Map. Designers Hope Business Stays Brisk." *Charleston Daily Mail*, November 4, 1997: D5.

"Protecting Di Image." *The Hollywood Reporter*, January 23–25, 1998: 6.

"Psychic Predicted Di's Death." *The Globe*, January 6, 1998.

"Queen Elizabeth's Christmas Message Recalls Diana's Death." *Los Angeles Times*, December 26, 1997: A18.

Quinn, Judy. "Still No Letup in Flow of Princess Diana Books." *Publishers Weekly*, No. 46, Volume 244, November 10, 1997: 16.

Quintanilla, Michael. "The Stuff: Move Over, Barbie." *Los Angeles Times*, December 21, 1997: E1.

Ratnesar, Romesh. "Outside Looking In." *Time*, September 15, 1997: 60–62.

Rayment, Tim. "Diana, The Princess Who Would Be Kingmaker." *Sunday Times,* November 26, 1995.

Reeves, Richard. "'Our Lady of Perpetual Celebrity'; Opinion: Richard Reeves," *Los Angeles Times,* September 5, 1997.

Robb, David and Josh Chetwynd. "Diana Death Brings Flash of Paparazzi Legislation." *The Hollywood Reporter*, September 3, 1997: 1–35.

Robertson, Geoffrey. "Privacy Matters." *The New Yorker*, September 15, 1997: 38–40.

Robertson, Mary. *The Diana I Knew.* New York: HarperCollins, 1998.

Robson, Louise. "UK: Paparazzi Set for Court Appearance." AAP Newsfeed, September 2, 1997.

Rosenberg, Howard. "1961–1997: A 'Masterpiece Theatre of Pomp and Puff." *Los Angeles Times*, September 7, 1997: A22.

_____. "What If Murrow Could Comment?" *Los Angeles Times*, February 2, 1998: F1.

Rosenblum, Trudi M. "Following Princess's Death, Diana Audios Hit the Stores This Month." *Publishers Weekly*, October 6, 1997: 34.

Rosser, Nigel. "I Heard Diana Calling Out His Name, Claims Bodyguard." *Evening Standard*, March 2, 1998: 5.

Royko, Mike. "Media Have Made Diana What She Is: Princess of Hype." *Chicago Tribune*, June 6, 1996: 3.

Sancton, Thomas. "Just Follow That Car." *Time*, January 19, 1998: 40.

_____. "The Dossier On Diana's Crash." *Time*, October 13, 1997: 50–56.

Sancton, Thomas and Scott MacLeod. *Death Of A Princess*. New York: St. Martin's Press, 1998.

Sanz, Cynthia. "Some Kind of Magic." *People*, June 17, 1996: 42–47.

Sauer, Mark. "Diana Artifacts Flood Market: Collectibles Worth More Sentiment than Money." *San Diego Union-Tribune*, October 9, 1997: E1.

Sawer, Patrick. "Delay At Crash Scene 'May Have Killed Diana.'" *Evening Standard*, February 9, 1998: 4.

"Scenes From a Marriage: The Story of a Love That Didn't Last." *Life*, February 1993: 28–39.

Schama, Simon. "The Problem Princess." *The New Yorker*, September 15, 1997: 62–65.

"75 Years of Miscellany." *Time*, March 9,1998: 177.

Seward, Ingrid. *Diana: An Intimate Portrait*. Chicago: Contemporary Books, 1988.

Shales, Tom. "The Royal Wedding; The TV Coverage: How Lovely It Was; Lovely, Lovely, Lovely." *Washington Post*, July 30, 1981: C1.

Sharkey, Jacqueline. "The Diana Aftermath." *The American Journalism Review*, November 1997: 18–25.

Shaw, David. "Hunger for Heroes, Villains Rooted in American Psyche." *Los Angeles Times*, February 17, 1998: A1.

_____. "The Simpson Legacy: Obsession: Did the Media Overfeed a Starving Public?; Chapter Three: Tabloid Tornado, Mainstream Mania: 'The Godzilla of Tabloid Stories.'" *Los Angeles Times*, October 9, 1995: S4.

Shrimsley, Robert. "Wakeham Hopes His Press Code Will Head Off Privacy Law." *Daily Telegraph*, December 9, 1997: 12.

Skelton, George. "Maybe 'Paparazzi Politicians' Have a Point." *Los Angeles Times*, September 4, 1997: A3.

Smith, Liz. "A Career Woman at Heart." *Newsday*, October 1, 1997: A13.

Smith, Sally Bedell. "Dodi's Life in the Fast Lane." *Vanity Fair*, December 1997: 138–146.

Solomon, Marion F. *Narcissism and Intimacy: Love and Marriage in an Age of Confusion*. New York: W. W. Norton & Co., 1989.

Sorkin, Andrew Ross. "Diana's Death Expands Web's New Role." *New York Times*, September 8, 1997: D3.

Spoto, Donald. *The Decline and Fall of the House of Windsor*. New York: Simon & Schuster, 1995.

Swardson, Anne. "French Inquiry on Diana Accident Moving Cautiously." *Washington Post*, February 12, 1998: E1.

Swardson, Anne and Charles Trueheart. "Headlong Flight From Paparazzi Ends in Carnage." *Washington Post*, September 1, 1997: A25.

Tendler, Stewart. "Police Ready For a Million Mourners." *The Times*,
September 2, 1997: 2.

"Teresa, Diana Equal Billing." *Tyndall Weekly*, September 13, 1997.

"13 Million Hits on Diana Website." AP Worldstream, September 5,
1997.

Thomas, Evan, Stryker McGuire, and Daniel Pederson. "A Prince as Parent."
Newsweek, November 17, 1997: 43–46.

Time, September 8, 1997: cover.

"Too Close for Comfort." *People*, September 15, 1997: 70–71.

Tuttle, Beth and Ann Rauscher. "70 Front Pages Show How Newspapers
Report Death of Princess Diana." U.S. Newswire, August 31, 1997.

"The 25 Most Intriguing People of the Year." *People*, December 29, 1997 and
January 5, 1998.

Tye, Larry. "Doctors Had Little Hope of Success." *Boston Globe*, September 1,
1997: A6.

Varadarajan, Tunku. "Hardbitten Bronx Thrills to Saga of Nun and Princess."
The Times, June 19, 1997.

Vester, Linda. "Princess Diana's Dress Sold for $36,800 at June Auction
Resold for $200,000 at Another Charity Auction." NBC News,
September 30, 1997.

Victor, Peter and Colin Brown. "Diana Accepts Charles's Divorce Terms;
Frosty Exchanges as Palace Says, 'Details Remain to Be Discussed.'" *The
Independent*, February 29, 1996: 1.

Walker, Dave. "Did Paparazzi Chase Princess to Her Death?" *The Arizona
Republic*, September 1, 1997: A1.

Wallace, Carol. "Letter From the Editor." *People*, September 15, 1997: 8.

Welkos, Robert. "Paparazzi Guilty in Schwarzenegger Case." *Los Angeles Times*,
February 3, 1998: B1–2.

_____. "Two Photographers Sentenced to Jail." *Los Angeles Times*, February 24,
1998: B3.

Whitaker, James. "Diana Would Have Hated People Paying to Be Close to
Her." *Mirror*, January 12, 1998: 3.

White, Tim, Art Harris, Wolf Blitzer, and Brian Jenkins. "Rees-Jones Speaks
From His Memory." CNN *Showbiz Today*, March 2, 1998.

Will, George F. *Suddenly: The American Idea Abroad and At Home,
1986–1990*. New York: The Free Press, 1991.

_____. *The Woven Figure*. New York: Scribner, 1997.

Willcocks, Carole. "A Royal Reunification." *National Catholic Register*, August
30, 1981: 6.

Wilkins, Emma. "Two Most Trusted Servants Remain at Their Post." *The
Times*, September 8, 1997.

Wilson, A. N. "The Danger of Charles Playing Up to the Hype." *Evening
Standard*, February 10, 1998: 11.

Wingett, Fiona and Dennis Rice. "I'll Cry on Your Shoulder, You Cry on Mine . . . Diana's Heartbroken Butler and the Troubled TV Funnyman." *Sunday Mirror*, September 21, 1997: 4–5.

Wolf, Naomi. *The Beauty Myth: How Images of Beauty Are Used Against Women*. New York: Anchor Books 1992.

Woods, Audrey. "Press Role in Princess Diana's Death Angers British." Associated Press, August 31, 1997.

"World Media Bid High on Photos of Fatal Crash; Huge Sums Offered, Picture Agency Says." *Toronto Star*, September 4, 1997: A17.

Worthington, Christa. "Going, Going, Gone . . . Diana's Dresses Raise 3.5M Pounds." *The Independent*, June 27, 1997: 9.

Wynn Davies, Patricia. "£17M Divorce for Charles and Diana." *The Independent*, July 13, 1996: 1.

"The Year in Pictures." *Life* (Collectors' Edition), January 1998: 24–124.

Zachary, Pascal G. "Junk History: It's Bigger than Big; It's More . . . " *Wall Street Journal*, September 19, 1997: A1.

Zoglin, Richard. "Hey, Wanna Buy Some Pix?" *Time* (Commemorative Issue), September 15, 1997: 56–57.

Interview Sources

The following people were interviewed for this book:

Floyd Abrams
22 March 1998

Cindy Adams
2 February 1998

Peter Bart
6 January 1998

Marilyn Beck
*10 November 1997
& 16 January 1998*

Myrna Blyth
2 March 1998

Leo Braudy
17 January 1998

Dr. Joyce Brothers
20 November 1997

Philip Elmer-DeWitt
9 February 1998

Howard Dickman
29 December 1997

Alan Entin
1 November 1997

Mitchell Fink
5 March 1998

Stuart Fischoff
7 November 1997

Nancy Friday
9 January 1998

Ellen Goodman
5 January 1998

Richard Greene
*10 November 1997
& 8 January 1998*

Carla Hall
14 March 1998

Bruce Handy
28 February 1998

Don Hewitt
10 February 1998

Warren Hoge
19 February 1998

Cathy Horyn
13 January 1998

Barbara Hower
19 January 1998

Karen Jackovich
12 February 1998

Landon Jones
4 November 1997

Leopold Katz
3 November 1997

Howard Kurtz
13 January 1998

Clemm Lane
2 March 1998

John Leo
7 January 1998

Martin Lewis
6 November 1997,
8 January 1998,
& 13 January 1998

Kim Masters
14 December 1998

Michael Medved
15 November 1997

Dick Morris
18 November 1997

Jay Mulvaney
4 April 1998

Cable Neuhaus
28 December 1997

Dan Okrent
9 February 1998

Norman Pearlstine
25 February 1998
& 2 March 1998

Jonathan Rader
14 January 1998

Anthony Robbins
5 March 1998

Richard C. Robertiello
25 May 1998

Howard Rosenberg
18 December 1997

Richard Sanders
5 February 1998

David Shaw
16 December 1997

Martha Smilgis
3 February 1998

Liz Smith
17 January 1998

Richard Stolley
2 November 1997

Margaret Trudeau
Kemper
16 January 1998

Heather Vincent
8 January 1998

Bernie Weinraub
7 March 1998

Judy Wieder
13 January 1998

Carole Willcocks
8 November 1997

Bob Woodward
19 February 1998

Richard Zoglin
9 February 1998

Index

A&E 71, 82, 118, 144, 151, 156

Abrams, Floyd 273

Adams, Cindy 90, 215, 279

AIDS 38, 96, 116, 118–20, 122, 162, 170, 191, 196

al Fayed Mohammed 204–06, 210, 213, 258–64

al Fayed, Dodi 9–11, 204–10, 211–16, 252, 254, 258–60, 268, 288, 298–301

Alter, Jonathan 255, 312

Althorp 44, 46, 224–25, 287, 312

American Civil Liberties Union 272

Andrew, Prince 69, 84, 116, 122, 124, 129, 131

Anne, Princess 69, 84, 124, 175

Archbishop of Canterbury 72, 180

Association of German Journalists 256

Atkinson, Jane 179

Attenborough, Sir John 113, 145, 158

Baldacci, Leslie 195

Barry, Stephen 46

Bart, Peter 296, 300, 305

Bartholomew, Carolyn 26–27, 53, 132

Bashir, Martin 158–60

Beck, Joan 195

Beck, Marilyn 239

Belsky, Dick 255

Betty Ford Center 170–71

Blair, Tony 122, 178, 197, 228, 264, 266, 269, 298

Blyth, Myrna 279

Boorstin, Daniel J. 15, 281–282

Boxer, Barbara 271

Braudy, Leo 15, 64, 80, 98, 103, 111, 170, 171–72, 238, 250, 275, 283, 302, 305, 309, 315

Brenna, Mario 207

British Press Commission 59

British Red Cross 139, 192

Broadcast Standards Commission 268

Brothers, Dr. Joyce 107, 234

Brown, Tina 88, 122–23, 209, 311

Buckley, William F. Jr. 276, 278

Burrell, Paul 156–158, 224–226

Burton, Richard 73

Campbell, Lady Colin 34, 56–58, 61, 120, 128,

Carling, Julia 151–52

Carling, Will 34, 150, 151–52, 159

Carlson, Margaret 254

Cartland, Barbara 46, 97

Chapman, Victor 101–103

Charles, Prince of Wales *(See also specific topics under* Diana)

    architecture 112

    "Camillagate" 137

    overspending 147

    public service 112

    wedding 71–76

Chess game 22–36

Clifford, Max 164

Clinton, Bill 18, 22, 87, 88, 98, 122, 149, 164

Clooney, George 270

Cocks, Jay 73, 75, 85

Codrescu, André 15

Cole, Michael 252, 263

conspiracy theory 253, 259-260, 262-264
Cook, Robin 192, 195, 266
Coz, Steve 255
Cruise, Tom 269

Davies, Nicholas 154, 159, 173
Deedes, Lord W. F. 99, 194
de la Billiere, Sir Peter 193
Dempster, Nigel 23–24
Dershowitz, Alan 276
Diana Princess of Wales
　Angola tour 192
　Argentina tour 176–77
　Australia-New Zealand tour
　　101–103, 107
　Bosnia visit 139, 194
　bulimia 24, 101–104, 128, 134,
　　165–66, 183, 190, 233
　Chicago visits 38–39, 194–95
　Christie's auction 196, 286
　courtship 20, 31, 51–62, 215
　dancing 114–116
　depression 47, 102
　Diana "loon attack" 144
　divorce 21, 26, 34–35, 39–42, 99,
　　124, 128, 130–34, 136, 149,
　　152, 155, 168, 171, 173–4,
　　178–79, 180, 185, 203, 206,
　　210, 240, 253, 287,295
　Egyptian tour 148
　fashion 109–111
　funeral 11–12, 58, 96, 201,
　　223–249, 295–298
　India and Nepal tour 139
　memorabilia 285–87
　memorial fund 288, 311
　"nervous breakdown" 134
　overspending 147
　Panorama interview (*see also* Bashir)
　　38, 159–162, 172
　parents' divorce 44
　relations with press 30, 100, 106,
　　121–22, 132 (and throughout)
　separation from Charles 28, 29, 84,
　　131, 134, 136, 139, 140–41,
　　168, 178, 212
　Sloane Ranger 48, 136

　"Squidgygate" 135
　wedding 71–76

Dickman, Howard 79, 293
Dimbleby, Jonathan 28, 32–33, 136,
　148, 150, 154, 166, 168
Disney World 141
Drescher, Fran 270
Drudge, Matt 249
Duchovny, David 270
Dunne, Philip 128

Edward VIII 67
Elizabeth II 27, 31, 44, 50, 64–68,
　77, 79, 84, 99, 119, 150, 160, 176,
　242
　annus horribilis 121, 137
　Christmas Address 137
　relations with Fleet Street 99
Elmer-DeWitt, Philip 246
Emmanuel, Rahm 307
Entin, Alan 43, 48, 128
Erikson, Erik 39–43, 198

Fallows, James 275
Feinstein, Diane 271–272
Fellowes, Robert 26, 50, 160
Ferguson, Sarah 24, 123, 131, 159
Fermoy, Ruth 44
Fink, Mitchell 91, 229, 295
Fischoff, Stuart 235, 239, 248, 273
Folkers, Richard 243
Franklin Mint 196, 286
Friday, Nancy 79, 86, 199–200, 233,
　242, 246, 279, 290, 298, 315
Frost, David 159

Galella, Ron 271
Gilbey, James R. 27, 135
Glover, Stephen 181
Goldsmith, Sir James and Annabella 155
Goleman, Daniel 189–91, 304
Good Samaritan Law 218, 260–261
Goodman, Ellen 294, 301, 310
Goodman, Walter 229
Goyette, Charles 252
Gray, Francine du Plessix 234

Greene, Richard 152, 156–158, 161, 164, 169 186, 188, 205, 209, 225, 243, 310
Greenfield, Jeff 307
Greenfield, Meg 281

Haley, Tom 254
Hall, Carla 229, 247
Hallett, E. Bruce 80, 90
Handy, Bruce 90, 247
Harding, Tonya 9
Harbor Gym Club 187
Harry, Prince 24, 30, 127
Harrods Department Store 130, 205, 231, 258–59, 301
Harvey, Anna 107
Harvey, Glenn 144
Harvey, Paul 250
Hastings, Max 130, 133, 145
Hauptfuhrer, Fred 148
Hewitt, James 23–24, 27, 33, 129, 148, 150, 165, 168, 173, 214–15, 290, 294
Higgins, Stuart 166
Hitchens, Christopher 197, 245–46, 250
Hoare, Oliver 147, 149
Hoey, Brian 166, 179
Hoge, Warren 232, 253, 263, 268–69, 309
Honigsbaum, Mark 182–83, 207
Horyn, Cathy 108, 166, 168, 170, 172–73, 200, 242, 306
Hotel Ritz 207, 212
Hower, Barbara 153, 172, 284
Huffington, Arianna 228, 312, 316
Hussey, Marmaduke 160

Il Tampanini 138
International Red Cross 180, 193
IRA 140
Irons, Jeremy 144

Jackovich, Karen 290
Jackson, Michael 9
James, Clive 155, 159, 313
Jenkins, Simon 85, 134, 136
John, Elton 224

Johnson, Paul 181
Jones, Landon 148–50, 170, 275, 277
Juan Carlos, King of Spain 128
Junor, Penny 166

Kahn, Hasnat 183
Kantrowitz, Barbara 309
Katz, Leopold 295
Kay, Richard 34, 56, 146, 152, 208, 210
Kelley, Kitty 25, 53, 101, 108, 111, 116, 117, 129, 131, 141–42, 166, 171, 197, 287
Kemper, Margaret Trudeau 113, 201–204, 234
Kennedy, Helena 174
Kerrigan, Nancy 9
King, Kay; Young England School 56
Knight, Stuart 132, 135
Kissinger, Henry 177, 188
Krauthammer, Charles 297
Kübler-Ross, Elisabeth 265
Kurtz, Howard 91–2, 149, 242, 275, 307
Kydd, Peter Shand 44

Lacayo, Richard 258–59
Lacey, Robert 133
LaFerla, Ruth 305
landmines 192–4, 210, 260, 310
Lane, Clemm 228
Langevin, Jacques 217, 254
Lapham, Lewis H. 296, 301
Lasch, Christopher 283
Lennox, Ken 132, 136, 138
Leo, John 170
Lewis, Martin 59, 78, 118, 166–67, 170, 188, 232, 308
Lindbergh, Charles 282

MacLeod, Scott 260
Madonna 39, 182, 270, 310, 265, 270
Mailer, Norman 248
Major, John 28, 177, 180, 204
Mannakee, Barry 128
Margaret, Princess 59, 69, 84, 96

Martin, Jack 212, 311
Masters, Kim 253–54, 311
Maxwell, Robert 125
McCartney, Paul and Linda 274
McGregor, Lord 26–27, 132–133
McKnight Sam 144
McLuhan, Marshall 15, 249
Medved, Michael 166
Mirror Group (withdraws from PCC)
    32, 142
monarchy 22, 63–70
Monckton, Rosa 181, 188, 209
Morris, Dick 21, 121, 165–67, 293, 316
Morrow, Lance 86, 292
Morton, Andrew 25–26, 28, 40–41,
    46, 48, 53–55, 102, 123, 129, 131,
    136, 151, 173, 175, 181, 191, 299,
    315
Mountbatten, Earl 52
Murdoch, Rupert 26, 49, 83, 85–87, 95,
    125, 148, 268

Neale, Greg 194
Neuhaus, Cable 168
Nordland, Ron 261

Okrent, Daniel 89, 229, 306
Onassis, Jacqueline Kennedy 271
Orbach, Susie 155, 158

pageantry 74–75
Paglia, Camille 308
Palmer-Tomkinson, Patti 52
Parker-Bowles, Camilla 25, 28–29, 114,
    129, 136, 138, 145–46, 151, 160–61,
    172, 209
Parry, Vivienne 156
Pasternak, Anna 33, 148
Paul, Henri 10, 213–26, 262
Pearlstine, Norman 89, 227–28, 238,
    273, 292
Peck, M. Scott 43, 53, 115, 198
Penn, Sean 270
Pew Research Center 237
Philip, Prince 27, 30, 68, 84, 123, 132,
    150, 176, 180, 223, 297
    documentary on his life 32

Powell, Colin 177, 188
Prager, Dennis 233, 310, 312–13
Press Complaints Commission 142, 175,
    267
Puttman, Lord 106, 146, 158, 176

Rader, Jonathan 104
Rees-Jones, Trevor 9, 13, 212–17, 242,
    258, 264
Reese, Gordon 158
Reeves, Richard 235, 308
Reiser, Paul 270
Riordan, Richard 271
Riou, Bruno 219
Robbins Anthony 154, 158, 236
Robertiello, Richard C. 314
Robertson, Geoffrey 142, 266–267
Robinson, Mary 140
Rosenberg, Howard 88, 226–27, 245, 247
Royko, Mike 87, 195

SAMU (Urgent Medical Aid Service)
    218, 263
Sancton, Thomas 260
Sanders, Richard 89, 291, 306
Sawyer, Diane 248
Schwarzenegger, Arnold 272
Schwarzkopf, General Norman 193
Screen Actors Guild 270–71
Selleck, Tom 270
Serota, Angela 155
Settelen, Peter 145
Seward, Ingrid 41, 44
Shales, Tom 80
Sharkey, Jacqueline 236, 293
Shaw, David 291, 305
Short, Clare 193
Simpson, O. J. 10
Smilgis, Martha 306
Smith, Liz 172, 235
Smith, Sally Bedell 205, 287
Snowden, Lord 199
Sola, Laurent 256
Solomon, Marion 44, 47, 62, 104,
    107
Spencer family 43–44, 48, 128, 224,
    226, 288, 298

Spencer, Charles 12, 253, 286, 298, 210,
   214, 299
Spencer, Francis (Shand Kydd) 40–42,
   44–45, 154, 163–64
Spencer, Jane 51
Spencer, John 41–46, 128
Spencer, Raine 46
Spencer, Sarah 51
Spoto, Donald 205
stalkerazzi 32, 144–45, 271, 275
Stamp, Terence 145
Starkey, David 58
Steele, Valerie 306
Stephan, Hervé 260
Stolley 38, 74, 172, 238, 280, 285,
   297, 310, 312
Stott, Richard 70, 138

Taylor, Bryce 31, 38, 140–141, 200
Taylor, Elizabeth 269
Teichner, Martha 308
Teresa, Mother 129, 194, 242, 291,
   312–313
Testino, Mario 198–99
Thatcher, Margaret 60, 84, 118, 158,
   232, 308
Tiffany Theory 14–15, 135, 316
Trudeau, Margaret (*see* Kemper)
Trudeau, Pierre Elliot 113, 201–203
Trump, Donald and Marla 177
Turow, Joe 235

United Cerebral Palsy of New York
   Foundation 177, 188

Versace, Gianni 200–201
Vincent, Heather 279, 290, 314

Wakeman, Lord 175, 266, 269
Walters, Barbara 141, 159, 188,
   244
Warhol, Andy 203
Weinraub, Bernie 90
Wieder, Judy 119
Whitaker, James 52, 55, 56
Will, George 148
Willcocks, Carole 60, 76, 77
William, Prince 30–33, 65, 87,
   94, 98, 102, 109, 127–28,
   148, 162, 166, 175, 182,
   196, 222, 224, 264, 268, 286,
   310
Windsor Castle 137
Winfrey, Oprah 141, 159, 169–170
Winn, Marie 249
Woodward, Bob 246, 250
Worsthorne, Sir Peregrine 130
Wyatt, Lord 28

yellow journalism 125

Zachary, G. Pascal 248
Zoglin, Richard 275

Permissions

These organizations have generously given permission to use extended quotations from the following copyrighted works:

From "The Interview: Princess Diana: Queen of Hearts," Martin Bashir, BBC *Panorama.*

From *The Frenzy of Renown: Fame and Its History* by Leo Braudy; copyright © 1986 by Leo Braudy. Used by permission of Oxford University Press, Inc.

From "The Talk of the Town" by Francine du Plessix Gray, *The New Yorker* Magazine, Inc. Reprinted by permission; copyright © 1997. All rights reserved.

From "Tea With Diana," with the permission of Landon Jones. *Princeton Alumni Weekly.* October 8, 1997.

From *The Royals* by Kitty Kelley; copyright © 1997 by H. B. Productions, Inc. Reprinted by permission of Warner Books, Inc., New York, New York, U.S.A. All rights reserved.

From *Diana, Her True Story—In Her Own Words* by Andrew Morton; copyright © 1997. Reprinted with the permission of Simon & Schuster.

From "Princess Diana: Why So Much Grief?" with the permission of Dennis Prager *The Prager Perspective*, September 1, 1997, edition.